"Life is a process. For some people, it seems the breadth of their life is required to heal a painful beginning. For others, it is a process of learning to embrace the people and the needs of the day, rather than dealing with the shadows of the past. But for all of us, the process is founded on the same principles. I have never read a book that so clearly defines the profound yet simple means of embracing life. Stormie's honesty and the clarity with which she writes drew me in, making me want to dig deeper into her book, dig deeper into my relationship with God, dig deeper into life."

—Amy Grant

"Stormie Omartian's new book truly is a step in the right direction and I endorse her words enthusiastically. Her practical approach to emotional health will be a blessing to all who care enough to take the first step."

—Florence Littauer
Author and Speaker

"Stormie's book is both unique and powerful. With it, hurting people will learn principles to allow God's grace to transform trouble into triumph. It's a delight to read."

—Debby Boone

"What a tool of God's mercy and grace this message gives. This book not only puts within my hand something to help those I know, but it helps me. By opening up and becoming vulnerable through sharing her own struggles and victories, Stormie gives hope for wholeness to us all."

—Neva Coyle
Author of *Free to Be Thin*

"If you find yourself staggering down the road of life due to emotional injury and emotional starvation, you'll find that Stormie Omartian is exactly the kind of person you've been longing to meet. Like the Good Samaritan, she'll see your wounds and take them seriously, pour on the oil and the wine and help bind up the wounds."

—Rich Buhler
Author of *Pain and Pretending*
Host of "Tabletalk"

"This book is rooted in a workable reality: There *is* a way to lasting happiness. And I've watched this reality *happen*—wholly, powerfully, beautifully—in Stormie's life, family, and career. Let her tell you how to take the right step, the best way."

—Jack Hayford
The Church On The Way

A
STEP
IN THE
RIGHT
DIRECTION

YOUR GUIDE TO
INNER HAPPINESS

Stormie Omartian

A JANET THOMA BOOK

THOMAS NELSON PUBLISHERS

NASHVILLE

The names of persons who came to Stormie for counsel have been changed to protect confidentiality.

Published in Nashville, Tennessee, by Thomas Nelson, Inc., and distributed in Canada by Lawson Falle, Ltd., Cambridge, Ontario.

Unless otherwise noted, Scripture quotations are from the NEW KING JAMES VERSION of the Bible. Copyright © 1979, 1980, 1982, Thomas Nelson, Inc., Publishers.

Scripture quotations noted NIV are from The Holy Bible, NEW INTERNATIONAL VERSION. Copyright © 1978 by the New York International Bible Society. Used by permission of Zondervan Bible Publishers.

Library of Congress Cataloging-in-Publication Data

Omartian, Stormie.
    A step in the right direction : your handbook for inner happiness
/ Stormie Omartian.
      p.   cm.
    "A Janet Thoma book."
    ISBN 0-8407-7479-6
    1. Mental health—Religious aspects—Christianity. 2. Omartian,
Stormie. 3. Christian life—1960— 4. Consolation. I. Title.
BT732.4.044 1991
248.8'6—dc20   91–29008
                                      CIP

Printed in the United States of America
1 2 3 4 5 6 7 — 96 95 94 93 92 91

To all who suffer
with any kind of emotional pain
or the frustration
of unfulfillment.
Through this book may God comfort your hearts,
give you renewed hope,
grow you into all you can be,
and help you to find wholeness
and total restoration.

CONTENTS

By Saying No to Sexual Immorality
By Cleaning Out Your House
By Taking Charge of Your Mind
By Taking Care of Your Body
By Spending Time with Other Believers
By Watching What You Say
By Giving Yourself Away
By Feasting at the Lord's Table
By Walking in Faith

Of Anger
Of Believing Lies About Yourself
Of Blaming God
Of Child Abuse
Of Confusion
Of Criticism
Of Denial
Of Depression
Of Destructive Relationships
Of Divorce
Of Envy
Of Fear
Of Lust

ACKNOWLEDGEMENTS

With special thanks:

TO my husband, Michael, for his faithfulness to God and to me.

TO my son, Christopher, and daughter, Amanda, for deciding unanimously and without hesitation that they don't want a new mom who doesn't write books.

TO Pastor Jack Hayford, for telling me about Jesus in a way that I could understand and for teaching God's Word in such power that it has changed my life forever and made possible the assembling of the biblical basis for this book.

TO my editor extraordinaire, Janet Hoover Thoma, for being not only brilliant, but compassionate as well.

TO Bruce Barbour and Bob Zaloba of Thomas Nelson for their support, encouragement, and expertise.

TO my secretary and long-time friend, Janet Hinde, for her hard work and sweet spirit throughout even the toughest times. Her efficiency and dedication have been an invaluable contribution to this project.

TO my dear prayer partners, without whose daily support this book would not have been written: Patti Brussat, Susan Howard Chrane, Debby Boone Ferrer, Pamela Deuel Hart, Priscilla Navarro, Patti Raffy, and Constance Zachman.

TO our monthly prayer group who gave no indication of being bored with my same prayer request month after month: Bob and Sally Anderson, Tom and Patti Brussat, Calvin and Susan Chrane, Russ and Renee Ellis, Tony and Pamela Hart, David and Priscilla Navarro, and Patrick and Patti Raffy.

TO my aunt, Jean Davis, for a lifetime of understanding, encouragement, and support.

TO my dad for all the great dinners he cooked to give me time to finish this book.

PREFACE

The purpose of this book is to bring hope, healing, and growth to anyone who is emotionally hurting or unfulfilled and to show practical steps to take to find a way out of pain and frustration. This is not a book to *define* problems, but to show the *solution* to *any problem*.

People who are emotionally needy are busy people. They are trying to cope with their hurt, fill their emptiness, meet their needs, struggle with their weaknesses, rise above their limitations, and survive as best they can. Even if they don't appear especially active in things they do, their minds, emotions, and bodies are busy fighting the effects of depression, unforgiveness, low self-worth, abandonment, anger, hopelessness, boredom, fear, anxiety, rejection, feelings of failure, and other negative emotions, which are constantly depleting them. Sometimes just doing the bare necessities for life requires as much as they are able to give. Because of the continual drain and the effort it requires just to maintain, they don't have time to read volumes, and they don't want technical terms and complex verbiage to wade through. They need truth—clear and simple—and steps to take that are easily understood and accomplished. The Seven Steps to Emotional Health are exactly that.

Under each of the seven steps are different subjects upon which I could write an entire book. But there isn't space nor time to do that. So I'm giving an overview, touching on key points to help people move a step at a time in the right direction. Don't allow the brevity with which I approach each topic to minimize its importance. They are *all* vital.

If you are emotionally hurting or you know someone who is or you counsel those who are, I pray this book may be a tool in your hands to help bring healing and restoration. If you are frustrated with your life, may this book help you to find fulfillment beyond what you dreamed possible.

For I know the thoughts that I think toward you, says the LORD, thoughts of peace and not of evil, to give you a future and a hope. Then you will call upon Me and go and pray to Me, and I will listen to you. And you will seek Me and find Me, when you search for Me with all your heart. I will be found by you, says the LORD, and I will bring you back from your captivity.
(Jeremiah 29:11–14)

CHAPTER 1

Seven Steps to Emotional Health

Y ou're worthless, and you'll never amount to anything," my mother said as she pushed me into the little closet underneath the stairway and slammed the door. "Now stay in there until I can stand to see your face!" The sound of her footsteps faded as she walked down the small hallway back to the kitchen.

I wasn't really sure what I had done to warrant being locked in the closet again, but I knew it must be bad. I knew *I* must be bad, and I believed that all the negative things she had ever said about me were surely accurate—after all she was my mother.

The closet was a small, rectangular storage area underneath the stairs where the dirty laundry was kept in an old wicker basket. I sat on top of the pile of clothes and pulled my feet in tight to eliminate the possibility of being touched by the mice that periodically streaked across the floor. I felt lonely, unloved, and painfully afraid as I waited in that dark hole for the seemingly endless amount of time it took for her to remember I was there or for my father to return. Either event would mean my release from the closet and from the devastatingly closed-in feeling of being buried alive and forgotten.

As you can probably tell from just this one incident, I was raised by a mentally ill mother, and, among other atrocities, I spent much of my early childhood locked in a closet. Although certain people were aware of her bizarre behavior from time to time, her mental illness wasn't clearly identified until I was in my late teens. During all my growing up years, my mother's extremely erratic behavior left me with feelings of futility, hopelessness, helplessness, and deep emotional pain. So much so that by the time I was a young woman I was still locked in a closet—only the boundaries were emotional rather than physical. I was walled in by a deep, ever-present pain in my soul, which expressed itself through certain acts of self-destruction, and a paralyzing fear that controlled my every breath.

I threw myself into anything I thought would help me get free of all that—Eastern religions, occult practices, psychotherapy, unhealthy relationships, and a short, ill-fated marriage. When it became obvious that each of these things fell far short of meeting my desperate needs, I sank deeper into depression. I turned to drugs and alcohol with dangerous frequency in hopes of momentarily transcending this chronic emotional torture. Through it all I was determined to find a way out of the pain if it killed me. A few times it nearly did. By the time I was twenty-eight, suicide was the only solution I could see.

I revealed the details of this life of devastation and journey to emotional restoration in my autobiography called *Stormie* (Eugene, OR: Harvest House, 1986). After I wrote this book, I was deluged with letters from people telling me of their similar emotionally traumatic circumstances.

"You've shown me for the first time that it is possible to be free of emotional pain. But now that I know there is hope for my life, what steps can I take to experience the same healing you've found?" I was asked that question time and again, and I tried to answer each individual as best I could. But the confines of a letter frustrated me because there wasn't enough time or space to address the questions adequately. Telephone calls and personal contact also proved far too time consuming and infringed on my family time. I knew I needed to put all the information I had on the subject in a book, which could be read and referred to as the desire presented itself. This is that book.

WHAT IS EMOTIONAL HEALTH?

Many people see their emotional state with resignation: "This is just the way I am" or "I guess I'll have to live with it because this is as good as it gets." Others believe that while there may be a way to make essential changes, one has to be either very spiritual or wealthy enough to afford the best professional help. "Emotional health," one girl told me, "is a remote ideal that many people want but very few people achieve."

My definition of emotional health is having total peace about who you are, what you're doing, and where you're going, both individually and in relationship to those around you. In other words, it's feeling totally at peace about the past, present, and future of your life. It's knowing you're in line with God's ultimate purpose for you and being fulfilled in that. When you have that kind of peace and you no longer live in emotional agony, then you are a success.

In contrast to what many people think, emotional health is just as practical and attainable as physical health. If you don't feed your body the right food, you will become ill and die. Spiritually, emotionally, and mentally, you have to be fed and cared for properly, or that part of you gets sick and dies a slow death. Proper exercise for the mind and emotions is just as beneficial as exercise for the body, but most people tend not to think of it that way.

In my first book *Greater Health God's Way* (Chatsworth, CA: Sparrow), I wrote about what I learned regarding proper care of the physical body. I'm not a nutritionist, a doctor, physical therapist, or health expert. I'm simply a person who was very sick and weak for twenty-eight years of my life and then discovered a way of living that worked. In *Greater Health God's Way* I laid down seven steps to health and instructed the readers to take one step at a time in each of the seven areas, reminding them that "Everything you do counts. It will either count for life or it will count for death." I have found that the same is true for emotional health. Just as I have a physical health plan, I have a plan for emotional health. I am not a psychiatrist, psychologist, professional counselor, or pastor. I am simply a person who lived with depression, fear, suicidal thoughts, hopelessness, and intense emotional pain every day. I no longer live with any of those things. Like my health book, with its seven steps to physical health, this book suggests seven steps to emotional health.

WHAT ARE THE SEVEN STEPS TO EMOTIONAL HEALTH?

Your mind and emotions, like your physical body, need to be freed from stress, fed properly, exercised, cleansed, nurtured, retrained, exposed to freshness and light, and given rest. The seven steps that will help you to do all these things are:

Step One: Acknowledge God
Recognize that God is on your side and acknowledge Him as Lord over every area of your life.

Step Two: Lay a Foundation
Recognize that your relationship with God is the sure foundation upon which emotional health is established, and then strengthen

that relationship by spending time in God's Word, prayer, praise, confession, and ongoing forgiveness.

Step Three: Live in Obedience

Recognize that God's rules are for your benefit, and try to the best of your knowledge to live His way, knowing that every step of obedience brings you closer to total wholeness.

Step Four: Find Deliverance

Recognize who your enemy is, and separate yourself from anything that separates you from God or keeps you from becoming all He made you to be.

Step Five: Receive God's Gifts

Recognize that God has provided gifts for you, and take the steps necessary to receive them.

Step Six: Reject the Pitfalls

Recognize and get free of the negative traps and deceptions that rob you of life.

Step Seven: Stand Strong

Recognize that as long as you stand with God and don't give up, you win.

These seven steps are really natural laws, which work for our benefit when we live in harmony with them. Living the right way generates life, no matter who we are or what our circumstances. Likewise, doing the wrong thing leads to death.

You don't learn the seven steps in a week; they are a way of life. Understanding them with your mind will influence the state of your heart, which will affect your emotions and ultimately your entire life. Please know that I didn't master these steps overnight—and you won't either. In fact, I still work on it the same way I work toward physical health. But I have tested this plan repeatedly over the past twenty years, and I have seen these steps operate successfully in my life and the lives of countless others. The plan will be as reliable and consistent as you are in following it. I will walk through the seven steps with you just as I did on my journey toward emotional health. Together we will take it a step at a time.

WHAT YOU SHOULD EXPECT

In the following chapters you will find three types of information. One type is *familiar* and seems obvious, but don't be deceived by that. The familiar and obvious are often overlooked for just that reason. You may be tempted to say, "I already know I'm supposed to forgive." But the question is, are you thorough and persistent in doing it? Do you realize that it is sometimes a *process?* Did you know that you can never have emotional wholeness as long as there is unforgiveness in *any* part of your life?

The second type of information is *unfamiliar.* You've never heard it before. Or if you *have* heard it, you didn't understand its significance for your own life or that it is a requirement for emotional restoration. Did you realize that you are hindering your emotional healing by having in your house things that carry negative mental or emotional attachments? Letters from an old boyfriend, for example, can subtly perpetrate feelings of failure, sadness, hurt or depression. It may be that such information is keeping you from the peace and fulfillment you desire.

The third type of information is *uncomfortable.* It's the kind you don't want to hear. You may react to it by saying, "I don't want to know about this because I don't want to do it." Remember how hard it was to learn you couldn't have all the candy bars and ice cream you wanted and how you paid for it when you went ahead and ate them anyway? Believe me, I understand how hard certain things are to hear and how difficult their accomplishment seems to be. But I would be less than a help to you if I were not to give you the *whole* truth. If I left some of the pieces out, you would have an incomplete plan for emotional restoration, and you'd live in frustration trying to find the missing piece. So I'm going to tell it to you as straight as I know how, and it's up to you to choose to do it or not. *Remember, you do the choosing. God working in you, as you allow Him entrance, makes it happen in your life.*

It takes awhile to put these seven steps into practice and make them a way of life. How long it takes depends on how committed you are to doing what's necessary to see it happen. It also depends on how deep your emotional damage is. The degree of pain we live with today is determined by the degree of hurt we've had in our past and how early in life it occurred. The earlier it happened, the more foundational it is, and the more difficult it is to rectify. However, you have not been put on this earth just to exist or survive. You are here to have a life of purpose and meaning. No matter how much has happened to you, how young you were when it happened, or how old you are now, you can be made whole.

The healing and restoration I found is there for you too. Whether it be from scars from as far back as early childhood abuse or from this week's untimely severing of a precious relationship, from today's shattered dream or the ravages of a lifetime of wrong living, you can be a whole person. You don't have to live in fear; you don't have to be depressed; you don't have to feel inadequate, stupid, untalented, or rejected. You don't have to put up with chronic emotional pain. It's possible to be free of all that. Whatever has been injured can be repaired.

But once you *are* healed, don't be misled into thinking you will never have a problem again. It just isn't so. Problems are a part of life in this world. They can be devastating, or they can be met head-on to make them work for you or else to minimize the discomfort they cause. That's why even after you are free of damaged emotions, you still must be on a maintenance program.

My journey from brokenness to wholeness didn't happen overnight. In fact, it took fourteen years from the time I began until I was pain-free and able to help others with the same problems. I believe it could have happened much faster had I figured out what I was supposed to be doing a lot sooner. Hopefully this book will speed up the process for you.

As you move into the Seven Steps to Emotional Health don't wait until you have mastered Step One before you move on to Step Two. It doesn't work that way. Rather, begin to take a step at a time in each of the seven areas. When you do, you'll see that other than the choices you make and the simple steps you take, you don't even have to be the one to make it all happen.

And keep in mind that emotional wholeness is a process which involves changing habits of thinking, feeling, or acting. That takes some time. The seven steps are not a quick fix but a way to find permanent transformation of your inner self. Don't expect to do everything in one leap. *Do it step by step, one step at a time in the right direction.*

■ ———————— *What the Bible Says About* ———————— ■

Emotional Health

The preparations of the heart belong to man.
Proverbs 16:1

"For I will restore health to you
And heal you of your wounds," says the LORD.
Jeremiah 30:17

I am feeble and severely broken;
I groan because of the turmoil of my heart.
　Psalm 38:8

He restores my soul.
　Psalm 23:3

He heals the brokenhearted
And binds up their wounds.
　Psalm 147:3

CHAPTER 2

Step One:
Acknowledge God

I took the handful of sleeping pills a friend had just given me and added them to my growing collection in a little gold box in the back of the bottom drawer of my bedroom dresser. "I have nearly enough to do the job right this time," I told myself. Deliberately and methodically I planned my suicide. I wanted to make it look like an accidental overdose so my sister and dad wouldn't bear any guilt.

I had tried to kill myself when I was fourteen by downing an odd combination of drugs in our bathroom, but they only succeeded in making me very sick. Since that failed attempt, I had thrown myself into everything I could possibly find to get out of my dark emotional prison cell. Unfortunately, every so-called "key to life" I tried only led me closer to death and further from the freedom, peace, and release I so desperately sought.

I'd had plenty of good psychiatric and psychological counseling, especially if measured in terms of how much money I paid for it, and I was grateful for each doctor as he kept me from destroying myself. Yet at twenty-eight, fourteen years after my suicide attempt, I still felt as if I were down in a dark hole, not unlike the closet of my early childhood, and I couldn't produce the strength to pick myself up one more time. Death was again the only solution I could see. I was amazed that in all those years of struggle my life had still come to nothing.

At that low point, my friend Terry said, "I can see you're not doing well, Stormie. Won't you come with me and talk to my pastor?" Sensing my reluctance, she quickly added, "You've got nothing to lose."

I silently bore witness to her accurate assessment of my situation and agreed to go even though I wanted nothing whatsoever to do with any kind of religion. My experience with churches had been that they made me feel more dead than I was already.

Terry took me to meet Pastor Jack Hayford from a nearby church called The Church on the Way, and it turned out to be like no other meeting I'd ever had. We met him at a restaurant for lunch, and from the moment he started talking, he had my full attention. He asked me a little about myself, but I was not open to revealing anything of my desperate circumstances. Even at this late hour in my life, I wanted to appear successful. For over an hour, Pastor Jack talked about God the way someone talks about a best friend. He said that at my invitation, God would come to live within me and transform my life from the inside out.

"If you receive Jesus, the relationship you can have with God will be so personal that every part of your being can be shared with Him and His with you," Pastor Jack explained. "You would never be without hope or purpose again."

I had no trouble listening to him talk about God because I knew there was a spirit realm. I had seen enough supernatural manifestations through my delving into the occult to convince me of their reality. But when he started talking about receiving Jesus and being born again, I winced.

I had frequently seen people standing on street corners, waving black books and screaming, "Jesus saves!" and "You're all going to hell!" to everyone passing by. Because of them, I feared that accepting Jesus meant having an intellectual lobotomy, which would turn me into an unthinking, self-righteous, coldhearted, beat-people-over-the-head-with-your-Bible kind of person with whom the reality of other people's true pain and circumstances never registered. I had noticed, however, that neither Pastor Jack nor Terry was anything like that.

Fortunately, Pastor Jack saw through my fears and didn't push me for any commitment. Instead he sent me home with three books: the first, about the life of Jesus, was the Gospel of John in book form; the second one, *The Screwtape Letters* by C. S. Lewis, was about the reality of evil; and the third was a book about the working of the Holy Spirit of God in people's lives.

"Let's talk again next week in my office and you can let me know then what you think of these books," Pastor Jack said as we ended our meeting. We agreed, and I went home to start reading. Something about what Terry and Pastor Jack said and did that day made me want to find out what they knew that I didn't.

As I read the pages of each book, I realized that for years I had believed lies about Jesus, judging Him from what I'd heard of Him without really *knowing* Him. His name and reputation had been so maligned, mocked, misinterpreted, misconstrued, joked, and lied about for so long that I dismissed Him from any possible connection with my life. As I read I also realized that God was not the cold and distant force I had thought, but rather a loving and powerful Father, who sent us a means of total restoration through Jesus, His Son.

The more I read, the more I saw that my Science of Mind belief that there is no evil in the world except what exists in people's minds was a deception. As C. S. Lewis's book dramatized the activity of Satan, the source of the horrible things that happen to people became obvious. There *is* an evil force intent on our destruction, and Satan, the head of that force, is real and very much our enemy.

As I seriously pondered all I read, I also thought about Terry and about Pastor Jack and how much I admired them. They were not phony, stupid, or unloving. They had an inherent simple beauty and a bold confidence that radiated God's power.

When Terry and I met with Pastor Jack the following week, he asked me directly, "Well, what did you think of the books I gave you?"

"I think they are the truth," I responded with uncharacteristic confidence.

"So would you like to receive God's life in you?" he asked openly.

"Yes," I said without hesitation. "I want that, and I want all that God has for me."

That day in October of 1970, I decided to believe Jesus was who He said He was and receive Him into my life. I canceled my suicide plans and never seriously thought of rescheduling them. I had taken my first step in acknowledging God. Upon that step my ultimate restoration as an emotionally whole person would be built.

The Most Important Step You'll Ever Take

The first step to emotional wholeness is simply to acknowledge God, recognize that He is on your side, and let Him be Lord over your life.

The prophet Jeremiah asked God a question we all ask:

"Why then is there no healing for the wound of my people?" (Jer. 8:22 NIV)

And God answered,

"They go from one sin to another; they do not acknowledge me." (Jer. 9:3 NIV)

One of the main reasons people are emotionally broken is that they have not acknowledged God as Savior, as Father, as Holy Spirit, as Lord in every area of life, and as the Name who answers every need.

Until we have aligned ourselves properly with God, nothing in life will fall into place as it should, and we will never know what it means to be emotionally whole.

Not long after I acknowledged God's presence in my life, I was browsing in a Christian bookstore and came across a charming children's book called *Three in One* by Joanne Marxhausen (St. Louis, MO: Concordia). The author used the example of an apple with its three parts—the peel, the flesh, and the core—to point out that those three parts were still just one apple. Likewise, she described three aspects of God: the Father, the Son, and the Holy Spirit. Three parts, but only one God. The message of this simple illustration was so clear that I realized we can never truly know God until we know Him in all those ways.

■ ————————— *What the Bible Says About* ————————— ■
Acknowledging God

In all your ways acknowledge Him,
And He shall direct your paths.
Proverbs 3:6

The fear of the LORD is a fountain of life.
Proverbs 14:27

For whatever is born of God overcomes the world.
1 John 5:4

You are my LORD,
My goodness is nothing apart from You.
Psalm 16:2

If God is for us, who can be against us?
Romans 8:31

ACKNOWLEDGE GOD AS
JESUS CHRIST, YOUR SAVIOR

As I read the books Pastor Jack gave me, I could immediately see two reasons to acknowledge Jesus as my Savior. *The first was to be completely free of guilt.*

My sense of guilt was overwhelming, but for all the wrong reasons. I had no remorse for things I *did* that were wrong. I saw actions like lying and love affairs as means of survival and refused to allow myself to feel bad about them. Whenever I did feel guilty, I assumed it was because my mother had instilled it in me with her constant anger. She had a way of making everything I did seem evil; some days I even felt guilty for being alive.

Everyone has some kind of guilt for mistakes of the past. Sometimes it's for things we know we've done, sometimes it's deep regret over what we fear we could have prevented, and sometimes it's for violation of certain natural laws we're not even aware of violating. Whatever the reason, the load of guilt sits on us with crushing weight, and unless it's eliminated it separates us from the fullness of life.

What can ever take our guilt away? Consider, for instance, the man who accidentally backed a car over his two-year-old daughter and killed her. Or the woman who took drugs when she was pregnant and gave birth to a brain-damaged child. What about the mother who accidentally shot and killed her teenage son when he came home late one night and she thought he was a robber? How do these people find freedom from guilt over such devastating and irreparable damage?

Or how do you and I live with painful regrets? "If only I'd . . ." "If I just hadn't . . ." These thoughts echo the agony of situations that can never be changed. It's done! And there's no way to live with the truth of it unless you push it down deep and never allow yourself to feel it again. Don't talk about it. Don't bring it up. The trouble with that is you think you're getting away with it until it starts to surface on its own. But then it comes out in the form of a disease. Or perhaps it affects your mind and emotions, making you angry or withdrawn or phobic or depressed like an infection of a deep wound that was quickly bandaged over without being cleaned and properly treated.

Or how do you and I live with our guilty feelings over things that aren't our fault, but we fear they *might* be: "If I'd been more obedient, maybe my dad wouldn't have left us." "Did I drive my husband to have that affair?" "If only I hadn't let my teenage daughter go out that night, she'd never have been hit by a drunk driver." Guilt upon guilt piles up to become a burden that is literally *unbearable*.

Finally, what about our guilt over things we've done that violated God's laws, laws of which we weren't aware at the time? No matter how much a woman who has had an abortion believes her decision was right, I've never heard one say, "I've been fulfilled and enriched by this experience." She may feel relieved of a burden, but she never thinks, "What a wonderful thing I've done. I know I have truly realized God's purpose for my life and I am a better person because of it." Acknowledged or not, the guilt is there because she has violated a law of nature.

What and who can take this guilt away? A friend's saying "Don't worry about it. . . . It wasn't your fault. . . . You can't blame yourself" never gets rid of what you feel inside. Only God's forgiveness can do that. When we receive Jesus, we are immediately released from the penalty for our past mistakes. For the first time in my life I felt free from having to face the failure of my past on a moment-to-moment basis.

The second important reason to receive Jesus is to have the peace of knowing that your future is secure. And not only is your eternal future secure—Jesus said anyone who believes in Him will have everlasting life (John 6:40)—but your future in *this* life is also secure. God promises that if you acknowledge Him, He will guide you safely where you need to go (Prov. 3:6). This doesn't mean that we will instantly have all our problems solved and never again know pain, but we will have the power within us to reach our full potential. We can never find any greater security than that.

Life Before Death

When Jesus died on the cross, He also rose from the dead to break the power of death over anyone who receives His life. Jesus conquered death—whether at the end of life or in the multiple ways that we face death daily. In the death of our dreams, finances, health, or relationships, Jesus can bring His life to resurrect any dead place in us. Therefore we don't have to feel hopeless. He also gives to everyone who opens up to Him a *quality* of life that is meaningful, abundant, and fulfilling. He transcends our every limitation and boundary and enables us to do things we never would have been capable of aside from Him. He is the only one with power and authority over the emotions or bondage that torture us. He is the only one who can give us life *before* death as well as life hereafter. Without Him we die a little every day. With Him we become more and more alive. You can try to make it happen yourself or pay someone else to do it for you, but I'm not talking about finding temporary relief or a way to cope. I'm talking about total freedom from emotional torment. Only *you* know if you want badly enough to make a commitment to Him.

Christianity is a living relationship with God through Jesus, His Son. *Salvation* is not just something Jesus did for us; it is Jesus living *in* us. You may have been born into a Christian family or have attended a Christian church all your life, but if you haven't told God that you want to receive Jesus, you haven't been born into the kingdom of God. You can't inherit it; get it by osmosis, transplant, or implant; or wish upon a star for it. You have to declare your faith before the Lord.

If you want Jesus' life in you, just say, "Jesus, I acknowledge You this day. I believe You are the Son of God as You say You are. Although it's hard to comprehend love so great, I believe You laid down your life for me so that I might have life eternally and abundantly now. I ask You to forgive me for not living Your way. I need You to help me become all You created me to be. Come into my life and fill me with Your Holy Spirit. Let all the death in me be crowded out by the power of Your presence and this day turn my life into a new beginning."

If you don't feel comfortable with this prayer, then talk to Jesus as you would to a good friend, and confess you've made some mistakes. Tell Him you can't live without Him. Ask Him to forgive you and come into your heart. Tell Him you receive Him as Lord, and thank Him for His eternal life and forgiveness.

After I prayed that prayer with Pastor Jack, Terry and I were leaving the office when he caught the arm of a young man walking by.

"Stormie, I want you to meet Paul, my assistant pastor," he said. "Tell him what just happened."

I was uneasy as I shook Paul's hand and said sheepishly, "I just received Jesus."

I half expected him to laugh and say, "You've got to be kidding!'' But much to my amazement he said with a reassuring combination of sincerity and seriousness, "Praise God. That's wonderful." I smiled in response and it felt good.

There is release in telling someone you have received Jesus. It doesn't matter who. All that matters is that you have acknowledged Jesus to someone else so that it is firmly established. Even if you've known the Lord for a long time, it's good to do that frequently. Your belief in Him needs to be reconfirmed periodically. Remind yourself that the resurrection life of Jesus lives *in* you and that He is able to raise up any dead areas of your life.

It's also good to write the date you received the Lord in your Bible or a record book that will not be thrown away. This records your new birth date so that if you ever have doubt or confusion about whether it really happened, you will have it written in black and white. One of my friends was born again six or seven times because her emotions were fragile and her mind so clouded with oppression that she was never sure she had done it well enough the first time. That isn't necessary.

You are never born again by chance. When you receive Jesus, it is because God the Father is drawing you in. Jesus said, "No one can come to Me unless the Father who sent Me draws him" (John 6:44). Once God draws you in, it's done. You are released from guilt, your future is secure, and you are saved from death in every part of your life.

■ ———— *What the Bible Says About* ———— ■
Acknowledging God as
Jesus Christ, Your Savior

And we have seen and testify that the Father has sent the Son as Savior of the world. Whoever confesses that Jesus is the Son of God, God abides in him, and he in God.
1 John 4:14–15

Jesus said to him, "I am the way, the truth, and the life. No one comes to the Father except through Me."
John 14:6

Nor is there salvation in any other, for there is no other name under heaven given among men by which we must be saved.
Acts 4:12

Unless one is born again, he cannot see the kingdom of God.
John 3:3

If you confess with your mouth the Lord Jesus and believe in
your heart that God has raised Him from the dead, you will
be saved.
Romans 10:9

ACKNOWLEDGE GOD AS FATHER

Acknowledging God as heavenly Father is sometimes difficult
for people, especially if they didn't have a father, or have been mistreated by a male parent or guardian.

One young woman told me, "Don't talk to me about God being
a father. My father forced me to have sex with him until I left home,
and now I'm unable to have a normal relationship with any man at
all." Another confided to me, "My father beat me every time he
came home drunk, and now I hate him. How can I think of God as
a father?" A middle-aged man said, "My father never did anything
for me. He was a weakling. He contributed nothing to my life and
then eventually deserted us. Don't mention the word *father*."

I never had a dad who abused me, and for that I am very grateful. Yet my dad never unlocked the closet or rescued me from my
mother's insanity, and he was the only one with the power and
authority to do so. Because of that experience, I subconsciously felt
God would not help me either. I didn't openly rebel against or re-
sent God, but felt that I might be forgotten.

Your life experiences may cause you to feel as these people did.
But let me assure you that God will never be a father who comes
home drunk, hides behind a newspaper, beats you, molests you,
lies to you, betrays you, deserts you, or is too busy for you. He is
different. He is a father who "knows the things you have need of"
(Matt. 6:8), and will "give good things to those who ask Him"
(Matt. 7:11). He will never leave or forsake you, He will unfailingly
have your best interest in mind, and He will always have more for
you than you ever dreamed of for yourself.

Examine your relationship with the heavenly Father and see if
any of the following statements apply to you:

_____"I doubt that I am a beloved son or daughter to my heavenly
Father."

___"I feel distant from Him."

___"I am afraid of Him."

___"I am angry with Him."

___"I feel abandoned by Him."

___"The thought of my heavenly Father brings tears of pain rather than tears of joy."

If you checked any one of these statements, you definitely need a greater understanding of your heavenly Father's love for you and view of you. Ask Him to make it clear. Say, "God, I acknowledge You as my heavenly Father today. Heal my heart's misconception of You. Where my earthly father has failed me and I have blamed You, forgive me and take away that hurt. I long to receive the inheritance that You have promised Your children." Determine that you will not close yourself off from the Father who loves you. Give Him a chance to prove Himself faithful and show His power in your behalf.

In my new relationship with God, I was strongly aware of His love, especially His love for *other* people. I didn't believe that He loved *me* as much as He loved *them*. The enormity of residual hurt and unforgiveness from the past, along with guilt, sadness, fear, and hopelessness, all served as a giant barrier that kept me from feeling His love. Because of these things, acknowledging God as *Father* took a great step of faith.

■ ——————— *What the Bible Says About* ——————— ■
Acknowledging God as Father

"I will be a Father to you, and you shall be My sons and daughters," says the LORD Almighty.
2 Corinthians 6:18

As a father has compassion on his children,
so the LORD has compassion on those who fear him.
Psalm 103:13 NIV

Do not fear, little flock, for it is your Father's good pleasure to give you the kingdom.
Luke 12:32

You, O LORD, are our Father;
Our Redeemer from Everlasting is Your name.
   Isaiah 63:16

For the Father judges no one, but has committed all judgment to the Son.
   John 5:22

It's one thing to know Jesus; it's another to know the Father. Salvation's purpose is not only to get us to Christ, but also to get us to the Father where we understand our relationship with our Creator. We may have distorted images of Him because of everything that has happened to us, but we will not be able to see who *we* really are until we are able to see God as *He* really is. Then, out of the context of a relationship that secures and satisfies us, we can begin to grow. There is much healing ahead for us when we do.

ACKNOWLEDGE GOD AS HOLY SPIRIT

When I first heard the names Helper and Comforter in reference to the Holy Spirit, I knew immediately I wanted those attributes of God in my life. I realized that to get them, I first had to acknowledge the Holy Spirit's existence and then invite Him to reside within me. When I did that, I learned three important reasons to be filled with God's Holy Spirit:

- to worship God more fully
- to experience and communicate God's love more completely
- to appropriate God's power in my life more effectively

I have discovered over the years, however, that infilling of the Holy Spirit is ongoing and ever deepening. We have to be willing to open up to each new level and dimension so that He can enable us to accomplish what we could never do without this full measure of His love, power, and life.

If you acknowledge Jesus as Savior and God as Father, you have to acknowledge the Holy Spirit. I've heard certain Christians speak of the Trinity as Father, Son, and H-H-L-L-S-S-P-P-S-S-H-H. They can hardly say "Holy Spirit" without choking, let alone acknowledge His working in their lives. Perhaps it's because they know too little about Him. Or maybe they were in a situation in which odd things were done in the name of the Holy Spirit. (Or perhaps they heard the term Holy Ghost and were afraid of ghosts!) Whatever the reason, let me assure you that the Holy Spirit is the Spirit of God sent by Jesus to give us comfort, to build us up, to guide us in all truth, to bring us spiritual gifts, to help us pray more effectively, and to give us wisdom and revelation. Are there people who can honestly say they don't ever need those things?

The Holy Spirit cannot be ignored. We can't pretend He doesn't exist or say that Jesus didn't mean it when He promised He would send the Holy Spirit to us or suggest that God was just kidding when He said He was pouring out His Spirit on all humankind. The Holy Spirit is not a vapor or a mystical cloud; He is another part of God. (Remember the peel, the flesh, and the core of the apple?) He is God's power and the means by which God speaks to you. If you ignore or reject Him, you will cut off this power and communication from working in your life.

If you can get your lips to say, "Jesus is Lord," you can be sure the Spirit of God is working in your life already. Being filled with the Spirit is mentioned in many Scriptures. Since there seem to be just as many interpretations of them as there are denominations, I'm not going to confine you to mine. Simply ask the Holy Spirit what those Scriptures should mean to you, and leave it in His hands to tell you.

No matter how long you have known the Lord, it's good to say to Him frequently, "God, help me to understand all I need to know about You and the workings of Your Spirit in my life. Fill me with Your Holy Spirit in a fresh new way this day, and work powerfully in me."

When you pray that way, you have just opened up the channel by which God will enable you to do all that you need to do to restore your emotional health. The Bible says, "I will put My Spirit within you and cause you to walk in My statutes, and you will keep My judgments and do them" (Ezek. 36:27). The Holy Spirit works the wholeness of God into us. And there need be no fear or mystery about this because we alone of God's creation have a special place built in us where His Spirit can reside. That place will always be empty until it is filled with Him.

We don't want to have "a form of godliness" but deny "its power" (2 Tim. 3:5); denying God's power limits what God can do in our lives and prevents emotional restoration. Nor do we want to be "always learning and never able to come to the knowledge of the truth" (2 Tim. 3:7). Unless the Holy Spirit coaches us from within, our knowledge of the truth will always be limited, and emotional health will be impossible. Don't limit what God can do in you by failing to acknowledge His Holy Spirit in your life.

■ ————————— *What the Bible Says About* ————————— ■

Acknowledging God as Holy Spirit

Repent, and let every one of you be baptized in the name of Jesus Christ for the remission of sins; and you shall receive the gift of the Holy Spirit. For the promise is to you and to your children, and to all who are afar off, as many as the Lord our God will call.
Acts 2:38–39

If you then, being evil, know how to give good gifts to your children, how much more will your heavenly Father give the Holy Spirit to those who ask Him!
Luke 11:13

However, when He, the Spirit of truth, has come, He will guide you into all truth; for He will not speak on His own authority, but whatever He hears He will speak; and He will tell you things to come.
John 16:13

And I will pray the Father, and He will give you another Helper, that He may abide with you forever—the Spirit of truth, whom the world cannot receive, because it neither sees Him nor knows Him; but you know Him, for He dwells with you and will be in you.
John 14:16–17

ACKNOWLEDGE GOD AS LORD OVER EVERY AREA OF YOUR LIFE

Once I'd begun to know God as Savior, as Father, and as Holy Spirit, I found I needed to expose many areas of my life to His influence. This was difficult because it called for my deepening trust. Until then I'd had few positive experiences with someone other than myself being in control of my life.

In every house I lived in when I was growing up, we always had rooms that no one was allowed to see. They contained a confusing clutter of items rendered useless by their overwhelming number and lack of order. One reason my mother never wanted anyone to come to our house (aside from the fact it was too exhausting for her to keep up a front of normalcy) was that she was afraid someone would see the secret rooms. Those rooms were reflective of our family life. The secret of my mother's mental illness had to be hidden at all costs. When I grew up, it was as if those secret rooms in our home became secret places in my heart. I kept so many parts of me hidden that I lived in terror they would be discovered and I'd be rejected.

When I first received Jesus into my heart, I showed Him into the guest room. The problem was He wasn't content to stay there. He kept knocking on one door after another until I was opening doors to rooms I had never even known were there. He exposed every dark corner of each room to His cleansing light. I soon realized that He wanted me to acknowledge Him as Lord over *every* area of my life.

One such room in my heart was the issue of having children. I married my husband, Michael, about three years after I received Jesus, and because so much was happening in our lives at that time, we never really discussed children. I had a million reasons for not wanting any, not the least of which was the fear that I would perpetuate my own crippled upbringing. I couldn't bear to watch myself destroy an innocent life. As God knocked on one door after another—finances, marriage, attitudes, appearance, friendships—I opened up to His Lordship. Yet I turned a deaf ear as He tapped relentlessly at the door of motherhood, which was dead-bolted by my selfishness and fear. The knocking persisted, however, challenging my daily "Jesus, be Lord over every area of my life" prayer.

One morning about a year after we were married, friends stopped us before church to show off their new son. As I held him briefly, I had a vision of holding a child of my own. As I thought about the incident later in church, the possibility of having a baby suddenly seemed not dreadful but pleasant.

Okay, Lord, I thought, *if we're really supposed to have a child, let me hear something to that effect from Michael.* With that I put the matter totally out of my mind.

Later that afternoon, Michael turned to me and said, "That baby you were holding this morning before church was so cute. Maybe we should have one of our own."

"What?" I said in disbelief. "Are you serious?"

"Sure. Why not? Isn't that what people do?" He asked.

"Yes, but I've never heard you say anything like that before." I remembered my quick prayer that morning. *Lord, it's frightening how fast You can work sometimes,* I thought to myself.

Even though I was still fearful and apprehensive, I knew the time had come when God was going to bring life to a place in me that had died years before. I sensed that allowing Him to be Lord over this area would be a major part of the redemption of all that had been lost in my life.

Giving Him the Run of the House

It's one thing to invite Jesus into the home of your being (being born again); it's another to give Him the run of the house (making Him Lord over your life). Acknowledging Jesus as Savior takes just a moment. Acknowledging Him as Lord takes a lifetime.

The Bible says,

> Trust in the LORD with *all* your heart,
> And lean not on your own understanding;
> In *all* your ways acknowledge Him,
> And He shall direct your paths. (Prov. 3:5–6, emphasis added)

Notice that word *all*. It's very specific. If we want things to work out well, we have to acknowledge Him as Lord over *all* areas of our lives. I had to be willing to give God the right of way by frequently saying, "Jesus, be Lord over every area of my life." Then as He pointed to places where I had not opened the door to His rulership, I let Him in.

I know now that God does this with all people who invite Him to dwell in their lives. Some people give Him total access to the home of their being right away. Others leave Him standing in the entry-way indefinitely. Many people do as I did and allow Him to gain entrance slowly. When He knocks on different doors inside you, just know that He will never bulldoze His way in and break down the walls. He will simply knock persistently and quietly and, as He's invited, will come to gently occupy each corner of your life to clean and rebuild.

In Jesus' time on earth He touched dead bodies and restored them to life. He also touched lepers and restored them to health. He will do as much for you right now. He will never say, "You are untouchable to me; you are too far gone; you smell too bad; your failure is too great; your circumstances are too dead." If something has died in you or your life, God is moved by compassion for it.

Wherever there are dead places in you, He will breathe life into them. He cares about your feelings and weaknesses. He desires to touch you with healing and life, but He will not do it unless you first acknowledge Him as Lord over those areas and invite Him into the situation. The fact that He won't touch those areas without an invitation from you is not an indication that He doesn't care; rather, He has given you a choice. Will you choose to open up and share every part of yourself with Him and let Him reign in your life?

Today my husband and I live in a house that is open, with few walls on the inside. People tell me, "When I come into your house, I can't just stay in the entryway. I have to walk into the living room, kitchen, or den." Because of the lack of barriers, the home itself invites them to move through it. I believe this reflects my relationship with God. My barriers are down, and He is not restricted from going into any area He desires. That doesn't mean I'm perfect. It means I am open to whatever God wants to do in me, no matter how uncomfortable it may feel at the time. The happiest people I know put all of their lives into God's hands, knowing that wherever He is enthroned, no threat of hell can succeed against them.

Acknowledging God over every area of your life is an ongoing act of will. You must get up each morning and say, "God, I acknowledge You as Lord over my life this day and Lord over any troubled or wounded area of my soul." Then God can take all that you have and turn it into all that you need.

■ ——————— *What the Bible Says About* ——————— ■

Acknowledging God as Lord Over Every Area of Your Life

Therefore God also has highly exalted Him and given Him the name which is above every name, that at the name of Jesus every knee should bow, of those in heaven, and of those on earth, and of those under the earth, and that every tongue should confess that Jesus Christ is Lord, to the glory of God the Father.
Philippians 2:9–11

You call Me Teacher and Lord, and you say well, for so I am.
John 13:13

For if we live, we live to the Lord; and if we die, we die to
the Lord. Therefore, whether we live or die, we are the
Lord's.
   Romans 14:8

Jesus said to him, "You shall love the LORD your God with
all your heart, with all your soul, and with all your mind."
   Matthew 22:37

Trust in the LORD with all your heart,
And lean not on your own understanding.
   Proverbs 3:5

■ _____ ■

ACKNOWLEDGE GOD AS A NAME
THAT ANSWERS TO EVERY NEED

A few weeks before I had that talk with Terry about meeting her
pastor, I woke in the middle of the night choking back sobs and
gasping for breath. Feelings of desperate loneliness swept over me
like that of being lost in the dark as a child, and I had a sense of
some strange overpowering and suffocating deathlike presence in
the room with me. I jolted to a sitting position to see, much to my
relief, that I was safe in my own bed.

"Thank God, it's not real," I cried into my hands as I tried to
massage away memories of the all-too-familiar dream.

Part of the emotional torment of the years before I came to the
Lord was recurring nightmares so genuine that when I awoke from
them it took time to determine what was reality and what was not.
In these frightening dreams, I was in a big, dark, empty room that
grew larger and larger until I was overwhelmed and engulfed with
paralyzing fear. The gripping despair I felt from these nightmares
became so intense that gradually it carried over into the daytime as
well.

When I shared these events with Terry, she gave me what
seemed at the time to be very odd advice.

"When that happens," she instructed me, "just speak the name
of Jesus over and over. It will take the fear away."

"That's it?" I replied, doubtful yet willing to do anything she
said if it would help. We had never really discussed the Lord before, so this suggestion seemed very foreign.

I didn't think much about our conversation until the next time I woke out of a nightmare and immediately remembered Terry's advice.

"Jesus," I whispered as I gasped for air. "Jesus!" I called louder and held my breath for a moment. "Jesus, Jesus, Jesus," I said again and again as though clinging for life to the sound of that word. In a few minutes the fear lifted.

It's just as she predicted, I thought to myself in amazement as I rolled over and went back to sleep.

That was my first experience with the power of Jesus' name and I have never forgotten it. If His name had that much effect over the realm of darkness for someone who was not even acquainted with Him, imagine the power of His name for those who know and love Him.

A Name for All Seasons

Certain guarantees and rewards are inherent in simply acknowledging the name of Jesus. For example the Bible says,

> The name of the LORD is a strong tower;
> The righteous run to it and are safe. (Prov. 18:10)

There is a covering of protection over anyone who turns to the name of the Lord. That's why my saying His name over and over, not in a mindless chanting but crying out to Him for help, brought the kingdom of His life to bear upon mine. It's true I had not at that point received Him as Savior, but I was being drawn to Him as the events of several weeks later proved.

The Lord has many names in the Bible, and each one expresses an aspect of His nature or one of His attributes. When we acknowledge Him by those names, we invite Him to be those things to us. For example, He is called Healer. When we say "Jesus, You are my Healer" and mix it with faith, it brings this attribute to bear upon our lives.

One of the reasons we do not have the wholeness, fulfillment, and peace we desire this day is that we have not acknowledged God as the answer to our every need. We think, "He may have given me eternal life, but I don't know if He can handle my financial problems." Or we think, "I know He can lead me to a better job, but I'm not sure if He can mend this marriage." "He healed my back, but I don't know if He can take away my depression." The truth is He is *everything* we need, and we have to remember that always. In fact, it's good to tell yourself daily, "God is everything I need," and then say the name of the Lord that answers your specific need at that moment.

Do you need hope? He is called our Hope. Say, "Jesus, You are my Hope."

Are you weak? He is called our Strengthener. Say, "Jesus, You are my Strengthener."

Do you need advice? He is called Counselor. Say, "Jesus, You are my Counselor."

Do you feel oppressed? He is called Deliverer.

Are you lonely? He is called Companion and Friend.

He is also called Emmanuel, which means God *with* us. He is not some distant, cold being with no interest in you. He is Emmanuel, the God who is with you right now to the degree you acknowledge Him in your life.

I have listed thirty of the names of the Lord in the Bible that would definitely be applicable to someone needing emotional restoration (page 27). There is a name which answers to every need in your life, even if I haven't listed it here.

Read that list over, keeping in mind that God desires to be all those things to you. Add the words "He is my" before each name. Or choose one name applicable to your needs and frequently thank God He is that for you. Acknowledging He *is* these things is the first step toward the realization of His becoming them in your life. Keep in mind that everything about *His* personality is stronger than anything negative in *yours*.

To Develop the Relationship Further

Another good reason to acknowledge the name of the Lord is that Jesus says if we acknowledge Him, He will acknowledge us. And there is an intimacy that grows as long as this acknowledgement is sustained.

When I was locked in the closet for hours at a time I felt helpless and afraid. "They've forgotten me," I cried to myself. "No one remembers I'm here." Because of this experience, I later became fearful that God would forget me too. In the Bible, King David said,

> For there is no one who acknowledges me;
> Refuge has failed me;
> No one cares for my soul. (Ps. 142:4)

This is the way I felt.

Thirty Attributes of the Lord

He is my Restorer (Psalm 23:3)
He is my Comforter (John 14:16)
He is my Strength (Isaiah 12:2)
He is my Redeemer (Isaiah 59:20)
He is my Hope (Psalm 71:5)
He is my Patience (Romans 15:5)
He is my Truth (John 14:6)
He is my Resting Place (Jeremiah 50:6)
He is my Overcomer (John 16:33)
He is my Light (John 8:12)
He is the Power of God (1 Corinthians 1:24)
He is my Bread of Life (John 6:35)
He is my Fortress (Psalm 18:2)
He is my Refuge from the Storm (Isaiah 25:4)
He is my Everlasting Father (Isaiah 9:6)
He is the Author of my Faith (Hebrews 12:2)
He is my Deliverer (Psalm 70:5)
He is my Counselor (Psalm 16:7)
He is my Peace (Ephesians 2:14)
He is my Rewarder (Hebrews 11:6)
He is my Healer (Malachi 4:2)
He is my Shield (Psalm 33:20)
He is my Wisdom of God (1 Corinthians 1:24)
He is my Purifier (Malachi 3:3)
He is my Hiding Place (Psalm 32:7)
He is my Shade from the Heat (Isaiah 25:4)
He is my Refiner (Malachi 3:2–3)
He is my Resurrection (John 11:25)
He is the Lifter of my Head (Psalm 3:3)
He is my Stronghold in the Day of Trouble
(Nahum 1:7)

Emotionally hurting people often feel that no one knows or cares who they really are. But God knows and cares. One common question from people who have been abused is "Where was God when the abuse happened?" The answer is that God is where He is asked to be. He knew and cared that I was locked in that closet. Yet it wasn't until years later when I asked Him to that He released me and healed me of its effects. It would've happened sooner if I had acknowledged Him and made Him Lord over my life sooner. No matter who has deserted or failed us in one way or another in the past, the Lord will always be there for us today. The Bible says,

> When my father and my mother forsake me,
> Then the LORD will take care of me. (Ps. 27:10)

He will never forget us.

Jesus said when you know the truth, you will be set free. I always thought that meant knowing the truth of a situation, but actually it is knowing *God's* truth in *any* situation. And our eyes will never be opened to His truth until our hearts are fully opened to Him.

God is the supreme intellect who created us and knows us better than we will ever know ourselves. He is powerful in our behalf and loves us to the fullest possible measure. Without Him, complete healing won't happen in our lives. All the things that need to be worked in us will never come about. Acknowledging Him as the answer to every need is the very foundation upon which wholeness is built and the first step toward emotional health. But there are many ways to do that; if you want it all you have to do it all in terms of what He requires.

■ ——————— *What the Bible Says About* ——————— ■

Acknowledging God as a Name That Answers to Every Need

Whoever calls upon the name of the LORD shall be saved.
Romans 10:13

Our help is in the name of the LORD.
Psalm 124:8

They will call on My name,
And I will answer them.
I will say, "This is My people";
And each one will say, "The LORD is my God."
   Zechariah 13:9

Therefore God also has highly exalted Him and given Him the name which is above every name.
   Philippians 2:9

Whoever acknowledges me before men, I will also acknowledge him before my Father in heaven.
   Matthew 10:32 NIV

CHAPTER 3

Step Two:
Lay a Foundation

I'm still on shaky ground," I said to myself as I drove to church one Sunday morning nearly a year after coming to know the Lord. Even though my life was much improved, I still had this uneasy feeling that at any moment I could lose the stability I'd gained. I feared that my glimpses of hope for the future would all come to nothing.

It was obvious that I had made *some* progress since that day in October with Terry and Pastor Jack. After all, in the beginning of my relationship with the Lord, I wasn't even able to get myself to church. For months Terry and her husband woke me on Sunday mornings with a phone call and then drove out of their way to pick me up, knowing I wasn't strong enough to get there on my own. After they stopped taking me, my attendance was sporadic for a time until I resolved to get myself to church regularly *without* their assistance. Now as I was driving myself there for the fifth consecutive Sunday morning, I thought about what I had been learning.

I'd heard Pastor Jack preach every week about "moving on with the Lord," and it was finally starting to register. Each time he mentioned it, he waved his arm slowly across the congregation, like a shepherd trying to move his sheep in a certain direction. *Oh, so you don't just stay in one place after you receive the Lord. You have to start growing*, I realized one morning as he waved his arm over the congregation again.

I thought after you received Jesus into your life, that was it. You'd made it. No more problems. But I was finding that wasn't the case. The truth is, I *had* made it into eternity by securing life after death. However, my life here on earth still needed work. I had to do certain things daily to sustain life and become spiritually and emotionally healthy. What a revelation! Having pursued physical fitness and the concept of proper body care for many years, I quickly related to this discipline—doing something good for yourself, no matter how much you *didn't* feel like doing it, so that you would be able to enjoy good health and well being. I began to understand that just as the physical body needs to be fed, exercised, and cleansed, so the spirit and soul need replenishing.

My foundation isn't as strong as it should be, I thought in church that morning. *That must be why I have times of doubt and feel like I'm on shaky ground. God, show me how to strengthen my relationship with You so that my foundation becomes solid.*

Over the next eight months I discovered five key elements that can be put together to strengthen our relationship with God, unlock any hidden emotional closet, and make an unshakable foundation upon which to build emotional wholeness. These five rocks of spiritual building are: the Word of God, prayer, praise, confession, and ongoing forgiveness. *The more thoroughly these foundational steps become a way of life, the more profound and speedy the healing process will be.* By neglecting even one of them, we end up with cracks in our foundation.

Some people do "get by" never doing any of these things, but I wasn't interested in getting by. I'd been doing that for years. I wanted to be restored to wholeness. To do that, I had to nurture my relationship with God, and spend quality time in His presence. This key—His presence—is the foundation for emotional health.

■ —————— *What the Bible Says About* —————— ■
Laying a Foundation

For no other foundation can anyone lay than that which is laid, which is Jesus Christ.
1 Corinthians 3:11

Rooted and built up in Him and established in the faith, as you have been taught, abounding in it with thanksgiving.
Colossians 2:7

When the whirlwind passes by, the wicked is no more,
But the righteous has an everlasting foundation.
Proverbs 10:25

Whoever hears these sayings of Mine, and does them, I will liken him to a wise man who built his house on the rock.
Matthew 7:24

Nevertheless the solid foundation of God stands, having this seal: "The Lord knows those who are His," and, "Let everyone who names the name of Christ depart from iniquity."

2 Timothy 2:19

■   ■

LAY A FOUNDATION IN GOD'S WORD

First, Pastor Jack asks us to bring our own Bible; now he wants us to read it ourselves? I thought incredulously as he encouraged us to "move on" once again, this time in the Word of God. I had purchased a Bible in a translation that I could understand just as he requested, but I thought that *he* would teach us from it and we would follow along.

I had given up trying to read the Bible years ago when several unsuccessful attempts brought discouragement and frustration. I found the writing so foreign I couldn't understand it at all. But Pastor Jack taught from the Scriptures with amazing clarity, and I hung on every word. It was like watching a movie so reflective of my own life that I became involved in the action.

Could it be, I asked myself, *that I might feel that same way when I read the Bible at home alone?*

The next morning I began reading in Psalms and Proverbs, which had short chapters and seemed to be safe enough for me to tackle. Over the following weeks I branched out in the Gospels of Matthew, Mark, Luke, and John. I was surprised at the way every word came alive with new meaning. Soon I had such a desire to know the whole story that I started at the beginning of the Bible and read straight through to the end. When I finished months later, I felt as if I knew the heart of the Author and my life had been changed.

While I was reading semi-faithfully each day, I noticed distinct and undeniable benefits. For example, I had been experiencing difficulty in thinking clearly, yet I found that I had noticeable mental clarity after I read the Bible. I discovered it was especially beneficial to read Scripture the first thing in the morning because it set my heart and mind on the right course for the day. Also reading the Bible before I went to bed at night insured that I would sleep without nightmares, which had been a problem for as long as I could remember.

Gradually the Bible became God's voice in my ear. When I heard

certain old, familiar words in my mind, such as *You're worthless.*
You'll never amount to anything. Why try? I also heard the words of
God saying, *You are fearfully and wonderfully made. I will lift you up*
from the gates of death. You will be blessed if you put your trust in Me
(Ps. 139:14, Ps. 9:13, Ps. 2:12).

The more I read, the more I saw that God's laws were good.
They were there for my benefit, and I could trust them. It became
clear to me that conscience wasn't an adequate indicator of right or
wrong. I could see that things can really only be found right or
wrong in the light of God's Word. Such guidelines, rather than re-
stricting, were actually liberating to me.

Even when His Word did not specifically say this is right or this
is wrong, my spirit became so aligned with His that I could sense
what was correct thought and action. For example, while the Bible
did say not to be drunk, I no longer felt it was even a good idea for
me to drink alcohol for a "relaxed" feeling, especially in light of my
history of alcohol and drug abuse. Besides, the high I was getting
from being in the presence of the Lord was far greater than any I
could derive from other sources. This was just one of many beginning signs of emotional maturity and wholeness that were being
worked in my soul, the foundation of which was laid in the Word of
God.

What? Me Read?

You may be thinking, *I can't afford the time it takes to read the*
Bible every day. But let me assure you that anyone who has deep
emotional hurts cannot afford to let a day go by without absorbing
at least a few verses of the Word into their heart and mind. This
doesn't mean that reading the Word will instantly heal your
wounds. It may do that or it may not. But it will always create a
favorable climate in your spirit and soul in which that can happen.

Good relationships, good health, being good at what you do—
they all require some sacrifice, some discipline, some discomfort,
and even some pain. Emotional health is like that, too. Reading
God's Word must become a daily discipline because we need a solid
grasp of the way God intends us to live. The Bible says, "Man shall
not live by bread alone, but by every word that proceeds from the
mouth of God" (Matt. 4:4). Regular feeding on God's Word satisfies the hunger of our souls and keeps us from emotional depletion
and spiritual starvation.

Perhaps you feel as I did at one point, *How can I be sure that the*
Bible is really God's Word? I reply to that question by asking an-

other. How can you be sure it isn't? The only way you can know about a book for certain is to read it straight through. You can't judge the Author unless you've read His book.

Don't let *other* people tell you what God's Word says (even if they're great Bible teachers like Pastor Jack); read it for yourself, keeping in mind that it was written for *you*. Get up early to read the Bible in the morning, if at all possible, in order to set the tone for the day. If you can't read then, decide when you can. Midmorning? Lunch hour? After dinner? Before bed? Make this an appointment with God and write it down on your calendar. Lock yourself in the bathroom if necessary.

If the Bible you're reading is difficult to understand, then get hold of another translation. I have used the New King James and New International Version in this book; other versions, such as the New American Standard, the Amplified, or the Living Bible, are also easy to read. If you can't afford to buy a more readable translation, ask around for one. Make a bold request of the pastor or chaplain. There are people all over the world who would like nothing better than to give you a Bible if you just let them know your needs.

What If I'm Hurting?

At times in my battle with fear and depression I sat down to read the Word of God feeling so depleted, numb, or preoccupied with my mental state that I could hardly even comprehend the words. I not only didn't feel close to God but felt it futile to hope He could ever change me or my life in any lasting way. In spite of that, as I read I was struck by a remarkable lifting of those negative emotions. Afterward I may not have been able to pass a Bible school quiz on the passage, but I felt renewed, strengthened, and hopeful.

When you feel confused, fearful, depressed, or anxious, take the Bible in hand and say, "This book is on my side. My soul is starving, and this is food for my spirit. I want to do the right thing and reading the Bible is always the right thing to do. Lord, I thank You for Your Word. Reveal Yourself to me as I read it and let it come alive in my heart and mind. Show me what I need to know for my life today. Let Your Word penetrate through anything that would block me from receiving it." Then begin to read until you sense peace coming into your heart.

While the Bible was written to give you knowledge of the Lord, it takes the Holy Spirit to bring a particular Scripture alive to your heart. When that happens, take it as God speaking words of comfort, hope, and guidance directly to you. The Bible says, "For

Fifteen Reasons to Read the Bible Daily

To be rid of anxiety and have peace (Psalm 119:165)

To set things right when life feels out of control
(Psalm 19:7–8)

To have direction and guidance (Psalm 119:105)

To experience healing and deliverance (Psalm 107:20)

To grow in the Lord (1 Peter 2:2)

To have strength, comfort, and hope
(Psalm 119:28, 50, 114)

To shape yourself and your life correctly (Psalm 119:11)

To be able to see clearly (Psalm 119:130)

To know what's really in your heart (Hebrews 4:12)

To build faith (Romans 10:17)

To have joy (Psalm 19:8)

To understand God's power (John 1:1)

To have more life in this life (Psalm 119:50)

To distinguish good from evil (Psalm 119:101–102)

To understand God's love for you (John 1:14)

whatever things were written before were written for our learning, that we through the patience and comfort of the Scriptures might have hope" (Rom. 15:4).

If you find that no matter how much you read you still don't feel any of the effects I have listed on page 35 happening in your life or you feel as if nothing is getting through, then you probably need deliverance. There may be a cloud of bondage and oppression between God's Word and your heart. It could be that major strongholds of unforgiveness, fear, doubt, suicidal thoughts, bitterness, or disobedience are separating you from all God has for you. I'll go into detail about that in Chapter 5. For now, just keep reading the Word because something of God's nature is getting through to your spirit whether you feel it at the moment or not.

I Already Know All That!

Don't say, "I've already read the Bible, I've memorized a hundred Scriptures, and I even teach Bible classes, so I don't need to read it every day." This is dangerous thinking. Whenever you eat food or drink water, you don't say, "I won't have to do that again," do you? Of course not. Your body needs to be fed daily. The same goes for your spiritual and emotional self. And because you're not the same person today as you were the day before, you will receive from God's Word in a new and different way today. In fact, if you've read your Bible many, many times, buy a *new* Bible in a different translation or the same translation in a different form, and read through it again. You'll be surprised how new and fresh the Word is to you.

Some groups of people reject God's Word by setting for themselves a lifestyle that opposes God's design for our lives. They believe they know it all and don't need His truth. However, if you watch long enough, you'll eventually see them destroy themselves. It may appear to be working for a time, but don't be deceived into thinking it always will. Anyone who *rejects* God's truth will always wind up the loser. We also lose part of our protective armor when we *know* God's truth but don't allow it regular opportunity to penetrate our lives in new and fresh ways.

It helps to keep in mind that the Bible is God's love letter to *you*. When you receive letters from someone you love, you don't just read them once and never look at them again. You pore over them time after time, drinking in the very essence of that person, looking between the lines for any and every possible message. God's love letters to you are full of messages. They say, "This is how much I love you." They do *not* say, "These are the things you need to do to *get* Me to love you." The Bible is not just a collection of information, it is a book of life. It's not to be read like a ritual or out of fear that something bad will happen if you don't. It's to be read so God can build you up in His love from the inside out, and brand His nature into your heart so that nothing can keep you away from His presence.

■ —————— *What the Bible Says About* —————— ■
God's Word

If you abide in Me, and My words abide in you, you will ask what you desire, and it shall be done for you.
John 15:7

For the word of God is living and powerful, and sharper than any two-edged sword, piercing even to the division of soul and spirit, and of joints and marrow, and is a discerner of the thoughts and intents of the heart.
Hebrews 4:12

He sent His word and healed them,
And delivered them from their destructions.
Psalm 107:20

The testimony of the LORD is sure, making wise the simple;
The statutes of the LORD are right, rejoicing the heart;
The commandment of the LORD is pure, enlightening
the eyes.
Psalm 19:7–8

The grass withers, the flower fades,
But the word of our God stands forever.
Isaiah 40:8

LAY A FOUNDATION IN PRAYER

During the first couple of years I walked with the Lord, my prayers went something like this:

- "God, help me to get that job."
- "Jesus, please heal my throat."
- "Lord, send enough money to pay these bills."
- "Father, take away my fear."

It took me a while to realize that those spur-of-the-moment prayers were not accomplishing much. I guess I thought the idea was to do the best I could on my own, and then if I needed a lifeline from God, I grabbed for it. The only problem was I needed a lifeline every other minute.

I loved the Scripture that says, "Ask, and it will be given to you; seek, and you will find; knock, and it will be opened to you" (Matt. 7:7). I took God at His Word and was asking, seeking, and knocking on a pray-as-you-go basis. I also took to heart the Scripture that says, "You do not have because you do not ask" (James 4:2). *Great! I can easily remedy that,* I thought, and I proceeded to ask for everything. But I was still not happy, and I didn't see the kind of answered prayer I desired.

One day as I was again reading that same verse, my eyes were opened to the next verse, "You ask and do not receive, because you ask amiss, that you may spend it on your pleasures" (James 4:3). Could it be that the "God-give-me-this, do-that, wave-your-magic-wand-here, get-me-out-of-this-mess" kind of praying was not what God desired for my prayer life? In utter frustration I said, "Lord, teach me how I'm supposed to pray."

He did exactly that!

I came to understand that prayer is not just asking for things—although that certainly is part of it. Far more importantly, prayer is talking with God. It's getting close to and spending time with the one you love. It's seeking Him first, touching Him, getting to know Him better, being with Him, and waiting in His presence. It's acknowledging Him as the source of power upon whom you depend. It's taking the time to say, *Speak to my heart, Lord, and tell me what I need to hear.*

When I came across the Scripture that says, "For your Father knows the things you have need of before you ask Him" (Matt. 6:8), I was puzzled.

"If God already knows what I need, why do I even need to ask for anything?" I questioned Pastor Jack.

In his usual clear manner, he explained, "Because God has given us a free will. He has set it up so that we always have a choice about everything we do, including whether or not we choose to communicate with Him. He will never intervene where man does not want Him."

Of course! I thought. *God wants us to desire to be with Him. There is no love relationship if one person has to dictate how the other must think, feel, and act toward them.*

"God *knows* our thoughts," Pastor Jack continued, "but He *responds* to our prayers. We have to come to a place of realizing that prayer is a *privilege* that is always *ours*, but the *power* in prayer is always *His*. *Without God, we can't do it. Without us, God won't do it.*"

That put a whole new perspective on the subject. Things wouldn't happen in my life unless I prayed. And I was no longer just asking for things, I was partnering with God. I was aligning my spirit with His, and together we would see that *His* perfect will would be done.

One significant example of this was my prayer for a husband. After the failure of my first marriage, I seriously doubted I could ever be happily married. Yet that was what I wanted most.

Will there ever be someone with whom I can share my life? I wondered, *someone I can love without being rejected? Someone who loves God and me and will be faithful to both of us?*

I had only known the Lord about two years when I started dating Michael Omartian, and I was desperately afraid of making another mistake. But God had taught me how to pray about such matters, so that's what I did.

"Lord, I thank you for Michael," I prayed every day, "but if he is not the husband You have for me, take him out of my life. Close the door on our relationship. I don't want to live my way anymore. I want *Your* will to be done in my life. I seek You first, knowing You will provide all that I need."

The more I prayed that prayer, the closer Michael and I became until finally we were both certain we were to be together. Now, in the eighteen years we've been married, neither of us has wondered if we married the wrong person, even during the toughest times. That's because our relationship was covered and committed to God in prayer from the beginning. And we know that prayer has held us together. Being able to come into God's presence with our hearts open to being changed kept us growing together instead of falling apart. Prayer and our commitment to doing things God's way have kept us out of divorce court when our flesh might have welcomed it in weak moments.

From an issue as major as marrying the right person, to something as minor as preparing a meal (which can be major to someone with emotional damage), everything I did was covered in prayer. Little by little the fabric of my life began to change, and wholeness crept into it the way damaged cells repair themselves in response to a healing ointmemt.

How to Pray Effectively

You know how friends can become emotionally separated when they don't see each other and communicate frequently. Well, it's the same with you and God. If you don't keep in touch with Him, you begin to feel distant from Him even when you're not. This is why you must pray daily. Also, when you spend time with someone you respect, the character of that person rubs off on you. When you are in the presence of God, His character is formed *in* you.

People with deep emotional wounds are especially vulnerable to the enemy's attack on their self-worth. It doesn't take much to push them over the edge into despair, and feeling distant from God will do it. That's why it's important to start the day first thing with some kind of prayer. We have to establish ourselves and our lives as being connected to Him.

We can't receive God's best for our lives, and we can't push back the things that were never God's will for us, except through prayer. We have to remember the many reasons to pray (see page 41) and get in the habit of not making prayer a last resort. We have to learn that we can't leave our life to chance. We have to pray about everything all the time, not just when things go wrong. We have to pray over anything that concerns us, no matter how big—"With God nothing will be impossible" (Luke 1:37)—or how small—"The very hairs of your head are all numbered" (Matt. 10:30).

Do whatever you have to do to secure a place and time to pray. When I was single and during the first few years of marriage, that was not a problem. However, after our first child was born it was much more difficult. When our second child arrived, the only way I could spend time with the Lord was to get up at 5:30 A.M. The only place I could go at that hour and not disturb anyone was a small walk-in closet off the master bath. What a contrast with my early years of being locked in the closet for punishment! Now I went there to commune with God. This went well for a while until I was discovered. First I was visited regularly by my eighteen-month-old daughter, who learned to climb out of her crib and come looking for me. Soon she was followed by her six-year-old brother. One morning, when both of them, plus my husband, two dogs, and

Fifteen Reasons to Pray

To seek the face of the Lord and know Him better
(Psalm 27:8)

To get your eyes off your problems and on to the Lord
(Psalm 121:1)

To speak to God (1 Peter 3:12)

To unburden your heart (Psalm 142:1–2)

To make your requests known to God (Matthew 21:22)

To hear God (Proverbs 8:34)

To be free of suffering (James 5:13)

To resist temptation (Matthew 26:41)

To be rescued from distress (Psalm 107:19)

To receive God's reward (Matthew 6:6)

To withstand evil (Ephesians 6:13)

To have joy (John 16:24)

To get close to God (Isaiah 64:7)

To be healed emotionally (James 5:13)

To have peace (Philippians 4:6, 7)

several hamsters, ended up in the closet, I knew it was time either to get up earlier or to find a new location. Sometimes we have to revise our plans, but securing a time and place to be alone with God is worth any effort.

Without reducing prayer to a formula, I found that it is good to include certain key points in each prayer time:

- Tell the Lord how much you love Him.
- Thank Him for all He has done for you.
- State how dependent you are upon Him.
- Tell Him everything that's in your heart.
- Confess anything that needs to be confessed.
- Give Him all your requests.
- Wait for Him to speak to your heart.
- Praise Him for working powerfully in your life.

Don't ever feel inhibited because you think you can't pray. If you can talk, you can pray. And don't be concerned about prayer talk, church talk, or Christianese talk—the Bible tells us the only qualification: "He who comes to God must believe that He is, and that He is a rewarder of those who diligently seek Him" (Heb. 11:6).

The more you pray, the more you will find to pray about, and the more you'll be led to pray for others: family members, friends, enemies, and all those in authority in any area of your life (pastor, teacher, boss, governor, president). You'll pray for them not only because they influence your emotional health and part of the peace you experience will result directly from that type of praying, but because Jesus asked us to do it.

What If God Won't Listen?

You can never be disqualified for prayer so don't be discouraged by negative thoughts like

- *You're not good enough to come before God's throne.*
- *You've failed again, so don't come crying back to God.*

Lies, lies, lies! Don't listen to any of them. Picture a Father who never works late, never ignores or rejects you, is never too busy, and is always waiting for you to come and talk with Him. And even though you have many brothers and sisters, you are never in competition with them because He has no favorites. I know that kind of love is hard to receive if you've never been loved like that as a child, but that's your heavenly Father's availability for you. As Pastor Jack Hayford so succinctly puts it, "Your heavenly Father is waiting to hear from you. Call home!"

Don't allow discouragement over unanswered prayer to cause you to doubt that God has heard you. If you have received Jesus and are praying in His name, then God hears you, and something is happening whether you see it manifested in your life now or not. In fact, every time you pray, you're advancing God's purposes for you. Without prayer, the full purpose God has for you can't happen.

Power in Numbers

It's important to understand that emotional restoration depends upon two kinds of regular prayer. One is deep, intimate prayer alone—just you and God. The other is prayer together with other believers—praying for one another. The battle to confront evil and push hell back from our lives becomes far too overwhelming to fight entirely alone. We need others praying with us to give us strength, to help us think straight, to lift our vision above our circumstances.

The Bible says, "Where two or three are gathered together in My name, I am there in the midst of them" (Matt. 18:20). There is power in two or more people praying together because God's presence attends it. This is one of His promises, and when He promises something, He doesn't *try* to keep His promises, as you and I do; He *does* keep them. Having one or more regular prayer partners is especially crucial to anyone coming out of a background of deep emotional wounds. I don't believe you can find the degree of restoration you want until people are standing with you in prayer.

Diane, my best friend since high school, came to know the Lord within a year after I did and started attending the same church. Because we had similar dysfunctional family situations, we understood each other's prayer needs and fell into the habit of praying regularly together over the phone several times a week. Through each low time of discouragement, each difficult decision, our prayers for one another were instrumental in our spiritual growth and emotional healing. I found you can only pray so much for yourself without getting bored or frustrated because of being too close to your own situation. It was actually easier to pray for *her* than it was to pray for myself, because there was no end to the possibilities I could see for her.

Gradually my prayer partners increased from one to three, then five, and now seven. We meet in my home one morning a week, and also seven couples meet with Michael and me once a month. With that many people united in prayer for one another, someone is praying for each member all the time. I can't imagine facing life without that support.

You need one or more persons with whom you can pray and agree every month, every week, or every day if need be. This must go two ways, though. *You* must be praying for *them*, also. Don't be afraid, shy, or hesitant to take this crucial step. Ask God to lead you to at least one other believer, and be bold enough to ask that person if he or she wants to pray with you regularly. If the first person you ask can't do it or doesn't work out, don't feel rejected or get discouraged, just keep looking for the right one. And don't hesitate to pray for someone because you fear your prayers won't be answered, as I did in the beginning. *Remember your job is to do the praying; it's God's job to answer the prayers.*

If you are blessed enough to have a husband or wife who will pray with you regularly, that's excellent. However, if your spouse seems less than enthusiastic about the idea, don't fret, badger, or nag. We can never dictate how other people are supposed to act, *especially* husbands and wives. Just let it go. Your healing, wholeness, and happiness doesn't depend on them. It depends on God. Don't allow disappointment in your spouse's spirituality to deter your own healing. This is a trap of the enemy to cause strife in the home and keep you from moving into all the Lord has for you.

Whether you pray with others or you pray alone, it's beneficial to read the Word of God *before* you pray because it prepares your heart to pray according to God's will. Have a pencil and paper with you so you can write down anything the Lord speaks to your heart. If you need an ability to pray beyond your own capabilities because you are too weak, too upset, or too frightened, ask the Holy Spirit to help you.

Once you pray about anything, put it in God's hands. That doesn't mean you don't pray about it again; it just means that you have laid that burden at the Lord's feet. It might not be the way you expect or according to your timing, but the answer will *always* come. Most importantly, you have spent time in the Lord's presence, which lays a foundation for your total restoration.

What the Bible Says About
Prayer

The effective, fervent prayer of a righteous man avails much.
   James 5:16

"And whatever things, you ask in prayer, believing, you will receive."
   Matthew 21:22

I cry out to the LORD with my voice. . . .
I pour out my complaint before Him;
I declare before Him my trouble.
   Psalm 142:1-2

Is anyone among you suffering? Let him pray.
   James 5:13

"For the eyes of the LORD are on the righteous,
And His ears are open to their prayers."
   1 Peter 3:12

LAY A FOUNDATION IN PRAISE

"I can't do it!" I cried to God in prayer shortly after Michael and I were married. "I can't handle the dishes—I can't handle the house—I can't handle my work—I can't handle the loneliness of being a wife of someone who works all the time—I can't deal with my own emotional ups and downs, let alone his! I can't do any of it, God, not any of it." I wept before the Lord with a mixture of frustration and guilt over the fact that I was feeling this way about my husband, my home, and my life. God had rescued me from the pit of hell and death just three years before and had given me hope and a future. How could I—who knew what it was to be hungry and poor and feel there was no love or purpose in my life—tell God I couldn't handle these answers to my own prayers?

Fortunately, the Lord did not strike me with lightning; instead He waited quietly until I was finished and then softly reminded me,

You are trying to do everything in your own strength. As I sat there in my discouragement, I sensed the Holy Spirit speaking to my heart saying simply, *All you have to do is worship Me in the midst of what you are facing and I will do the rest.*

"Oh, thank you, Lord," I prayed through my tears. "I think I can at least handle doing that much."

I lifted my hands and said out loud, "Lord, I praise You in the midst of my situation. Thank You that You are all powerful and there is nothing too hard for You. Thank You for who You are and all You have done for me. I worship You, Jesus, Almighty God, Holy Father, Lord of my life." As I continued to praise and thank God for all that He is, that hopelessly out-of-control feeling diminished.

"Lord, I give You my home, my marriage, my husband, and my work. They are Yours," I said as my shoulders relaxed, the knot in my stomach left, and I sighed with tears of relief. The pressure was off. The burden now was *His.* I didn't have to try to be perfect anymore, and I didn't have to beat myself up when I wasn't.

Since that time, praise has become an habitual attitude of my heart that says, "No matter what is going on in and around me, *God is in charge!* I trust Him to bring good out of this situation and work things out for my highest blessing."

Praise is not always my first reaction to things, so I often have to remind myself of Pastor Jack Hayford's teaching on praise: "It's not your saying, 'I'll give it everything I've got and the Lord will bless it,' but rather it's the Lord saying to you, 'You just bless My name and *I'll* give it everything *I* have.'" Now, when I come to the place where my flesh can't go any further, I stop where I am and worship God. This key has unlocked even the heaviest of closet doors and illuminates the darkest of nights.

A Key to Transformation

Worship is powerful because God's presence comes to dwell in our midst when we praise Him. In His presence we find healing and transformation for our lives. In fact, the more time we spend praising the Lord, the more we will see ourselves and our circumstances grow in wholeness. That's because praise softens our hearts and makes them pliable. It also covers us protectively. The more the pliability and covering are maintained, the more quickly our hearts can be molded and healed.

Please read the preceding paragraph again. Underline it, circle it, draw arrows pointing to it, commit it to memory, write it on your hand, or do whatever you have to do to remember it. It is the first thing we forget and the last thing we remember because our flesh doesn't naturally want to do it.

Praise and worship of God are always acts of will. We have to *will* to praise God even when we don't feel like it. Sometimes our problems or the burdens we carry choke out our good intentions, so we have to make the effort to establish praise as a way of life. And it becomes a way of life when we make it our *first* reaction to what we face and not a last resort. *Now* is the time to start being thankful to God for everything in your life. Thank Him for His Word, His faithfulness, His love, His grace, His healing. Thank Him for what He has done for you personally. If you have trouble thinking of something, then thank Him that you're still breathing and you can read. Keep in mind that whatever you thank the Lord for—peace, financial blessing, health, a new job, an end to depression—will start the process of its being released to you at that time.

In the Old Testament, the people who carried the Ark of the Covenant stopped every six steps to worship. We also have to remind ourselves not to go very far without stopping to worship. For emotional healing and restoration, we have to be six-step persons and continually invite the presence of the Lord to rule in our situations.

The reason people don't give thanks to God in praise is because they don't know Him well enough. The more you know of Him, the more you perceive His goodness, the more you can't help but thank, praise, and worship Him for who He is and what He has done. The more you do that, the more joy you will have in your heart. Pastor Jack Hayford describes joy as "that inner happy confidence that there is nothing that can successfully resist the inevitability of Christ's certain triumph in me." What a wonderful thing to know about yourself. Such knowledge of the Lord is the foundation for your healing.

Worship, God's Way

To have the healing and wholeness we desire, we must worship God *His* way. However, *His* way often doesn't fit our schedule or style. I have found several ways to praise God, ways that don't always come easily but are crucial to emotional healing. Pliability in praise brings a powerful release.

Fifteen Reasons to Praise the Lord

To enthrone God and acknowledge His greatness
(Psalm 95:1–5)

To increase our awareness of God's presence
(Psalm 103)

To have the joy of the Lord (Psalm 30)

To acknowledge God's hand in every area of our lives
(Psalm 91)

To release God's power into our situations (Psalm 144)

To know God better (Psalm 50:23)

To break our chains of bondage and bring deliverance
(Psalm 50:14–15)

To be under His covering of safety and protection
(Psalm 95:6–7)

To strengthen the soul and be transformed
(Psalm 138:1–3)

To receive guidance and establish God's purposes in our
lives (Psalm 16:7–11)

To thwart the devil's plans for our destruction
(Psalm 92)

To dissipate doubt and increase faith (Psalm 27)

To be delivered from fear (Psalm 34)

To bring a fresh flow of His Holy Spirit in us
(Psalm 40)

To possess all God has promised for us (Psalm 147)

1. *Praise is meant to be sung.* King David says in Psalm 147:1:

> It is good to sing praises to our God;
> For it is pleasant, and praise is beautiful.

This is often hard for us because at times singing is the last thing we feel like doing or we're so self-conscious about our voices that we don't open our mouths, even when we're alone. Yet in the Bible the singers went before the troops into battle. Their singing praises to God confused the enemy. It works exactly the same way for us today.

Many times my soul was tormented with such depression in the middle of the night that I got up, shut myself in my prayer closet so I wouldn't wake anyone, and sang softly to the Lord. I'd sing a hymn, or a chorus, or make up a song. Sometimes all I could sing was "Thank you, Jesus. Praise you, Lord" over and over until I felt the oppression leave and strength and life come into my soul.

You may be so depressed or hurting that you feel you can't even unclench your jaw. When that happens say, "God give me a song in my heart that I can sing to you" and begin to hum to the Lord any melody that comes to mind. Then put words to it that are from your heart to God. Don't worry about the pitch, the rhythm, the melody, or the sound of your voice. Sing it all on one note if you want. Remember, the true singer is the one who has God's song in his heart. The Lord thinks your voice is beautiful. He designed it for the purpose of praising Him. Continue to sing over your situation because, as you do, something is happening in the spirit realm and you will feel the heaviness lift.

2. *Praise is meant to be expressed with the lifting of your hands.*

> Lift up your hands in the sanctuary,
> And bless the LORD. (Ps. 134:2)

Lifting our hands to the Lord as we praise God is also an act of the will that is not second nature to us. It is really not the strength of our arms that lifts our hands, but rather it is the heart. When our hearts are full of thanks to God, it's far easier to lift up our hands and praise Him. However, when our hearts are heavy, sad, depressed, angry, discouraged, or tired, we still must make ourselves lift them up. Worship is the exercise of spirit overcoming our flesh. We have to talk to our spirit and say, "I *will* rejoice and be glad. I *will* lift my hands to the Lord." We can't wait for good feelings first. We have to lift our hands and let go of ourselves so the joy of the Lord can rise in our hearts.

The most important reason for you to do this is to let go of everything you're holding onto and surrender to God: "I give up, Lord." You can also think of it as taking your life in your hands and offering it up to Him. "I give You everything of myself, Lord."

The more you lift up to God in submission, the more freedom you will know. Remember, everything God asks you to do is for *your* benefit, not His. He doesn't ask you to do things that will embarrass you or make you feel stupid. He asks you to do things that will make you more whole.

3. *Praise is meant to be done together with others as well as alone.* "In the midst of the assembly I will sing praise to You" (Heb. 2:12). I used to hurry into the church twenty minutes late on Sunday mornings. By the time I found a seat and settled into it, the worship time was over and the pastor was preaching. I wasn't concerned about this because I was there for the teaching. Yet my mind wandered everywhere and didn't settle into the message until the sermon was half over.

On the days I arrived in plenty of time to get a seat *before* the service started and was a full participant through the entire worship time, I found I was open to receive the message as if God was speaking directly to me. My heart was made soft and receptive to what the Holy Spirit wanted to teach me because of the twenty or thirty minutes I had spent worshiping God in unity with other believers. Negative attitudes I had come in with were melted away and replaced with ones more in alignment with what God desired. I was made ready and open to receive from God.

Don't miss times of worship with other believers. Corporate worship is powerful to the point of breaking down strongholds in your life and allowing changes that might not take place otherwise. Many negative emotions will be released from your heart in group worship. And it will be a protection against all that steals life away from you.

A Weapon Against Futility

Without praise we experience an eroding that leads to bondage and death. The Bible says, "Although they knew God, they did not glorify Him as God, nor were thankful, but became *futile* in their *thoughts,* and their foolish *hearts* were *darkened*" (Rom. 1:21, emphasis added). *With* praise you and your circumstances can be changed, because it gives God entrance into every area of your life and allows Him to be enthroned there.

So any time you struggle with negative emotions, such as anger, unforgiveness, fear, hurt, oppression, depression, self-hatred, or worthlessness, thank God that He is bigger than all that. Thank Him that His plans and purposes for you are good. Thank Him that in any weak area of your life, He will be strong. Thank Him that He came to restore you. Remember the names of the Lord, and use them in your worship. "I praise You, Lord, because You are my Deliverer and Redeemer." "Thank You, God, that You are my Healer and Provider." Once you align yourself with God's purposes through praise, you can claim things that you can't see yet in your life as though they were there. "Lord, I have absolutely no way to make my healing come about, but You are all powerful and can make it happen. I thank You and praise You for Your healing power in my life." Doing this is your greatest weapon against the feelings of inadequacy, purposelessness, and futility that undermine all God has made you to be.

Those of us with deep emotional hurts can never find total restoration outside of the presence of God, and praise lifts us powerfully into His presence, where we will find healing and deliverance. Don't ever neglect this key in your foundation. Your life of wholeness will be supported by it.

■ ———————— *What the Bible Says About* ———————— ■
Praise

Let us continually offer the sacrifice of praise to God, that is, the fruit of our lips, giving thanks to His name.
Hebrews 13:15

But the hour is coming, and now is, when the true worshipers will worship the Father in spirit and truth; for the Father is seeking such to worship Him.
John 4:23

Rejoice always . . . in everything give thanks; for this is the will of God in Christ Jesus for you.
1 Thessalonians 5:16–18

I will render praises to You,
For You have delivered my soul from death.
   Psalm 56:12b–13a

That you may proclaim the praises of Him who called you
out of darkness into His marvelous light.
   1 Peter 2:9

■   ■

LAY A FOUNDATION IN CONFESSION

In spite of how much God's Word was feeding my soul and
alleviating my fear, and even though I was spending much time
in the presence of the Lord in prayer and praise, I was still experiencing the intense periodic depressions I had struggled with
for years. In fact, the entire first year I was married they seemed
to be getting worse instead of better. When I started feeling extremely suicidal, Michael suggested I call the church for
help. They instructed me to come in immediately and speak with
one of their counselors.

"I have these depressions that happen frequently, emotional
blackouts that last as long as two weeks at a time. I can hardly
function, and my thoughts often turn to suicide as the only way
out. I can't even get out of bed, except for the basic necessities of
life. What's the matter with me?" I asked Mary Anne, the counselor I was referred to at the church. Her beautiful, compassionate
face invited my complete trust. "I have the Lord, a good husband,
a home, and no financial worries for the first time in my life. I read
God's Word and I pray. Why is this still happening?"

"Tell me about your childhood, Stormie," she said softly. "What
was it like?"

Because I felt safe with her, I told more about my past than I had
ever revealed to anyone. She listened for nearly half an hour, speaking only to ask a question or two. When I was finished she said very
directly, "You have bondage, Stormie, and you need deliverance."

I have what? I need what? I thought to myself.

Mary Anne must have read my expression because she quickly
added, "It's nothing to be afraid of. Bondage is the oppression that
comes upon us when we don't live the way we're supposed to. Deliverance breaks that oppression."

Then she instructed me, "I want you to go home and write down
every sin God brings to your mind. Ask God to help you remember

each incident, and as you write it down say, 'God, I confess this before You and ask Your forgiveness.' "

"I thought I was forgiven of all my sins when I received Jesus," I said politely, not wanting to seem unwilling to cooperate.

"That's right, you have been. But often we live right in the middle of things from which God has liberated us. Jesus' death on the cross means He took all that we had coming to us (the consequence of sin, which is death) and in return He gave us all that He had coming to Him (the reward of sinlessness, which is eternal life). Receiving Him means being freed of this death grip. However, the bondage that accompanies each sin must have a point of severance—through confession. Whatever you confess before God will release you from the bondage that accompanies it. So go home, confess everything, and then come back in a week and we'll pray about all of it."

How well she must have me sized up, I thought to myself as I left her office, pondering all she instructed me to do. *She knows it's going to take a week of writing to get all my sins down on paper!* She had assured me that the paper would not be used against me at a later date, so I agreed to do it.

I'd had enough good teaching at The Church on the Way to know the word *sin* is an old archery term, meaning to miss the bull's-eye. Anything other than dead center is sin. So sin in our lives doesn't just mean robbing a liquor store, murdering someone, or playing cards on Sunday. It's much more than that. In fact, anything off the center of God's best and perfect will for our lives is sin. That takes in a lot of territory!

In those days of dark depression, I was so drained of energy that I had to take a nap before I could do anything. So I took a nap before I started making my list. Once I began, I was able to come up with a sizable number of obvious failures, even before I got around to asking the Lord to show me any *hidden* sins.

Just when I thought I surely had nothing more to confess, I read in the Bible, "If we say that we have no sin, we deceive ourselves, and the truth is not in us. If we confess our sins, He is faithful and just to forgive us our sins and to cleanse us from all unrighteousness" (1 John 1:8–9). In spite of the fact that I had confessed so much already, I knew I was kidding myself to think there wasn't more. In fact, God must have known I couldn't possibly do it all in one week, so on the morning I was supposed to return to Mary Anne's office, she called to say she was ill and asked if we could reschedule for the following week.

I was terribly disappointed about that as my depression had become unbearable. But with no other recourse, I continued listing and confessing. The pile of papers grew as incidents I hadn't thought of in years flooded my mind!

I soon realized that unconfessed sin is like carrying around heavy bags of garbage. The heavier they get, the weaker we become until we are crippled under the weight of it all. I was to know the full sense of that truth when I returned to the counseling office.

"Do you have your list?" Mary Anne asked as she smiled and held out her hand.

"Yes," I replied sheepishly. I showed her my mound of papers, embarrassed by the prospect of having her learn the full extent of the awful truth.

"Good," she said and summoned another counselor to the room. I immediately imagined that she was summoning reinforcements in case she gave out during the hours it would take to pray about it all. Much to my surprise and relief, she and the other counselor simply put one hand on me and one hand on the papers. They didn't show the slightest interest in reading them. "Did you confess each sin as it came to mind?" Mary Anne questioned.

"Yes, I did," I nodded.

"Then lift them up to the Lord, confess it all as sin, and ask for God's forgiveness. We are going to pray for God to release you from the destruction that all this has brought upon your life."

I did what they instructed, and as they prayed I felt a distinct physical release from my head, neck, and shoulders. The headache I'd had for days disappeared, new strength came into my body, and I felt lighter and cleaner than I ever remembered feeling in my life. Other things that happened in the counseling office that day had just as profound an effect (I will explain them in later chapters), but the immediate release I experienced in that time of confession was unique and unforgettable. The outcome of what turned out to be two hours of praying with the counselors was that I went home free of chronic depression and never experienced its paralyzing grip again.

The Weight of Unconfessed Sin

When sin is unconfessed, it becomes a subtle *growth*—wrapping its tentacles around every part of our beings until we are paralyzed. The agony of its weight is accurately described in the Bible by King David:

When I kept silent, my bones grew old
Through my groaning all the day long.
For day and night Your hand was heavy upon me;
My vitality was turned into the drought of summer.
I acknowledged my sin to You,
And my iniquity I have not hidden.
I said, "I will confess my transgressions to the LORD,"
And You forgave the iniquity of my sin. (Ps. 32:3-5)

When sin is left unconfessed, a wall goes up between you and God. Even though the sin may have stopped, if it hasn't been confessed before the Lord, it will still weight you down, dragging you back toward the past you are trying to leave behind. I know because I used to carry around a bag of failures on my back that was so heavy I could barely move. I didn't realize how spiritually stooped over I had become. When I confessed my sins that day, I actually felt the weight being lifted.

All of us with deep emotional wounds from the past already suffer from low self-esteem, fear, and guilt. We mentally beat up on ourselves, tend to think the worst about our situations, and feel responsible for everything that goes wrong. It's true we can have times of feeling guilty for things we have done, but we don't have to be tortured by living endlessly in guilt. God provided the key of confession to release us from that.

Often we fail to see ourselves as responsible for certain actions. For example, while it's not your fault that someone abused you, your *reaction* to it now is your responsibility. You may feel justified in your anger or bitterness, but you still must confess it because it misses the mark of what God has for you. If you don't, its weight will eventually crush you.

The Key Is Repentance

For confession to work, repentance must go along with it. Repentance literally means a change of mind. It means to turn your back, walk away, and decide not to do it again. It means getting your thinking aligned correctly with God. It's possible to confess without really ever conceding any fault at all. In fact, we can become simply good apologizers with no intent of being any other way. Confession and repentance mean saying, "This is my fault. I'm sorry about it, and I'm not going to do it anymore."

All sin has to be confessed and repented of for you to be free of bondage, whether you feel bad about it or not and whether you recognize it as sin or not. That day in the counseling office, I confessed the two abortions I'd had even though I still had no concept of how wrong abortion was. I always viewed abortion as a means of survival, not as a sin, but that did not make it right in God's eyes. I had read in the Bible about the value of life in the womb. I also read, "My conscience is clear, but that does not make me innocent" (1 Cor. 4:4 NIV). I was not free from the death grip of the abortions until I repented and received God's full forgiveness.

Every time you confess something, check to see if you honestly and truly do not want to do that anymore. And remember, God "knows the secrets of the heart" (Ps. 44:21). Being repentant doesn't necessarily mean you will never do it again, but it does mean you don't *intend* to do it again. If you find that you are committing the same sin over and over, you need to confess it each time. If you have committed a sin that you just confessed the day before, don't let that come between you and God. Confess it again. As long as you are truly repentant each time, you will be forgiven and eventually set free. The Bible says, "Repent therefore and be converted, that your sins may be blotted out, so that times of refreshing may come from the presence of the Lord" (Acts 3:19).

Because we are not perfect, confession and repentance are ongoing. There are always new levels of Jesus' life that need to be worked in us. We fall short of the glory of God in ways that we can't yet even imagine.

Confessing Hidden Faults

When you are building a foundation, you have to dig out the dirt. The trouble is, most of us don't go deep enough. While you can't see all your errors all the time, you *can* have a heart that is willing to be taught by the Lord. Ask God to bring to light sins you are not aware of so that they can be confessed, repented of, and forgiven. Recognize that there is something to confess every day and pray frequently as David did:

- See if there is any wicked way in me,
  And lead me in the way everlasting. (Ps. 139:24)
- Create in me a clean heart, O God,
  And renew a steadfast spirit within me. (Ps. 51:10)
- Cleanse me from secret faults. (Ps. 19:12)

Sometimes when we don't think we have anything to confess, praying for God's revelation will reveal an unrepentant attitude, such as criticism or unforgiveness, that has taken root in the heart. Confessing it keeps us from having to pay the emotional, spiritual, and physical price for it. It will also benefit our social lives since the imperfections in our personalities that we can't see are often obvious to others.

Sin leads to death; repentance leads to life. How much time passes between the sin and the repentance will account for how much death is reaped in your life. If you've reaped a lot of death, the problems don't go away immediately when you confess. But your confession has started the process of reversing what has taken place as a result of the sin.

There is also much healing when you confess your faults to another person for the purpose of prayer. The Bible says, "Confess your trespasses to one another, and pray for one another, that you may be healed" (James 5:16). Ask the Lord to show you when it is right to do that. But be sure the person you confess to is trustworthy and won't use the information against you.

Always keep in mind that God's ways are for your benefit. Confession is not for Him to find out something. God already knows. Confession is for *you* to be made whole. He is not standing over you, waiting to punish you for what you do wrong. He doesn't have to because the punishment is inherent in the sin. Because God knows this, He has given you the key of confession. People who confess find mercy and God's unlimited power.

■ ———————— *What the Bible Says About* ———————— ■
Confession

He who covers his sins will not prosper,
But whoever confesses and forsakes them will have mercy.
   Proverbs 28:13

Beloved, if our heart does not condemn us, we have confidence toward God. And whatever we ask we receive from Him, because we keep His commandments and do those things that are pleasing in His sight.
   1 John 3:21–22

Blessed is he whose transgression is forgiven.
   Psalm 32:1

There is no creature hidden from His sight, but all things are naked and open to the eyes of Him to whom we must give account.
    Hebrews 4:13

There is no soundness in my flesh
Because of Your anger,
Nor is there any health in my bones
Because of my sin.
For my iniquities have gone over my head;
Like a heavy burden they are too heavy for me.
My wounds are foul and festering
Because of my foolishness.
    Psalm 38:3–5

LAY A FOUNDATION IN ONGOING FORGIVENESS

Forgive someone who treated me with hatred and abuse? Someone who has ruined my life by making me into an emotional cripple? How can I? I thought to myself, overwhelmed at the prospect of so great a task. I had already confessed my sins, and now Mary Anne was asking me to forgive my mother—all in the same counseling session. *Shouldn't this take months, even years, of therapy?*

"You don't have to *feel* forgiveness in order to say you forgive someone," Mary Anne explained. "Forgiveness is something you do out of obedience to the Lord because He has forgiven *you*. You have to be willing to say, 'God, I confess hatred for my mother, and I ask your forgiveness. I forgive her for everything she did to me. I forgive her for not loving me, and I release her into your hands.'"

As difficult as it was, I did as she said because I wanted to forgive my mother even though I felt nothing close to that at the time. "God, I forgive my mother," I said at the end of the prayer. I knew that for me even to be able to say those words, the power of God must be working in my life. And I felt His love at that moment more than I ever had before.

The next morning after this counseling and deliverance time with Mary Anne, I awoke with no depression or suicidal thoughts. It felt odd because as far back as I could remember I'd always had them. Even more surprising was that on the next morning and the next and the next, I never suffered that level of depression again. I may have felt depression or had a suicidal thought, but they never controlled me or caused me to become dysfunctional.

I soon learned, however, that unforgiveness as deeply rooted as mine toward my mother must be unraveled, one layer at a time. This was especially true for me since my mother's verbal abuse continued to increase in intensity as time went on. Whenever I felt anger, hatred, or unforgiveness toward her, I had to take charge of my will and deliberately say, "Lord, my desire is to forgive my mother. Help me to forgive her completely."

Over the next couple of years, I did this more often than I can begin to count. One day as I was again asking God to give me a forgiving heart, I felt led to pray, "Lord, help me to have a heart like *Yours* for my mother."

Almost immediately I had a vision of her I had never seen before. She was beautiful, fun loving, gifted, a woman who bore no resemblance to the person I knew. My understanding told me I was seeing her the way God had made her to be and not the way she had become. What an amazing revelation! I couldn't have conjured it up myself. Nothing surpassed my hatred for my mother, except perhaps the depth of my own emptiness. Yet now I felt compassion and sympathy for her.

In an instant I put together the pieces of her past—the tragic and sudden death of her mother when she was eleven, the suicide of her beloved uncle and foster father a few years later, her feelings of abandonment, guilt, bitterness, and unforgiveness which contributed to her emotional and mental illness. I could see how her life, like mine, had been twisted and deformed by circumstances beyond her control. Suddenly I no longer hated her for it. I felt sorry for her instead.

Being in touch with the heart of God for my mother brought such forgiveness in me that when she died a few years later, I had absolutely no bad feelings toward her. Although her mental illness and irrational behavior had continued to worsen, which kept us from any kind of reconciled relationship, I harbored no bitterness, and I have none to this day. In fact, the more I forgave her, the more the Lord brought to mind good memories. I was amazed that there were any at all.

Stairway to Wholeness

Forgiveness leads to life. Unforgiveness is a slow death. It doesn't mean you aren't saved, and it doesn't mean you won't go to heaven. But it does mean you can't have all that God has for you and you will not be free of emotional pain.

The first step to forgiving is to *receive God's forgiveness* and let its reality penetrate the deepest part of our being. When we realize how much we have been forgiven, it's easier to understand that we have no right to pass judgment on one another. Being forgiven and released from everything we've ever done wrong is such a miraculous gift, how could we refuse to obey God when He asks us to forgive others as He has forgiven us? Easy! We focus our thoughts on the person who has wronged us rather than on the God who makes all things right.

Forgiveness is a two-way street. God forgives you, and you forgive others. God forgives you quickly and completely upon your confession of wrongdoing. You are to forgive others quickly and completely, whether they admit failure or not. Most of the time people don't feel they've done anything wrong anyway, and if they do, they certainly don't want to admit it to you.

Forgiveness is a choice that we make. We base our decision not on what we *feel* like doing but on what we *know* is *right*. I did not *feel* like forgiving my mother. Instead I *chose* to forgive her because God's Word says, "Forgive, and you will be forgiven" (Luke 6:37). That verse also says that we shouldn't judge if we don't want to be judged ourselves.

It was hard for me to understand that God loves my mother as much as He loves me. He loves *all* people as much as He loves me. He loves the murderer, the rapist, the prostitute, and the thief. And He hates all of their sins as much as He hates mine. He hates their murdering, raping, whoring, and stealing as much as He hates my pride, gossiping, and unforgiveness. We may sit and compare our sins to other people's and say, "Mine aren't so bad," but God says they all stink so we shouldn't worry about whose smell the worst. The most important thing to remember when it comes to forgiving is that *forgiveness doesn't make the other person right, it makes you free*.

Forgiving the Abuser

We often feel that the abusive person in our life is an obstacle to our freedom and healing, but we can never be completely released from or reconciled to a person we haven't forgiven. We have to be willing to say, "Lord, I choose to forgive this person completely." When we do that, the cleansing process has begun. That's because *the law of the Lord is to let go, not get even*.

If you forgive one day and the next day you find you are still angry, hurt, and intensely bitter toward that same person, don't be discouraged. Continue to take it to the Lord again and again. Sometimes we can forgive quickly, but usually forgiving a person who has caused deep wounds is an ongoing, step-by-step process, especially if there has been no reconciliation or the abuse is still going on in some way. You will know the work is complete when you can honestly say you want God's best for that person.

A young girl named Donna came to my office for help. "My father raped me many times," she cried as she told me about her past. "Because of him I'm an emotional cripple. I can never forgive him."

"Donna, you have every right to feel the way you do. What was done to you was horrible. If you've been so beaten down and destroyed by your dad that you can't even bring yourself to say the word *forgive* in the same sentence with his name, then tell God about it. Tell the Lord you need Him to give you the strength to say this prayer, and then say, 'God, I don't have any love for my dad, and I feel hurt when I even think of him. I don't want to forgive him or pray for him. In fact, part of me wants him to pay for what he has done. But because You have asked me to, I pray that You will bless him and lead him into full knowledge of You. Let him become the person You created him to be. I refuse to hold him to myself with unforgiveness. I release him to You and choose to forgive him this day. O Lord, work complete forgiveness in my heart.'"

Forgiving your parents is one of the most important things you can do: "Honor your father and your mother, that your days may be long upon the land which the LORD your God is giving you" (Ex. 20:12). Forgiving them is part of that honoring and will affect the length and quality of your life.

Pastor Jack Hayford said something that affected me profoundly with regard to forgiving my own mother. He said, "You grow up to hate yourself when you hate your parents because what you see of them in yourself you will despise." When you despise something in yourself, check to see if it's because it reminds you of one of your parents. If so, there may be an area of unforgiveness there.

I've found that the best way to turn anger, bitterness, hatred, and resentment for someone into love is to pray for that person. God softens your heart when you do. It also helps to remember that we will *all* stand before the same judgment seat and no one gets away with sin. We *all* eventually pay for it. If you feel that abusive person is not paying enough, remember that God extends to him the same mercy that is extended to you. In other words, God is not punishing you or me as much as we deserve either.

When you have been badly wounded it's important not only to forgive the person who hurt you, but to forgive each event as it comes to mind. In other words, be specific about addressing each one of your wounded places. I had to forgive every incident with my mother as I remembered it or as it was happening. Every time I forgave, it helped me to let go of more of the past and move on with my life.

You may feel that the abuse in your past has kept you from becoming all you were supposed to be. But it's really not forgiving the abuse that will keep you from becoming all that God made you to be. Not forgiving the abuse you suffered as a child can lead the way to your being an abusing parent, no matter how good your intentions to be otherwise. Or you may have a hard time dealing with your own anger if you don't forgive your father's angry outbursts toward you. Giving your life to God and living His way will insure that you become all you were created to be, no matter what has happened to you. That's because of God's miraculous ability to meet you right where you are and transform your life.

If *you* have done things to others that were hurtful and need to be forgiven, first ask for the Lord's forgiveness and then ask for forgiveness from the people you have hurt. Keep in mind, however, that while God never fails to forgive you, people might. You can't control what others do.

Confronting the Abuser

You're on touchy territory if you confront the person who abused you because you run the risk of a defensive response or complete denial. Linda, a young woman of twenty-eight, told me she went to her father and said, "Dad, I forgive you for all the times you sexually molested me." The father was embarrassed and enraged; he accused her of fabricating the whole story. This devastated Linda, and she felt worse than before.

"Let me give you a few suggestions about this," I told her. "First of all, your own healing does not depend on an admission of guilt or an apology from the offending person. Too many of us would still be crippled today if it did. You can be healed and set free from your unforgiveness without their help. In fact I believe more can be accomplished if you have received a certain amount of emotional healing *before* you confront them. The abuser should be confronted out of a forgiving heart and a longing for reconciliation; otherwise you're not making things better but stirring up an old problem and holding that person responsible.

When you go to an abusing or offending person, make sure you go humbly, not expecting *anything* in return. And make sure the only confessing you do is the kind that admits *your* fault, *not* the other person's. If you don't, you're automatically implying they are to blame, and this may put them on the defensive.

I didn't go to my mother and say, "Mom, I forgive you for all the times you abandoned me in the closet, struck me in the face for reasons I couldn't understand, and called me obscene names." I did, however, attempt to confess *my* faults to my mother and ask for *her* forgiveness. I said, "Mom, I know I was a terrible teenager. I was disrespectful and hateful to you, and I'm sorry. Please forgive me."

It would have been wonderful to hear her say, "Of course I forgive you, dear. Besides, you weren't all that bad, and I wasn't the best mother. Anyway, it's all forgotten, and look how wonderfully you've turned out." I didn't expect that, and therefore was only mildly disappointed when she went on and on about how horrible I'd been.

Beyond forgiving the people who have obviously hurt you, you need to ask God to show you where you have unforgiveness that you don't see. You need to forgive people who have let you down, neglected you, or failed you in some way.

One of the greatest revelations of my life came when I realized I harbored unforgiveness toward my father. Since he wasn't the abuser, I didn't even realize I was angry toward him until Mary Anne instructed me to ask God to reveal any hidden unforgiveness. When I did, rage surfaced in me over the fact that he had never once let me out of the closet and he had not protected me from my mother's insanity. I had always felt he was never there for me. I cried longer and harder over that than I had ever cried before, and afterward I felt a giant weight had been lifted from my shoulders. I had always loved my dad, but that day set me free to love him more. We see a person quite differently once we've forgiven them.

My dad is now eighty-three, has lived with Michael and me and the children for the last three years, and is a great blessing to all of us. Not only is he an avid encourager of my children and an enthusiastic sports companion for my husband, but he is now *always* there for me in a way that has been remarkably healing. He loves to cook and cooks wonderful meals for us when I get too busy to do it. He keeps an eye on the children if I have to leave. He takes care of many household chores that I hate—cleaning out the fireplace and taking out the trash. I don't believe this living arrangement would have worked so successfully if I hadn't been willing to forgive.

Forgiving Yourself and God

While forgiving others is crucial, forgiveness is also needed in two other areas. One is *forgiving yourself.* Emotionally wounded people often feel guilty about not being what they think they should be. Instead of beating ourselves up for that, we need to be merciful. We have to be able to say, "Self, I forgive you for not being perfect, and I thank You, God, that You are right now making me into all that You created me to be."

Besides forgiving others and yourself, you must also check to see if you need to *forgive God.* If you've been mad at Him, say so. "God, I've been mad at You ever since my brother was killed in that accident." "God, I've been mad at You since my baby died." "God, I've been mad at You ever since I didn't get that job I prayed for." Be honest. You won't crush God's ego. Release the hurt and let yourself cry. Tears are freeing and healing. Say, "Lord, I confess my hurt and my anger, and my hardness of heart toward You. I no longer hold that offense against You."

Forgiveness is ongoing because once you've dealt with the past, constant infractions occur in the present. None of us gets by without having our pride wounded or being manipulated, offended, or hurt by someone. Each time that happens it leaves a scar on the soul if not confessed and dealt with before the Lord. Besides that, unforgiveness also separates you from people you love. They sense a spirit of unforgiveness, even if they can't identify it, and it makes them uncomfortable and distant.

You may be thinking, "I don't have to worry about this because I have no unforgiveness toward anyone." But forgiveness also has to do with not being critical of others. It has to do with keeping in mind that people are often the way they are because of how life has shaped them. It has to do with remembering that God is the only one who knows the whole story and therefore we never have the right to judge. Being chained in unforgiveness keeps you from the healing, joy, and restoration that are there for you. Being released into everything God has for you today and tomorrow means letting go of all that's happened in the past.

What the Bible Says About
Ongoing Forgiveness

And whenever you stand praying, if you have anything against anyone, forgive him, that your Father in heaven may also forgive you your trespasses.
Mark 11:25

Let all bitterness, wrath, anger, clamor, and evil speaking be put away from you, with all malice. And be kind to one another, tenderhearted, forgiving one another, even as God in Christ forgave you.
Ephesians 4:31–32

Judge not, and you shall not be judged. Condemn not, and you shall not be condemned. Forgive, and you will be forgiven.
Luke 6:37

He who loves his brother abides in the light, and there is no cause for stumbling in him. But he who hates his brother is in darkness and walks in darkness, and does not know where he is going, because the darkness has blinded his eyes.
1 John 2:10–11

CHAPTER 4

Step Three:
Live in Obedience

When will I ever get to the point where I no longer hurt inside?" I asked God one day in prayer a few months after my counseling session with Mary Anne. Even though I had been set free from depression and my life was far more stable than it had ever been, I still lived on an emotional roller coaster. My questions to God during that time went on and on:

- "When will I stop feeling like a failure?"
- "When will I not be devastated by what other people say to me?"
- "When will I not view every hint of misfortune as the end of the world?"
- "When will I be able to go through the normal occurrences of life without being traumatized by them?"

There were no answers from God at that moment, but as I read the Bible the next morning, my eyes fell on the words, "Why do you call Me 'Lord, Lord,' and do not do the things which I say?" (Luke 6:46). The passage went on to explain that anyone who hears the words of the Lord and does *not* put them into practice is building a house with no foundation. When the storm comes, it will collapse and be completely destroyed.

Could it be that I'm getting blown over and destroyed by every wind of circumstance that comes my way because I'm not doing what the Lord says to do in some area? I wondered. I knew I was building on solid rock (Jesus), and I had been laying a strong foundation (in the Word, prayer, praise, confession, and ongoing forgiveness), but it appeared that this foundation could only be stabilized and protected through my obedience.

I searched the Bible for more information, and every place I turned I read more about the rewards of obeying God:

- "Blessed are those who hear the word of God and keep it!" (Luke 11:28)
- "No good thing will He withhold
  From those who walk uprightly." (Ps. 84:11)
- "Behold, I set before you today a blessing and a curse: the blessing, if you obey the commandments of the LORD your God which I command you today." (Deut. 11:26–27)

The more I read, the more I saw the link between *obedience* and the *presence of God*. "If anyone loves Me, he will keep My word; and My Father will love him, and We will come to him and make Our home with him" (John 14:23). I was already convinced by this time that I could only find wholeness and restoration in His presence, so this promise that my obedience would open the door to God's dwelling with me was particularly impressive.

I also saw a definite connection between *obedience* and the *love of God*. "If anyone obeys his Word, God's love is truly made complete in him" (1 John 2:5 NIV). According to the Bible, God doesn't stop loving us if we *don't* obey. Even if He doesn't love the way we live, He still loves *us*. But we are unable to feel or enjoy that love fully if we're not living as God intended us to live. Just as surely as living God's way leads to experiencing His love and life, doing things that are *opposed* to His ways will lead to separation from God's love, which is death to us. The Bible clearly says,

> As righteousness leads to life,
> So he who pursues evil pursues it to his own death.
> (Prov. 11:19)

The more I read about obedience, the more I realized that my disobedience of God's directives could explain why nothing happened when I prayed the same prayers over and over. The Bible says,

> One who turns away his ear from hearing the law,
> Even his prayer is an abomination. (Prov. 28:9)

If I'm not obeying, I shouldn't expect to get my prayers answered, I thought to myself.

Benefits of Obedience

How many times do we ask God to give us what we want, but we don't want to give God what *He* wants? We lack what we desire most—wholeness, peace, fulfillment, and joy—because we are not obedient to God.

Often we are not obedient because we don't understand that God has set up certain rules to *protect us* and work for *our benefit*. He designed us and knows what will fulfill us most. Even the Ten Commandments were not given to instill guilt, but as an umbrella of blessing and protection from the rain of evil. If we choose to live outside the arena of blessing, we suffer the consequences. Spiritual darkness and confusion then have access to our lives, and we are drained of God's best. When we obey, life has simplicity and clarity and unlimited blessing. We *need* God's laws because we don't know how to make life work without them. The Bible says, "If anyone competes in athletics, he is not crowned unless he competes according to the rules" (2 Tim. 2:5). If restoration is the name of the game, then obedience is one of the rules. The more I've searched the Scriptures, the more I've found that the Bible is full of promises for those who obey God:

- *There is the promise of healing.* Make straight paths for your feet, so that what is lame may not be dislocated, but rather be healed. (Heb. 12:13)
- *There is the promise of answered prayer.* If I had cherished sin in my heart, the Lord would not have listened. (Ps. 66:18 NIV)
- *There is the promise of God fighting our battles for us.*
  Oh, that My people would listen to Me,
  That Israel would walk in My ways!
  I would soon subdue their enemies,
  And turn My hand against their adversaries. (Ps. 81:13–14)
- *There is the promise of living a long life in peace.*
  Let your heart keep my commands;
  For length of days and long life
  And peace they will add to you. (Prov. 3:1–2)

There are many more promises like these, and just as many warnings of what will *not* happen in our lives if we *don't* obey. After reading them, I felt inspired to ask God to show me exactly what I needed to be doing. He was quick to answer that prayer.

The Choice Is Ours—The Power Is His

I've learned that God doesn't enforce obedience. We often wish He would because it would be easier, but He gives us the choice. I had to ask Him to teach me to be obedient out of love for Him and desire to serve the One who has done so much for me. If you want the same benefits, you have to do the same thing. It helps to understand that the Lord is on your side and the call to obedience is *not* to make you feel like a hopeless failure if you don't do everything right. Knowing that God asks you to live a certain way for your own benefit because He knows life only works out right for you when it is lived on His terms will help you to desire to know His ways and live in them.

The law was given in the Old Testament to show us that we can't possibly fulfill it in terms of *human* energy, but must depend on God. We need His power to escape the death syndrome that surrounds us. The Bible says that Noah was given new life because he did *all* that God asked him to do (Gen. 6:22). That word *all* seems frightening when it comes to obedience because we know ourselves well enough to doubt we can do it all. And the truth is we can't. But we *can* take steps in the right direction and watch *God* do it.

The minute we take one step of obedience, God opens up opportunities for new life. The minute we start to think it's not necessary to obey, we have opened the door for evil. Oswald Chambers says, "If [a person] wants insight into what Jesus Christ teaches, he can only get it by obedience. . . . spiritual darkness comes because of something I do not intend to obey" (*My Utmost for His Highest*, Westwood, NJ: Barbour & Co., 1984, 151).

For anyone who has been emotionally wounded in any way, a certain amount of deliverance and healing will happen in your life just by being obedient to God. The Bible says, "He who obeys instructions guards his soul" (Prov. 19:16 NIV). The more obedient you are, the more bondage will be stripped away from your life. There is also a certain healthy confidence that comes from knowing you've obeyed God. This confidence builds self-worth and nourishes a broken personality. You start the process by being willing to say, "God, I don't want to be a person who collapses every time something shakes me. I don't want anything to separate me from Your presence and love. And I really do have a heart that wants to obey. Please show me where I am not living in obedience, and help me to do what I need to do."

There are many different areas of obedience, but the ones I will mention in this chapter are important for emotional health. Don't be discouraged by how many there are. They are a guideline, not a threat. Just take one step at a time, remembering that the power of the Holy Spirit *in* us enables us to obey God.

It took me years to figure out I was supposed to be doing these things, and I still review them regularly to see where I've gotten off the mark. Hopefully, you will move into them more quickly than I did and begin to enjoy the benefits sooner.

■ ——————— *What the Bible Says About* ——————— ■

Obedience

Great peace have those who love Your law,
And nothing causes them to stumble.
  Psalm 119:165

If you are willing and obedient,
You shall eat the good of the land.
  Isaiah 1:19

Do not merely listen to the word, and so deceive yourselves. Do what it says.
  James 1:22 NIV

Therefore, to him who knows to do good and does not do it, to him it is sin.
  James 4:17

He who says, "I know Him," and does not keep His commandments, is a liar, and the truth is not in him.
  1 John 2:4

■ ■

LIVE IN OBEDIENCE BY SAYING YES TO GOD

When you buy a house, you first make a large down payment. Then, to keep the house, you must make a smaller payment every time it comes due. You can't change your mind and say, "I don't feel like making payments!" without serious consequences.

The same is true for your relationship with God. To make Him your permanent dwelling place, your initial down payment consists of making Him Lord over your life. After that, ongoing payments must be made, which means saying yes whenever God directs you to do something. They are all a part of the purchase, but one happens initially and the other is eternally ongoing. (Just like house payments!) The difference is that the Lord will only take as much from me as I am willing to give Him. And I can only possess as much of what He has for me as I am willing to secure with my obedience.

Taking the initial step of making Him Lord over your life is the same for everyone. Saying yes to God every day is an individual matter. God gives you personalized direction. He may ask you to do something He is not asking anyone else to do. For example, He may be directing you to leave a specific job or move to another city. You have to trust that God has your best interests in mind and be willing to do what He asks of you, even if you don't understand why at the time. Obedience starts with having a heart that says yes to God.

Releasing Your Dreams

I always wanted to be a successful entertainer. It sounds embarrassingly shallow even to mention it now, but it was a desperate drive at the time. I desired to be famous and respected, never mind the fact that I possibly didn't have what it might take to attain either. After I received the Lord and had been married just a few months, God clearly impressed upon my heart that I wasn't to be doing television or commercials anymore. I wasn't sure why, but I knew it wasn't right for me. Whenever my agent presented me with an interview I once would have died for, the thought of it gave me a hollow, uneasy, deathlike feeling. Because the peace of God did not accompany the prospect of doing it, I turned down every job that was offered.

Yes, God, I won't do that commercial. Yes, God, I won't accept another television show. Yes, God, I won't sing in clubs anymore. Yes, God, I'll leave the agency.

Gradually, all my work was gone. God had closed all doors and asked me to stop knocking on the ones that were not in His plan for me. The experience was scary, but looking back now I clearly see the reasons for it. Acting was an idol for me. I did it entirely for the attention and acceptance it would bring me, not because I loved the work. My identity was totally wrapped up in what I did. For God to change that, He had to take away my means of defining who I thought I was and help me to establish my identity in Jesus. He knew I couldn't be healed of my deep inferiority feelings if I was daily putting myself in a position of being judged by superficial standards.

The part we don't want to hear is that a time comes when each of us must place our desires and dreams in the hands of God so that He might free us from those that are not in His will. In other words, you secure your future by allowing your dream to die and God's plan to replace it. If you've always had a certain picture of what you think you should do, you have to be willing to let the picture be destroyed. If it really is what God has for you, He will raise you up to do that and more. If it isn't, you will be frustrated as long as you cling to it. Often the desires of *your* heart *are* the desires of *His* heart, but they still must be achieved *His* way, not yours, and you must know He is accomplishing them in you, not you achieving them yourself. *God wants us to stop holding on to our dreams and start holding on to Him so that He can enable us to soar above ourselves and our own limitations.* Whenever we let go of what we long for, God will bring it back to us in another dimension.

The Art of the Quick Response

Saying yes to God means being willing to obey *immediately* when we hear His voice, and not waiting until all else fails or we feel like it or we're at the end of ourselves. For God to transform us into whole people, we have to be totally available to Him. If He is saying to us to "Do this," then saying, "Yes, God" immediately, will bring the desired results more quickly.

Again, this is done a step at a time. If you can't trust God enough yet to say, "Anything You ask of me, I'll do," then keep working at it. I must admit that saying yes to God was difficult for me until I read God's words in the Scripture, "When *I* called, *they* did not listen; so when *they* called, *I* would not listen" (Zech. 7:13 NIV, emphasis added). That puts it all in perspective, doesn't it? If we want God to hear our prayer, we need to listen and respond to His voice.

Being willing to say yes to God made me a candidate for much healing and blessing. Of course, I don't always hear Him and I don't always say yes immediately, but my desire is to do that. Saying yes to God without reservation is the first step of obedience that begins to build the superstructure for emotional wholeness on the foundation you have laid down in the Word, prayer, confession, praise, and ongoing forgiveness.

■————— *What the Bible Says About* —————■
Saying Yes to God

Those who live according to the flesh set their minds on the things of the flesh, but those who live according to the Spirit, the things of the Spirit.
Romans 8:5

If anyone desires to come after Me, let him deny himself, and take up his cross daily, and follow Me. For whoever desires to save his life will lose it, but whoever loses his life for My sake will save it.
Luke 9:23–24

Delight yourself also in the LORD,
And He shall give you the desires of your heart.
Psalm 37:4

You shall worship the LORD your God, and Him only you shall serve.
Matthew 4:10

I delight to do Your will, O my God.
Psalm 40:8

LIVE IN OBEDIENCE BY BREAKING FROM THE WORLD

The first time I heard Dolores Hayford speak, I knew Pastor Jack had inherited his gift of teaching from his mother. In a clear, gentle voice she told a story of her youngest son, Jim.

"Why do some people get all the breaks with God?" Jim asked his mother one day, when he realized that certain people have blessing upon blessing and others don't.

After giving it some thought Mrs. Hayford said, "Son, those who get the breaks with God are the ones who first break from the world."

That piece of motherly advice stuck in my mind so strongly I pondered it for weeks afterward. *What exactly is the world?* I prayed to the Lord. *And how do I break away from it?*

Over the next few months of Bible study I came to see that the world is anything that sets itself against God and His ways. The Bible says, "Whoever therefore wants to be a friend of the world makes himself an enemy of God" (James 4:4).

I knew I didn't want to be God's enemy!

I also read, "Be sober, be vigilant; because your adversary the devil walks about like a roaring lion, seeking whom he may devour" (1 Peter 5:8). The Bible describes *Satan* as our *enemy*, the *ruler of this world,* and by aligning with the world's systems and ways of doing things, we are aligning with him.

In the past, I had rejected the idea of a personal devil as basically naive. Only the most foolish and ignorant people could support such nonsense. Besides, my occult practices had convinced me that evil existed only in people's minds. But the more I studied God's Word and saw its accuracy, the more I faced the reality of a dark and evil force controlling the lives of people who allow it. How could I deny that it existed when I could *see* it manifested in every form of evil in the world around me? I now recognize that the foolish and ignorant people are those who deny the satanic realm. *Breaking from the world means recognizing our enemy and refusing to be aligned with him in any way.*

The Ruler of This World

Time and time again in the Old Testament a king who served the Lord in all other things would not destroy the high places where pagan gods were worshiped. As a result, he and his people did not enjoy all the blessing, protection, healing, and answered prayer that God had for them. They, like us, did not clearly identify their enemy and break completely from the world.

Our enemy is Satan, the ruler of this world, who was originally created beautiful, wise, and without sin. He had access to the throne of God, but fell from this high position when he chose to exert *his* will over God's. No one tempted him; he decided on his own to rebel. When his rebellion led to his expulsion from God's kingdom, he set himself to oppose all that God is and does.

But Satan is limited. He cannot be everywhere, he is not able to do everything, he is not all-powerful, and he is not all-knowing. God, on the other hand, is *all* of those things. What Satan and God *do* have in common is that they both have a plan for our lives, which can only be made operative if we submit to it. We don't have to fear Satan because the Bible says that "He who is in you is greater than he who is in the world" (1 John 4:4). Jesus living in us will always be greater than the devil living in the world. Because Jesus' death on the cross has broken his power, we don't have to be intimidated by him.

There is no indication in the Bible that Satan can possibly win over God; God's power far surpasses his. The only success Satan can have comes through deception—getting us to believe he doesn't exist or that he is not our enemy, or instilling in us lies about ourselves, our situations, others, or God. Once we believe his lies, he controls our lives.

Satan is such a master of deception that he will even try to clothe himself as an angel of light and blind you to his very existence. I feel bad when people tell me there is no such thing as a devil. I reflect on their lives—a marriage that is falling apart or a son on drugs or a teenage daughter having her second abortion or a husband's drinking problem or a mother's depression or a secret affair—and I think, *Dear person, there is nothing in your life to convince me that there is no devil.* Their situations are worse because they have an enemy and don't even know it. He will lead them down the path of destruction, and they will follow him and then blame God for what happens. The devil's plans for your life will succeed if you believe that he doesn't exist or that he is in any way on your side.

Accepting the world's standards for our lives numbs our sensitivity to God's will. It separates us from what He has called us to be. We reserve a place in our hearts to be the exception. We think, "I'm above the Lord's ways. I don't need to obey." But that is what Satan said before he fell from heaven.

The way we combat this deception is simple. The Bible says, "Submit to God. Resist the devil and he will flee from you" (James 4:7). We need to separate ourselves from the world's habits and ways of thinking and to destroy the high places of our hearts. We must tell Satan we refuse to believe his lies or do things his way. When we refuse Satan, the promise is:

> The LORD will go before you,
> And the God of Israel will be your rear guard. (Isa. 52:12)

The Lord will protect us from anything we may face ahead, and He will guard us against any dangers sneaking up from behind.

Run a Check for High Places

Breaking from the world doesn't require you to live like a hermit for the rest of your life. But you do have to run a frequent check on your heart to make sure that you are not too attached to the world. Ask yourself these questions:

- Do I judge myself by the world's standard for beauty, acceptability, and success?
- Do I depend on worldly magazines and books to tell me how to live?
- Am I willing to ignore certain convictions I have in order to find favor with people?
- Am I drawn toward emulating the lifestyles of celebrities rather than becoming who God created *me* to be?
- Am I willing to compromise what I know of God's ways in order to gain something I want?

If you said yes to any of those questions, you are cutting off possibilities God has for your life. God asks, "Since you died with Christ to the basic principles of this world, why, as though you still belonged to it, do you submit to its rules?" (Col. 2:20 NIV). He clearly instructs us, "Do not be conformed to this world, but be transformed by the renewing of your mind, that you may prove what is that good and acceptable and perfect will of God" (Rom. 12:2).

Believe me, I know you can't lay down everything in your life at once. Many of our high places were erected for our own survival and we feel we still need them. But the more you allow God to reign in you, the easier it will be to let go of anything that exalts itself above Him.

I'm deliberately not making a list of "don'ts" because the point is for *you* to separate *yourself* in your heart. You will learn what particulars to eliminate as you seek God and pray. Say, "Lord, if there are things in my life that are not of You, I don't want them. Take them away. Release me from longing for them. Help me to draw on You for all my needs. Teach me to recognize my enemy and give me strength to resist him." As you speak that prayer and mean it, you set in motion the conditions of your request.

I never thought I opposed God, but I have learned that nearly everything I did before I received Jesus opposed His ways. We can make ourselves sick by being dissatisfied with what He gives us or by running after things that are not from Him. God wants to take all cravings for the world out of our hearts and replace them with a hunger for more of Jesus. God wants us to experience the peace and fulfillment of knowing that we have everything we need and everything we have is from Him.

The Bible says, "Come out from among them and be separate" (2 Cor. 6:17). You can't go forward if you cling to things that separate you from God. It's a step of obedience that happens in the heart and paves the way for your total restoration.

■ ─────────── *What the Bible Says About* ─────────── ■
Breaking from the World

Do not love the world or the things in the world. If anyone loves the world, the love of the Father is not in him. For all that is in the world—the lust of the flesh, the lust of the eyes, and the pride of life—is not of the Father but is of the world. And the world is passing away, and the lust of it; but he who does the will of God abides forever.
1 John 2:15–17

Let no one say when he is tempted, "I am tempted by God"; for God cannot be tempted by evil, nor does He Himself tempt anyone. But each one is tempted when he is drawn away by his own desires and enticed.
James 1:13–14

That they may come to their senses and escape the snare of the devil, having been taken captive by him to do his will.
2 Timothy 2:26

He who sins is of the devil, for the devil has sinned from the beginning. For this purpose the Son of God was manifested, that He might destroy the works of the devil.
1 John 3:8

■ ─── ■

LIVE IN OBEDIENCE BY BEING BAPTIZED

"We need to be baptized, Michael," I said late one evening shortly after he and I were married. We had been discussing Pastor Jack's sermon on baptism the day before and how Jesus himself had been baptized by John the Baptist (Matt. 3:13–16).

For months I had seen people being baptized at the church on Sunday nights but had dismissed it as a religious ritual I didn't need. Besides, I had been baptized as a baby, as were all children in our family. But at that Wednesday evening prayer meeting Pastor

Jack explained that baptism isn't just a ritual or optional meaningless tradition; it is a commandment of Jesus.

"Going against a tradition that is God-ordained brings trouble, and you jeopardize your fruitfulness by ignoring it," he said. "When you come to baptism, you are turning your back on your old life. You are saying, 'Lord, you have died for me, now I am dying to myself to receive your life.' His death on the cross sealed the covenant from His side. Your response in baptism is saying, 'Lord, I seal the covenant from my side, but it's Your power that makes it work.'"

The more Michael and I talked about the fact that we were limiting what God could do in us and possibly bringing trouble into our lives by not taking this step of obedience, the more urgent it seemed. "We should do it right away," he said to me.

"How right away do you mean?" I responded.

"Tonight," he said firmly.

"Tonight? Where are we going to find someone who will baptize us tonight? It's after ten o'clock."

"Pat Boone baptizes people in his pool," he said enthusiastically.

"Pat Boone? In his pool? Does that count? Doesn't it have to be in a church? With a pastor?"

"It can be anywhere. And Pat Boone is a church elder. They baptize people at their house all the time."

"But does he do it at this hour?" I questioned further. We had attended some Bible studies at Pat and Shirley's house, but I wasn't sure they would welcome an unscheduled visit from us this late in the evening. "Let's call him and find out," Michael said as he picked up the phone. Within ninety seconds the arrangements were made. We grabbed a change of clothes and were on our way.

The Boone house was a twenty-minute drive from ours, and on the way strong cold October winds whipped our small car. I started to feel anxious and afraid.

"We must be doing something important," I said. "I keep hearing this voice in my head saying, 'This is stupid. Go home and go to bed. It's late. It's cold. This isn't necessary.'"

We pulled in the circular driveway and parked near the front door. Once we were inside Pat's large, rambling two-story house, I felt safe. We had been in the enormous open den for prayer meetings or to hear visiting ministers speak, and I could always sense the presence of the Lord there.

The house was quiet, only a couple of rooms were lit, and Shirley and their four daughters were upstairs getting ready for bed. Pat didn't question the hour or give any indication that he was inconvenienced. The Holy Spirit who had prompted *our* hearts must also have prepared *his* as well.

Michael and I sat on the couch and Pat sat on the floor in front of us. He talked for nearly a half an hour about the significance of what we were doing, reiterating much of Pastor Jack's message. Once he was convinced that we understood, he showed us to the small house outside where we changed into appropriate clothing. As we walked to the pool, the cold wind became violent, and I could barely control the large terry cloth towel I had wrapped around myself. The baptism took less than a minute, and when I came up out of the water the wind had quieted. I felt there was a definite correlation in the spirit realm.

We had waited a long time to take this step of obedience because we hadn't understood its importance. I'm still not sure I understand it all today, but I *do* understand that right after that, our growth and deliverance proceeded more quickly. And I felt a new joy in my heart from knowing I had obeyed the Lord.

A Baby Step of Giant Significance

Baptism is a very simple first step in learning to obey God, and it only has to be done once if you understand what you're doing. But if the baptism had no meaning for you (either because you were a baby or had no relationship with the Lord), you need to be baptized now. While you are not negating anything you did as a child or when you didn't know the Lord, you are now saying, "I let my life as I have always lived it be buried in the water. I enter a stream where the power of the Holy Spirit carries me. I place God as captain over my life and desire that He navigate me where I should go. I now live in the power of His life."

Jesus Himself was baptized in order to do what was right and He commanded us all to do the same, saying, "He who believes and is baptized will be saved" (Mark 16:16). It can't be any clearer. Baptism in water is an act of obedience to declare the lordship of Jesus in your life.

While there is no magic in the water, you are not simply getting wet either. Whether you feel it at the time or not, the strongholds of your past have been broken in the spirit realm. You may not observe anything different about the weather as I did and you may not see a single dove or hear God's voice as Jesus did, but you can trust that the Holy Spirit of God has descended upon you and will open up the kingdom of God to you.

I've known some believers who suffer with horribly painful wounds from their past, but they refuse to take this simple step. I'm not even sure why. They come to me for advice, I go through the foundational steps with them, and they refuse to do this one. Year after year I see them still suffering, still having problems in their marriages, still dealing with anger and unforgiveness, still battling depression. They have still not made a *total commitment to living God's way.*

Don't let Satan rob you of what God has for you by convincing you, "It's not important." "You'll look silly." "This is a meaningless ritual." "There's no power in this." Reject those lies. Even if you've been a Christian for thirty years and a leader in your church, don't let pride keep you from receiving what God has for you. If you're an invalid or handicapped or in a hospital or nursing home, have someone call a pastor to come to you to baptize you. If you're in prison, tell the chaplain you want to be baptized or find a believer who has been baptized and have him pour water on your head and baptize you in the name of the Father, Son, and Holy Spirit. The power is not in the water, or whether you submerge yourself; it's in your desire to obey God's Word and the Lord Jesus' command. God doesn't take a magic wand and wave it over your life like a fairy godmother. He wants more for you than that. He wants to walk *with* you hand in hand and give you keys of authority to live victoriously in this life.

■ —————— *What the Bible Says About* —————— ■
Being Baptized

Then Peter said to them, "Repent, and let every one of you be baptized in the name of Jesus Christ for the remission of sins; and you shall receive the gift of the Holy Spirit."
Acts 2:38

Or do you not know that as many of us as were baptized into Christ Jesus were baptized into His death? Therefore we were buried with Him through baptism into death, that just as Christ was raised from the dead by the glory of the Father, even so we also should walk in newness of life.
Romans 6:3–4

Then Jesus, when He had been baptized, came up immediately from the water; and behold, the heavens were opened to Him, and He saw the Spirit of God descending like a dove and alighting upon Him.
Matthew 3:16

And now why are you waiting? Arise and be baptized, and wash away your sins, calling on the name of the Lord.
Acts 22:16

■ ─── ■

LIVE IN OBEDIENCE BY FASTING AND PRAYER

She wants me to fast? I gasped to myself upon hearing Mary Anne's assignment for me the very first time I met her in the counseling office. I'd heard about fasting from Pastor Jack, and the whole church was fasting every Wednesday, but I wasn't ready for that. Besides I was afraid of being hungry since I'd gone to bed too often that way as a child.

"There's a certain kind of release that will not happen without fasting and prayer, Stormie," Mary Anne explained. "It's an act of denying yourself and placing God at the center of your life, which breaks any hold that Satan has on you and destroys the bondage resulting from sin."

I need that, I thought to myself as I listened, *and if it might not happen unless I fast, then I've got to do it.*

Mary Anne suggested that I fast for three full days, drinking only water, and then return to her office with the list of sins I mentioned earlier. I did as she instructed, drinking water and praying every time I felt hungry. After the first day the hunger pangs weren't bad. In fact, it was much easier than I had anticipated. When it was time to see Mary Anne, she called to cancel our appointment and reschedule it for the following week. That meant I needed to fast three days again.

Nothing's going to happen, I thought. *I've been depressed for twenty years and it's never going to be any different. I was foolish to hope otherwise.*

Through the week, my depression grew in degree and intensity. The fasting was harder this time and I wanted to give up, but I obeyed anyway. On the day of my counseling appointment I prayed for a miracle, but I was afraid to really hope for one.

From the moment I entered the counseling office something was different. My mind was somewhat clearer, but most of all I sensed the presence and power of the Lord far more profoundly than ever before. After I confessed my sins and forgave my mother, Mary Anne and another counselor laid their hands on my head and shoulders and prayed for my deliverance from depression. As they prayed, a source of energy like electricity coursed through my body. The counseling session lasted two hours, and when it was done I felt tired but relieved and peaceful.

The next morning, I woke up without depression. Day after day I waited for it to come back, but it didn't. In fact, even though I was depressed at times later on, it was never that intense, nor was I ever controlled by it again. I believe that fasting helped me to be set free with greater speed and completeness.

Who, Me? Why Should I Fast?

God designed fasting to bring us into a deeper knowledge of Him, to release the Holy Spirit's work in our lives, and to bring us to greater health and wholeness. Fasting blesses every area of our mental, physical, spiritual, and emotional lives. It breaks down strongholds that we are not even aware the enemy has erected against us. In fact, the Bible says certain spirits can be broken only through fasting. When Jesus' disciples asked why evil spirits didn't submit to them, He replied, "This kind can come out by nothing but prayer and fasting" (Mark 9:29).

Fasting is like getting a holy oiling so the devil can't hold on to you. It's designed

> "To loose the bonds of wickedness,
>   To undo the heavy burdens,
>   To let the oppressed go free,
>   And that you break every yoke?" (Isa. 58:6)

If fasting accomplished no more than that, anyone seeking emotional wholeness would want to take that step of obedience.

Who doesn't desire to be free from any hold of the devil? Who doesn't need the power of God to penetrate his circumstances? Who doesn't want to be released from at least one negative emotion? We all do. So what's holding us back? Ignorance and fear. We are ignorant of what the Bible says about the subject, of what God wants from us, of what fasting can accomplish, and of the wonderful benefits. We are also afraid we'll die in the night if we go to bed without dinner. Or at least we fear the hunger, headache, nausea, weakness, and dizziness that often accompany infrequent fasts. But there are many good reasons to put up with this discomfort, a number of which I have listed on page 84.

There are over eighty references to fasting in the Old *and* New Testaments. Jesus Himself fasted. If fasting was dangerous or something to fear, why would it be mentioned throughout the Bible? Why would the greatest people of biblical history have done it, and why would Jesus have fasted for forty days?

Fasting is a spiritual exercise and discipline during which you give yourself completely to prayer and close communication with God. Discipline always has its rewards. A physical discipline, like exercising, has physical rewards. A spiritual discipline, like fasting, has spiritual rewards. (Fasting has physical benefits also, but for the purpose of this book I will only emphasize the spiritual.)

You don't fast to get God to love you. He already loves you, and He will love you just as much whether you fast or not. It is also not a time to get what you want from God. It *is* a time to draw closer to Him, to sensitize your soul to His Spirit, and see Him work mightily on your behalf.

How Should I Fast?

Once you are convinced of the rightness of fasting, you need to take the first step. Begin by simply skipping a meal, drinking water, and praying through it. Say, "God, I fast this meal to your glory and to the breaking down of strongholds in my life." Then lift up in prayer all the areas where you know you need freedom. Say, for example, "Lord, I fast this day for the breaking down of strongholds the devil has erected in my mind in the way of depression, confusion, unforgiveness, or anger."

The next time you fast, try skipping *two* meals, drinking water and praying through each one. See if you can work up to a full twenty-four- to thirty-six-hour water fast once a week. I do this every week and actually look forward to it as a time to hear God more clearly. Fasting is just like any other discipline in that if you fast regularly, it becomes easier. Also, the better you treat your body between fasts, the more pleasant the fast will be.

When you are able to do a thirty-six-hour fast without problems and are willing to try a three-day fast several times a year, then do so. If you have a physical limitation and cannot water fast, then go on a vegetable or fruit fast, denying yourself all else but vegetables or fruits for a day. Most people can do that.

Twenty Reasons to Fast

To purify and cleanse the spirit, soul, and body

To receive divine guidance and revelation

To seek God's face and have a closer walk with Him

To hear God better and to understand His will more fully

To invite God's power to flow through you more mightily

To establish a position of spiritual strength and dominion

To break any bondage that is on you

To receive clarity of mind

To be free of evil or debilitating thoughts

To break through depression

To weaken the power of the devil in your life

To stabilize you when life seems out of control

To be strengthened in your body and soul

To break the lusting of the flesh after anything

To discover gifts God has placed in you

To be released from heavy burdens

To establish a clean heart and right spirit within you

To be set free from negative emotions

To find healing

To gain strength for what you don't have the ability to do

If you are afraid of fasting, read a good Christian book on the subject. My own book, *Greater Health God's Way* (Sparrow), has a chapter on fasting to help you move into that discipline.

The Fasting God Chooses

In Isaiah 58, God describes the benefits of fasting. I've included a portion of it on page 86, but I recommend reading the whole chapter each time you fast to remind yourself of exactly why you are fasting (to be free), what you are to do (give of yourself), and what your rewards are (healing, answered prayer, deliverance, protection).

Be sure to accompany your fast with prayer. Fasting without praying is just starvation. This is a time to be close to the Lord and allow Him to guide you where you need to go. Sometimes you will have the clear leading of the Holy Spirit as to why you are fasting; sometimes you won't. Whether you do or not, it's good to have a prayer focus in mind.

God calls all who are able to fast and pray—not just pastors, not just elders, not just authors or teachers, not just men and women over fifty, but all adults who acknowledge Jesus as the Son of God. Ask God what He is saying to *you* about fasting, for he *is* saying something. Remember that "no discipline seems pleasant at the time, but painful. Later on, however, it produces a harvest of righteousness and peace for those who have been trained by it" (Heb. 12:11 NIV).

Because fasting is an instrument for defeating the enemy, it's a key to deliverance and emotional wholeness. Don't neglect it. Even after you have been set free, Satan will be looking for ways to put you back into bondage. Be determined to slip through his fingers by walking ongoingly in this step of obedience.

■ ——————— *What the Bible Says About* ——————— ■
Fasting and Prayer

Is this not the fast that I have chosen:
To loose the bonds of wickedness,
To undo the heavy burdens,
To let the oppressed go free,
And that you break every yoke?
Is it not to share your bread with the hungry,
And that you bring to your house the poor who are cast out;

When you see the naked, that you cover him,
And not hide yourself from your own flesh?
Then your light shall break forth like the morning,
Your healing shall spring forth speedily,
And your righteousness shall go before you;
The glory of the LORD shall be your rear guard.
Then you shall call, and the LORD will answer;
You shall cry, and He will say, "Here I am."
If you take away the yoke from your midst,
The pointing of the finger, and speaking wickedness,
If you extend your soul to the hungry
And satisfy the afflicted soul,
Then your light shall dawn in the darkness,
And your darkness shall be as the noonday.
The LORD will guide you continually,
And satisfy your soul in drought,
And strengthen your bones;
You shall be like a watered garden,
And like a spring of water, whose waters do not fail.
Those from among you
Shall build the old waste places;
You shall raise up the foundations of many generations;
And you shall be called the Repairer of the Breach,
The Restorer of Streets to Dwell In.
    Isaiah 58:6–12

LIVE IN OBEDIENCE BY
RENOUNCING THE OCCULT

"I want you to renounce all your occult involvement," Mary Anne instructed me in that same counseling and deliverance session in which I had fasted and confessed my sins.

My occult involvement? What's the big deal about that? I wondered. It never entered my mind that supernatural dabbling was anything worth confessing. I had started out slowly in the occult with Ouija™ boards, horoscopes, numerology, and transcendental meditation. Then I went full speed into astral projection, seances to summon the dead, hypnotism, Science of the Mind, and various Eastern religions. The occult was often frightening yet attractive. Books I read on the subject promised that these methods would help me find God and eternal peace.

Every occult practice I tried brought me an immediate high, but soon it was followed by a major letdown. None of it offered enough substance to sustain me for very long. Even so, I was so desperate for even a temporary respite from the emotional pain, unreasonable fear, and life-sucking emptiness I felt inside that I delved ever deeper.

"What do you mean exactly?" I asked Mary Anne. "I haven't been into the occult since I received the Lord."

"That's good, Stormie, but let me read from God's Word about the seriousness of occult involvement. The Bible says, 'There shall not be found among you anyone who . . . practices witchcraft, or a soothsayer, or one who interprets omens, or a sorcerer, or one who conjures spells, or a medium, or a spiritist, or one who calls up the dead. For all who do these things are an abomination to the LORD' (Deut. 18:10–12). You not only need to stop practicing these things," she continued, "but you must renounce them before God and cast out the satanic spirits behind them so they have no hold over your life."

I didn't want to believe that the occult was that bad, but I did believe the Bible was God's Word. If God said it was wrong, I was willing to disconnect myself from any association with it. So I confessed and renounced all my occult involvement, and Mary Anne prayed for me to be set free from it. As she did, I felt a distinct sensation like an electrical charge pulsing through my head, throat, chest, stomach, and even my hands. Immediately I felt as if I had been released from a vise that I hadn't even realized was there. My mind was instantly clearer, I felt renewed strength, and I had a sense of peace, security, and well-being like I had never known before.

Aligning with a Winner

What the Bible says about the occult is clear. If we are aligned with it, we cannot be aligned with God. Pastor Jack Hayford says, "The occult is real in its power, but wrong in its source. It derives its power from the realm of darkness." On the subject of astrology he says, "The danger of astrology is beyond a simple, superstitious misuse of time. Paying the trade of occult practices is to traffic with the demonic. It isn't the result of some cosmic influence radiating from the stars, but a hellish one emanating from Satan himself, who has found but one more way to steal, to kill, and to destroy."

People have often told me, "But these things are real. I had my fortune told once, and it all came true."

Yes, these things are real and people can sometimes predict accurately, but the power behind it can never know *all* the truth, and it doesn't know the mind of God. Satan has certain supernatural powers, but his wisdom is limited and he is a loser. God, on the other hand, is all-knowing and all-powerful. He allows us to choose whom we will serve, and when we decide to come to Him alone for everything we need, we are guaranteed to be winners. We can't afford to align ourselves with a loser.

You may think reading your horoscope and checking on someone's astrological sign is harmless or a Ouija™ board is merely a parlor game or transcendental meditation gives you a more peaceful day or palm reading is fun, but you're being deceived. It's not harmless, it's destructive. Each experience will contribute to your ultimate depression, fear, and confusion. If it's going to stand in the way of your unlimited blessing, healing, deliverance, and wholeness, why would you want it?

Mysticism won't fulfill its promise. You can sit in a lotus position till you're a hundred and never escape the curse on your life. You can have your palm read a thousand times, and you still won't find the deliverance you need. You can follow your astrological chart every day and never be free of your deep feelings of low self-worth. You can channel to ancient gurus and have out-of-body experiences until the end of your days, and you'll still have the same emotional pain in your gut.

Believe me. I know. I've been there. I have tried them all. They don't work. But the danger is not that they don't work. The danger is that they work just enough to make you think they do work, and they suck you in. The danger is that the power behind them is real and intends to destroy you. Even though you may be just playing around, the devil isn't. If you link yourself with the spirit of witchcraft, you may find out that you will someday have a new job and a tall dark stranger in your life. But that's hardly worth ending up on the road to hell.

Act Immediately

If you are involved in the occult now or have had any occult involvement in the past, you must renounce it all before God. You can't be aligned with Satan and expect God to set you free. Say to God, "I confess my involvement with spirits other than the Spirit of God." Then name each type of occult practice with which you have had dealings. "I renounce astrology, I renounce fortune-telling, I renounce Ouija™ boards, I renounce reincarnation, I renounce seances, I renounce numerology, I renounce tealeaf reading, I renounce horoscopes, I renounce automatic writing, I renounce sorcery, I renounce hypnotism, I renounce yoga, I renounce astral projection, I renounce satanism, I renounce spiritism, I renounce ESP, I renounce tarot cards, I renounce palm reading, I renounce mind control, I renounce transcendental meditation, I renounce levitation, I renounce false religions, I renounce channeling. I recognize these practices as satanic, and I bind the powers of darkness behind them. In Jesus' name, I break any hold they have had on me."

Get rid of any occult material you have in your possession—magazines, books, tools, or pictures. If you've been *heavily* involved in the occult, ask a pastor, a counselor, or another strong believer to pray for you to be set free from the bondage that accompanied it. Then continue to check for occult practices that can creep in.

Ask the Lord to bring to the surface anything in your life that is not of Him, and when He does, renounce it in the name of Jesus and desire to have nothing more to do with it. *Keep in mind that looking to anything other than God as a source of power in your life is occult.* You can *never* find restoration as long as the occult has *any* hold on you.

■ ———————— *What the Bible Says About* ———————— ■
Renouncing the Occult

Let now the astrologers, the stargazers,
And the monthly prognosticators
Stand up and save you
From these things that shall come upon you.
Behold, they shall be as stubble,
The fire shall burn them;
They shall not deliver themselves
From the power of the flame;
It shall not be a coal to be warmed by,
Nor a fire to sit before!
    Isaiah 47:13–14

And when they say to you, "Seek those who are mediums and wizards, who whisper and mutter," should not a people seek their God? Should they seek the dead on behalf of the living?
    Isaiah 8:19

I give you the authority . . . over all the power of the enemy,
and nothing shall by any means hurt you.
Luke 10:19

■ ————————————————————————————————— ■

LIVE IN OBEDIENCE BY SAYING
NO TO SEXUAL IMMORALITY

"It's especially important to include every sexual sin you have
ever committed," Mary Anne had instructed me the first time I saw
her and she asked me to go home and list my sins.

How embarrassing, I thought. My desperate need for love, approval, and closeness had been so strong that I'd fallen into one
wrong relationship after another. It would be mortifying to tell her
about all that.

"You don't have to go into any detail," Mary Anne added as if
she knew exactly what I was thinking. "Just put down the name,
confess your involvement, and ask God to restore you. We'll pray
over the whole list next time."

As I left her office I immediately started remembering various
instances, and each one made me cringe. I found it felt good to
write it on my "sin list," confessing it to God and asking forgiveness just as she told me to do, like the release that comes from telling a bad secret. By the time I returned to Mary Anne's office for
the deliverance counseling, I had listed and confessed every incident of sexual immorality I could remember. She prayed for me to
be cleansed and released from the effects of all the sin on the list and
then reassured me that the devil could never throw it up in my face
again. I had confessed it. God had forgiven it. As long as I didn't do
it again, it was done. I felt cleansed and new. I discovered that
sexual purity and responsibility contribute to a sense of well-being
and cause a person to feel good about himself.

Sex as a Soul Tie

Sexual immorality is having sex with anyone to whom you are
not married. People are usually sexually immoral because either
they believe there is nothing wrong with sexual immorality or they
are too insecure and in need of closeness, love, affirmation, and
power, to say no.

We all need love and, when desperate, will look for it wherever
we can find it. But sex outside of marriage will never be the com-

mitted, sacrificial, unconditional love that we really need. It's not that God is a prude. Sex is His idea, after all. But He made certain guidelines for our benefit, and we can only find total fulfillment within them.

The problem with sexual immorality is that it is not just a physical encounter; it invades the soul. Sexual joining unites one person with another. When the relationship is broken, a part of the personality of each person involved is chipped away. Many such involvements cost many chips. By the time these people find the persons they're *supposed* to be with, they are so fragmented that they don't have a whole person to offer them.

Sandi had experienced many hurtful relationships and a short failed marriage with a man who left her for another woman while she was pregnant. When she came to me she was broken, hurting, fearful, and well aware of how her promiscuity had destroyed her. After several months of meeting with me, she received Jesus, gave up her drugs and occult practices, and ended her affair with the young man she was seeing. She started attending church, and within months she had shed her insomnia, her fear of being alone, her unforgiveness toward her ex-husband, and her lack of self-worth. She was on the road to restoration. I was thrilled with the way she was allowing God to work in her life.

Then one day she went on a blind date with a tall, handsome, successful young man who appeared to be everything she ever wanted in a husband. She immediately fell in love with him and, in her loneliness and desperation for affection, ignored what the Bible says about sex outside of marriage. Instead, she fell for such lies as, "We love each other. . . . We're going to get married anyway. . . . How will we know if we're compatible. . . . It's not hurting anyone. . . . Everyone else is doing it."

The man stayed with her for little more than a year, during which time she stopped attending church, stopped reading the Bible, and stopped praying. After he left her, she became extremely fearful, depressed, and laden with guilt. She began having one serious physical problem after another, and when I next saw her, she looked old and drawn, as if she were dying. I took her back to church where she started counseling and is now on the road to recovery, but it will take her awhile to regain the healing she forfeited. She has lost years of her life and delayed finding God's restoration for her and possibly the godly husband she so earnestly desires. Don't let that happen to you.

When It Wasn't Your Fault

"I can't bear to hear anything about sexual immorality," a young girl named Caroline cried to me. "I feel irreparably dirty already, and this only makes me feel worse."

She related her horror story of repeated sexual intercourse with her father from the time she was nine and of a date rape she suffered in her teens. She became promiscuous after that and felt that sexual purity was forever out of her reach. She felt an overwhelming hopelessness.

"Caroline, sexual purity, like virginity, is something only you can *give* away. It's *not* something that can be *taken* from you. That's because sexual purity is a matter of the heart. Someone may forcibly penetrate your body, but they can't penetrate your heart, soul, and spirit."

"But you don't understand," Caroline sobbed. "I didn't try to fight off my father. I didn't even try to stop the date rape. I allowed myself to be promiscuous. Don't you see? I let it all happen."

"Tell me why you didn't fight them off or try to stop them, Caroline," I asked, knowing what her answer would be.

"I was afraid to fight," she explained, her voice filled with self-loathing and remorse.

"Caroline, let me explain something," I said. "You became afraid to fight the moment your own father forced himself upon you sexually. When someone is sexually abused as a child, their ability to make sound decisions is taken from them. Everything they do from that point on is for survival, or the opposite, self-destruction. From that first moment of unredeemed and unhealed sexual abuse, you were rendered incapable of doing anything different from what you did. There were no choices for you, only the illusion of choice. But God makes all things new, and that means the moment you let Jesus into your heart, give God all of your past, and commit to walking in sexual purity, you are as pure as anyone can be. Confession, forgiveness, deliverance, and the Lord's healing love are the processes that will cleanse you from the residue of what occurred in the past. Don't let the devil take that away from you by making you feel unclean."

Wounds as deep as Caroline's are not healed overnight. It has taken a lot of prayer, counseling, and love. But hope was ignited in her when she caught the vision of herself as pure.

If you feel tainted by sexual impurity because of acts that were not your choice, God wants you to be released from the burden of them. Speak to the Lord about *all* that has happened. Every incident of your memory needs to be spoken out to Him so that it loses its power to torment you. Then ask Him to cleanse you from every effect of it.

Building a Relationship That Lasts

Sex should *only* be associated with a relationship that is lasting, and without marriage you are not committed to anything lasting, only to lasting as long as it feels good. And we will always pay a steep price when we buy into the "whatever feels good, do it" philosophy. On the other hand, we gain in depth of friendship whatever we feel physical abstinence costs us. When you eliminate the physical side of the relationship, you find out what is really there. Also, you don't get destroyed when you break up. Sex before marriage means you have not established the relationship as a friendship *first,* and it's the very reason many relationships are not working out.

Sexual immorality scars our souls and damages our emotions more severely than any other disobedience. The road back from such devastation to the inner person is also slower because the fragmentation of the soul is deeper than any caused by other sins. The Bible says, "He who commits sexual immorality sins against his own body" (1 Cor. 6:18). We will *always* pay for it, and the price will *always* be way too high.

I know how difficult this step of obedience is, especially for someone who is emotionally needy or who has suffered hurt, rejection, or a lack of love. The fact that someone seems to care about you and makes you feel loved and good about yourself is irresistible. Fortunately, we have a God who understands how difficult it is. That's why He put His Spirit in us to overcome temptation. All He asks is that we have a heart that says, "I want to do what's right. God, help me to do it."

If you have any unconfessed sexual sin in your past, confess it immediately. Don't fall into the trap of thinking, "How can I confess this incident as sexual failure when that person made me feel so good?" or "How can I confess something I don't want to stop doing?" or "Why should I confess something that wasn't my fault?" Sin destroys your life, whether you enjoyed it at the time or not, whether you intended to do it or not, or whether it was your choice or not.

If you are now in a sexual involvement outside of marriage, you must ask the Holy Spirit to help you take the steps necessary to release you from it. Say, "Holy Spirit, take root in my personality and guide my actions according to God's ways. Open my eyes to the truth of Your Word. Help me to want to stand for what is right and strengthen me to say no to sexual disobedience. Help me to lay down the rules for my relationships and to resist anything that is not Your best for my life." If you fall again after you pray this prayer, don't withdraw from God. Confess it, pray again, and try harder. If you have a strong sexual addiction, you need to seek counseling. Something in your past has caused that, and God wants to heal you.

If you are already convinced that you want to live in sexual purity and you are dating someone who is pressuring you to violate that conviction, then that person's commitment level to God and to you is not what it should be, and you need to consider severing the relationship until this matter can be reconciled before the Lord. If the person truly loves you and this relationship is right, nothing will be lost and much will be gained.

Sexual immorality closes off the possibilities God has for your lasting fulfillment. Allowing it to chip life away is counterproductive for someone seeking to put the pieces of his life back together. Only an inflow of God's holiness can bring the wholeness you desire. See to it that it happens to you by saying "No!" to sexual immorality and "Yes!" to God's restoration.

■ ─────── *What the Bible Says About* ─────── ■
Saying No to Sexual Immorality

The body is not for sexual immorality but for the Lord, and the Lord for the body.
1 Corinthians 6:13

Whoever has been born of God does not sin, for His seed remains in him; and he cannot sin, because he has been born of God.
1 John 3:9

Put to death, therefore, whatever belongs to your earthly nature: sexual immorality, impurity, lust, evil desires and greed, which is idolatry. . . . You used to walk in these ways, . . . But now you must rid yourselves of all such things as these.
Colossians 3:5, 7–8 NIV

There must not be even a hint of sexual immorality, or of any kind of impurity.
Ephesians 5:3 NIV

For if we sin willfully after we have received the knowledge of the truth, there no longer remains a sacrifice for sins.
Hebrews 10:26

LIVE IN OBEDIENCE BY
CLEANING OUT YOUR HOUSE

After the deliverance counseling session with Mary Anne, I still wasn't sure exactly what had happened to me but I did feel remarkably peaceful and free of depression. Mary Anne instructed me to spend as much time as possible reading the Word in order to fill any empty space in me with the Lord's truth. I was eager to do that, so I decided to read straight through the Bible again. I had plenty of time on my hands as I was not working and my husband was very busy with his projects, so I read nearly a book a day. Each page came alive with meaning, and it drew me in like the best-selling novels I used to read.

I hadn't read more than a few minutes about the rewards of obedience in Deuteronomy 7 when I came across the words of the last verse: "Do not bring a detestable thing into your house, or you, like it, will be set apart for destruction" (v. 26 NIV).

Detestable thing? In my house? Do I have that, Lord? Show me if I do.

Almost before the words were out of my mouth, I thought of my sixty or seventy books on the occult, spiritism, and Eastern religions. I had stopped reading them when I received Jesus and had renounced my involvement, but I still had the books. I had noticed them briefly on one occasion, but the thought of throwing out expensive hard-cover books never crossed my mind. I thought I might give them all to one of my nonbelieving friends sometime.

I was suddenly embarrassed at the hypocrisy of that thought. Now that I was a believer, I was going to give my books on worshiping other gods to my unbelieving friends? What ignorance! Those books advocated the evil that had nearly destroyed my life, yet I was willing to let them influence someone else's life. I gathered twenty to thirty shopping bags and went to my bookshelves, a woman with a mission. I looked through each of my hundreds of books and discarded the ones about the occult or with any questionable material in them.

I didn't stop there, however. The more I thought about it, the more I recognized other offensive possessions. My search-and-destroy mission soon included paintings, sculptures, wall hangings, hand-painted trays, and miscellaneous artifacts that exalted other gods. I threw out records and tapes that were negative, satanic, or questionable in any way.

By then I felt so good that I thought, *Why stop there?* I threw out all clothes that did not glorify God. My low-cut dresses, see-through blouses, and too-tight jeans were quickly discarded. I also gave away all reminders of my first marriage and old boyfriends and unhappy times.

I might sound like a fanatic on a witch-hunt, but I was compelled by a sound decision to separate myself from anything that separated me from God. I had experienced enough of God's blessings to know that I wanted *all* He had for me. When I finished my spiritual housecleaning, I felt rejuvenated and exuberant. I sensed a spiritual and emotional breakthrough as if I had finally passed through some invisible barrier.

Since that time I do this type of housecleaning periodically—never to the extent of this first experience because I'm careful not to accumulate anything "detestable." But walking with the Lord fine-tunes our discernment, and things I've never seen as harmful before are now revealed as promoting destruction.

Years later, for instance, when my young son was having repeated nightmares, I prayed about them and felt specifically led to go directly into his room and check through his computer games. He had many, but I felt directed to pick up one that a Christian family had given him for Christmas. There was nothing suspicious in any way on the outside, but when I checked the instructions, I found the worst satanic garbage I could imagine.

When my son came home from school, I showed him the instruction booklet and explained how I felt his nightmares were associated with the game. He agreed that he didn't want it anymore, so we destroyed it immediately, and he and my husband and I prayed over his room. The nightmares stopped. Coincidence? I don't think so. There have been too many "coincidences" like this.

Discerning the Negative

There comes a point in everyone's walk with Jesus when it's time to do some housecleaning. Some things you need to be rid of will be obvious. Anything depicting sexual immorality, occult practices, or any kind of evil, for example, is clearly marked for the trash barrel. Other things may not be harmful in themselves, but can be destructive for you because of a negative association. For example, gifts from a former boyfriend—even if he was a great person and you had a happy relationship—have no place in your life now if you are married. In fact, anything you possess that reminds you of people, incidents, or things that are not of the Lord (or make you react negatively with depression, anger, anxiety, or fear) must be eliminated. Give them away if they are useful to someone who has no emotional tie to them.

To gain discernment, fill your heart and mind with God's Word and spend much time in the Lord's presence in prayer and worship. Then ask, "Lord, show me if there is anything detestable in my house." Go through your closets and cupboards. Check your walls and bookshelves. Throw out anything suspicious.

Decide that because you love God, you will part with that old Buddha ring with the ruby in his belly or the painting of a vampire swallowing a snake that Uncle Ned painted just for you or tapes and videos that exalt immorality or questionable books and magazines a friend gave you or anything that you know in your spirit is not right. Things that don't *build* you should not be part of your life.

I'm not trying to control you, make you irritated and miserable, or move you into censorship and book burning. But I know that possessions mean nothing if you don't have the peace of God in your heart. If you feel unrest in your spirit, have trouble sleeping, or feel oppressed in your home, see if you need to get rid of something and then do it.

Spiritual Cleaning

It is also a good idea to pray over your home to clean it out spiritually. Every time we've moved to a different house, we've asked a small group of believers to come over and help us pray through it. We walk the boundaries of the property and every room, praying for the peace and protection of God to reign supreme there. We bind up any hold the devil may have had on the property, and we cast the enemy out. Then we proclaim that the house and property are the Lord's.

If you have never prayed over your house, apartment, or room, then do it immediately. Don't live in a place that is not covered by the Lord. If you can, join with one or more believers to pray, and ask for these things:

- For God's peace and protection to be over it
- That nothing evil can enter in
- To break any point of bondage that has found a place there

You won't enjoy the peace and quality of life you desire until you clean your house thoroughly. Replace whatever you take out of your life with something of the Lord. I bought Christian books and music to replace what I threw out. I searched for God-glorifying art and clothing, neither of which is easy to find.

The less contact you have with what is not of God, the more of God you can have in your life. The more of God you have, the more you will know His love, peace, joy, healing, and wholeness.

■ ——— *What the Bible Says About* ——— ■
Cleaning Out Your House

Let us purify ourselves from everything that contaminates the body and spirit, perfecting holiness out of reverence for God.
2 Corinthians 7:1 NIV

I will set nothing wicked before my eyes.
Psalm 101:3

Keep yourselves from idols.
1 John 5:21

The curse of the LORD is on the house of the wicked,
But He blesses the habitation of the just.
Proverbs 3:33

I will walk within my house with a perfect heart.
Psalm 101:2

LIVE IN OBEDIENCE BY
TAKING CHARGE OF YOUR MIND

"I've started having uncontrollably bizarre, and frightening thoughts," I told Mary Anne nearly a year after my deliverance. I put my fingers to my temples and rubbed hard. "I've been doing so well, I don't know what happened. Sometimes I feel like I'm losing my mind. It's scary. I've always been afraid I'd go crazy like my mother."

"Let me assure you that you are not going to go crazy like your mother," she said with great confidence. "First of all, you are not your mother. You are a different person. Secondly, you are not mentally ill. But you *are* being mentally oppressed."

"What do you mean?" I questioned further.

"The Bible tells us we have the mind of Christ when we are born again, but we still have to allow this mind to be in us," Mary Anne explained. "You've been delivered from major oppression, but you still must choose to let the mind of Christ control you. You've started allowing yourself to listen to whatever thoughts come into your mind."

This was new information to me. I knew that God gives us a choice about how we live, but I had never realized I could choose my thoughts. I grew up with a mother whose every wild imagination and stray thought controlled her. From that I had determined we must all be victims of our minds.

"The Bible makes it clear we are not to conform to the world's way of thinking," Mary Anne continued. "It says we are to renew our minds by taking 'captive every thought to make it obedient to Christ' (2 Cor. 10:5 NIV). God has also made clear what we *are* to allow into our minds. 'Whatever is *true*, whatever is *noble*, whatever is *right*, whatever is *pure*, whatever is *lovely*, whatever is *admirable*, if anything is *excellent* or *praiseworthy*—think about such things' (Phil. 4:8 NIV emphasis added). God is very specific about this and *you* need to be too."

"But what about tormenting sexual thoughts?" I asked. "I'll be sitting in church and suddenly the most perverse sexual image flashes across my mind."

"Let me ask you something," she answered. "Do you choose to think these vile sexual thoughts?"

"Definitely not!" I responded immediately.

"So where do they come from?"

"Not God," I said with great surety.

"Of course not. They come from the enemy of your soul. Satan puts those thoughts there, and you've accepted them as yours. That's why you feel guilty about them. This is mental oppression, a ploy of the devil. When he starts to bring up things like that you have to tell him to leave you alone."

"You mean if I resist the thoughts they will leave?"

"Yes, eventually," Mary Anne assured me.

"Well, what about horrendously frightening thoughts? Last night quite unexpectedly I envisioned in vivid detail an airplane suddenly crashing into our house, exploding in flames and burning my children to death. I could hardly sleep because of it."

"Everyone has fear at one time or another," she said. "But is there any particular reason you should fear disaster coming upon your children?"

"No, not really?"

"Would you *choose* to be afraid?"

"Never!"

"Of course, you wouldn't. So where do fears come from? They are from the evil one. Recognize that and don't take fear upon you. Satan has bound people in the areas of *lust* and *fear* more than any other.

What a revelation! Suddenly all my tormenting thoughts didn't seem so overpowering. Nor did I have to feel guilty about them now that I was certain they were not coming from me. All I had to do was resist them in Jesus' name.

Immediately I set about doing just that. Whenever upsetting thoughts came into my mind and I identified them as not from me or God, I said aloud, "I will not be controlled by negative thoughts. I renounce these sexual images in the name of Jesus. I reject visions of disaster coming upon me and my family. I refuse the suggestion that I will go crazy like my mother. God has not given me a spirit of fear. He has given me a sound mind. I have the mind of Christ and I refuse any thoughts that are not of the Lord."

Although sometimes I had to pray like that for days, relief usually came right away when I resisted negative mental suggestions and spent much time praising God. I did the same thing whenever a memory of a past incident played itself over and over in my mind like a stuck record. "I give that memory to you, Jesus, and I refuse to think about it any more," I said every time it came to mind. That always stopped it. Now, though I'm just as vulnerable to an attack of mental oppression as anyone, I quickly identify it and refuse to give place to it.

I'm convinced we can never be totally healed of emotional damage when a war is constantly going on in our minds—especially if we are losing the battle. The Bible says, not to "walk as the rest of the Gentiles walk, in the futility of their mind, having their understanding darkened, being alienated from the life of God, because of the ignorance that is in them" (Eph. 4:17–18). We have to choose daily to allow the mind of Christ to be in us and the wisdom of God to guide us.

What Is Your State of Mind?

Considering that the state of your mind affects the state of your heart, which in turn affects your entire being, it's wise to evaluate the condition of your mind frequently by asking yourself these questions:

____ Do my thoughts make me feel sad, depressed, lonely, or hopeless?

____ Do my thoughts cause me to be angry, bitter, or unforgiving?

____ Do my thoughts cause me to feel self-hatred and self-doubt?

____ Do my thoughts bring feelings of anxiety or fear?

____ Do my thoughts constantly rehearse negative memories?

____ Do my thoughts become dominated by blatant sexual images?

____ Do my thoughts make me feel unclean or sickened?

____ Do my thoughts cause me to feel anything other than peace and well-being?

If you answered yes to any of these questions, you are living with needless torment, and it's time to take charge of your mind. Don't think you're alone, however. Anyone who has ever suffered from traumatic emotional hurts is highly susceptible to these feelings. Not only do we have bad memories to deal with, but the devil delights in taking the painful events of our past and sowing them as seeds of negativity in the mind.

The best way to control your thoughts is to control outside influences. Did you know that you can become fearful and anxious from simply watching the wrong TV shows, even when they don't seem upsetting at the time? Think about it. How many shows have you watched and gone away feeling uplifted, hopeful, energetic, full of love, and motivated to do good things? Not many, I'm sure. Usually we feel exhausted, empty, restless, uneasy, unclean, or fearful. That's because whatever goes into your mind affects your emotions. You have to be specific about what you allow into your mind and truly take *every* thought captive.

Don't just leave the television on for hours. Know for sure exactly what program you're watching and why you're watching it. Don't allow yourself the leeway of saying, "I don't really pay attention to the TV. I just leave it on all day for company." Get in the habit of asking the Holy Spirit, "Is this good for me?" If it leaves you depressed, fearful, or frustrated or causes you to fantasize about your life, turn it off immediately. Anything that comes from God will *never* make you feel that way.

What kind of magazines and books are you reading? Do they enrich your life? Or do they make you feel depressed, frustrated, unfulfilled, guilty, or dissatisfied with the life God gave you? If so, put them down. What about the movies you see or the videos you rent? Do they make you feel good about yourself, other people, and life in general? If not, walk away from them. What about the music you listen to? Does it leave you joyful, uplifted, or peaceful? If not, turn it off. Don't say, "It doesn't matter what I see, read, or hear— I can distinguish between right and wrong." That's not entirely true. Certain influences can filter into your spirit and erode your life without your even realizing it. Anything that isn't feeding you is depleting you. If it's not of God, it will make your heart numb to what *is* of God.

Fantasizing is a series of mental images, as in a daydream, which usually involves some unfulfilled desire. Don't fall for the misconception that you can fantasize about whatever you want because it's not real. It *is* real. When it's going on in the mind, that means it's going on. Many people's lives are crooked because they don't think straight, so turn off any thoughts that are not inspired by the Lord.

Take the same approach when things that have happened in the past come back to your mind. Unless you are trying to remember them for the specific purpose of being healed or set free (as would happen in a counseling session or in your time with the Lord), don't let your mind play continuous reruns. Don't let the enemy of your soul repeatedly fill you with regret and remorse over past events. Don't let your mind wander and race from one anxious and painful thought to another. Take each negative thought to the Lord immediately. Recognize that you need God's power to enable you to take charge of your mind, and ask Him to help you be rid of anything negative that has crowded in.

Tactics of War

The main weapon in mental warfare is deliberately to feed your mind on God's truth and power. Think about the greatness of the Lord. Fill your mind with His Word. Seek out Christian books and magazines. Play Christian music in your home and in your car. Put on worship music and turn it loud enough to drown out the negative voices in your head. There are movies, music, books, and television programs that may not be saying "Jesus is Lord," but they are based on Christian principles and have a Christian spirit behind them. Seek them out. Remember that whatever goes into your mind becomes a part of you. To control your emotions you have to control your mind.

Those who have been severely abused often struggle with the feeling that they are going crazy. If there is mental illness in your family, you may fear, as I did, that it will be passed on to you or another family member. If so, *you* must come to the full knowledge, *without any doubt*, that *anything other than a sound mind does not come from God*. Mental illness does not have to be passed along from generation to generation any more than the sins of the parents have to be visited upon the children to the third and fourth generation if you have the authority of Jesus and the power of the Holy Spirit to stop them. God gives us a sound mind. If you don't feel you have one, then ask Him for it and don't accept anything less.

If at any time you feel confused, disoriented, or mentally fragile, say, "Thank You, Lord, that You have given me love and power and a sound mind." Then praise God until those feelings lift. If you have to say that prayer a hundred times a day, then do it. At times I said over and over, "God has given me a sound mind. God has given me a sound mind. God has given me a sound mind." I refused the lie that I would end up like my mother. I refused to review the past and live in dread of the future.

There is no holding pattern for a believer. We don't live in a neutral state. We are either going forward or backwards. We are either being renewed or consumed. We are at war, and the war is being waged against us by an enemy who wants control of our minds. If you are hurting, he probably has too much access to your mind already. Don't relinquish any more territory to him. Walk in obedience by taking charge of your mind *now*.

■ ——————— *What the Bible Says About* ——————— ■
Taking Charge of Your Mind

And do not be conformed to this world, but be transformed by the renewing of your mind, that you may prove what is that good and acceptable and perfect will of God.
Romans 12:2

Casting down arguments and every high thing that exalts itself against the knowledge of God, bringing every thought into captivity to the obedience of Christ.
2 Corinthians 10:5

You should no longer walk as the rest of the Gentiles walk, in the futility of their mind, having their understanding darkened, being alienated from the life of God, because of the ignorance that is in them, because of the hardening of their heart.
Ephesians 4:17–18

To be carnally minded is death, but to be spiritually minded is life and peace.
Romans 8:6

But I see another law in my members, warring against the law of my mind, and bringing me into captivity to the law of sin which is in my members.
Romans 7:23

LIVE IN OBEDIENCE
BY TAKING CARE OF YOUR BODY

In my teens and early twenties, intense negative emotions provoked one stress-related disease after another in my physical body. I had everything from problem skin, falling hair, headaches, and chronic fatigue to infections and allergies. Several months before I received the Lord, I had become so weakened that I developed sores in my mouth and could barely eat or talk. The doctor I went to for help said I had a severe vitamin B deficiency. He plunged a needle into my right hip and emptied a large syringe of vitamin B, which hurt so badly I could hardly stand up.

"I know this hurts, but you need this strong dose to help clear up those sores," the doctor told me. "I want you to come back for a shot three times a week until you're on your feet, but you've got to start taking care of yourself. You must eat right, get plenty of rest, and I advise you to get rid of whatever is causing all the stress in your life before it kills you," he added with no smile whatsoever.

I paid the bill and walked painfully out to the car with the strong taste of vitamin B still in my mouth from the shot. By the time I started the engine, the pain in my head began to subside. As I pulled out of the parking lot, I sensed some relief from the anxious knot in my stomach. Ten minutes down the freeway, I started to feel like a new person. When I pulled into my driveway, I experienced a strange and amazing sensation of hope.

I took the doctor's advice and over the next few days went back to a routine of proper eating and exercise. When I first came to Hollywood and took regular dance classes, I discovered the benefits of physical exercise. The emphasis on youth and appearance in that town also drew me into eating health food. But all my good efforts were not enough to sustain me under the weight of ever-building emotional stress. Lately I had let them all go because I was exhausted from my depression. But when I had those B shots, I felt like a new person—from hopelessness to hope in twenty minutes. Granted, it wasn't lasting, and I had to return for another shot a few days later, but I did learn that physical health and emotional health are definitely connected.

We can't have good physical health without a certain amount of emotional health. Likewise, we can't have good emotional health without a certain amount of physical health. In fact, we can be suffering from depression or some other negative emotion simply because of physical depletion or imbalance. If I feel discouraged, depressed, overwhelmed, or fearful, I check first to see if I have been taking proper care of my physical health. There have been times, even in recent years, when I've felt I couldn't cope with my life and all it took was a good night's sleep, eating right, and getting back on my exercise routine to turn everything around.

Greater Physical Health God's Way

Physical health is no minor subject. It is a crucial link to emotional wholeness. In fact emotional health and physical health so affect one another it's difficult to perceive where one leaves off and the other begins. Do you realize that you can actually create emotional problems for yourself just by eating poorly, getting no exercise, and living with constant stress? Poor health can make even small problems seem monumental and hopeless. If your body is nutritionally starved, it's possible to have suicidal thoughts, feel you're going crazy, or abuse your children, all simply because your body is too depleted to cope. Physical health is important to emotional restoration.

No one gets away with neglecting their health. We may have temporary success, but we all eventually have to pay the price for our neglect. I know a doctor who was a practicing psychiatrist for a few years before deciding to become a nutritional specialist. He told me he realized early in his practice that people's minds and emotions were greatly affected by the condition of their bodies. He felt he could help people more on the physical side of things. Many doctors feel that most diseases are caused by mental and emotional stress. Some, like this doctor I mentioned, believe that emotional problems can be controlled through good physical health. Rather than rack your brain trying to decide which came first in your own case, just know that God made the body as well as the soul and the spirit. He expects us to take care of them all. Right alongside the steps you are taking toward emotional wholeness, you must be taking steps toward physical wholeness.

First of all, you should have regular checkups to make sure you are in good health. If you have specific physical problems, don't just let them go. Get a doctor's attention for them. Then take stock of the way you've been treating your body. This is not to make you feel guilty, because I understand how overwhelming body care can seem sometimes, especially when it is so closely associated with your emotions. But you can take certain basic steps that will have immediate benefits for you.

After I received the Lord, I studied the Bible regarding health and discovered that there is more to good health than just exercise and diet. In fact, seven important factors must be in proper balance in order to achieve consistently good health. If I neglect to tell you even one of them, I risk leaving out an essential factor. Below is a brief summary of the seven different areas I presented in my book *Greater Health God's Way* (Sparrow). Because taking care of your physical body is a very important step of obedience, ask God to show you any area you have neglected.

1. *Ask God to show you about the stress in your life.* Stress is the response of your mind, emotions, and body to whatever demands are being made upon you. Emotional pain and negative emotions are a *constant* major source of stress, and great emotional trauma can throw your physical body completely out of balance.

If you are experiencing rejection, hurt, unforgiveness, bitterness, anger, loneliness, fear, or any other kind of negative emotion, then your body is carrying a load it wasn't designed to carry. Each one of these is like a large siphon which is draining life.

What determines the effect of stress on your body is not so much what happens to you as it is how you respond to it. Once you identify stress, you can do one of two things: do something to change the situation, or learn to live with it, while fortifying yourself physically, mentally, and spiritually to survive.

Sometimes stress is so hidden that we don't realize we're being affected by it. Sometimes it creeps up on us. We think we are coping well so we don't see the signs. The important thing to remember is that the ultimate reaction to stress is death. That's why we must learn to recognize stress in our lives *before* it gets serious and then take specific steps to alleviate it.

2. *Ask God to show you about the food you are eating.* Are you eating too many impure, processed, or depleted foods? If so, toxic wastes can pile up in your body, causing physical stress that interferes with the body's functions. When you don't feed your body properly, you become physically depleted, your mind cannot process information accurately, and every decision is exhausting. Do you realize that you could be depressed right now, even feel like ending it all, because of the way you are feeding your body? We've all experienced times where a single incident can put us over the edge, while the same incident occurring at a different time may not affect us that way at all.

Those of us who have lived with severe underlying stress due to emotional damage are more susceptible to depletion through poor eating habits than other people are. Trauma or abnormal amounts of stress can throw the body out of balance. Without proper care, this damage is never repaired, which leads to unhealthy cravings and out-of-control food habits.

If you are suffering from an eating disorder of any kind, seek help immediately. Your changeable metabolism and out-of-control hormones will cloud any progress you make toward emotional restoration. If your eating disorder is a secret—and nearly all of them are at some time—you are carrying guilt along with it. Making food a ritual, a religion, or the center of your life causes it to become your enemy. It was never meant to be that, and you don't have to live with that kind of misery.

Try to stay away from all junk—sugar, white flour, soft drinks made with chemicals, fried fast foods, highly processed foods with preservatives and chemicals. Make an effort to replace the junk with foods that are as close to their natural state as possible. Fresh fruits, vegetables, whole grains, nuts, and seeds contain the perfect balance of vitamins, minerals, and digestive enzymes. Correct eating must become a way of life and not a last resort in the face of sickness or excess weight.

3. *Ask God to show you about exercise.* The main purpose of

exercise is to keep the body healthy by enabling it to do four extremely important things: eliminate poisons, increase circulation, strengthen muscles, and eliminate stress.

Everybody must do some kind of regular physical exercise. Ask God specifically what *you* should be doing. It doesn't have to be an added pressure to you. It should be a relief. It doesn't need to be anything fancy either. You don't have to pay hundreds of dollars for the perfect exercise outfit, the gym membership, the equipment, or the video recorder. Those things are nice, but don't feel bad if you don't have them. The greatest exercise you can do for your body, mind, and emotions is walking. Go out for a walk every day in a safe area, even if it's only ten to fifteen minutes, and see if it doesn't have a positive effect on your emotions.

Certain frustrations that build up body tension can be worked out in exercise. Toxic wastes and poisons that build up in your system and lower your emotional well-being will be flushed out by proper exercise. An aerobics class, a good Christian exercise tape, or a daily walk outside in the fresh air and sunshine could turn your life around.

4. *Ask God to show you about drinking water*. Water is involved in every single process in our bodies, including digestion, circulation, absorption, and elimination. It is a primary transporter of nutrients through the body and it carries poisons out of the body.

Thirst does not always adequately indicate the body's need for water, so we should make sure we drink about eight eight-ounce glasses of water a day. Buy bottled water from a reputable company if you need to. It's hard to flush impurities from your system with water that has more impurities than you have.

5. *Ask God to show you about prayer and fasting*. As I mentioned earlier, fasting with prayer is an important spiritual step. And it is also important for your body as a natural self-healing and cleansing process. During a fast the energy used to digest, assimilate, and metabolize is spent purifying the body.

6. *Ask God to show you about spending time daily in fresh air and natural sunlight*. Fresh air and natural light bring a certain amount of healing and rejuvenation to every part of the body and mind. Natural light is a powerful healer, germ killer, remedial agent, and relaxer. Scientists are now discovering that light has a significant effect on the immune system and the emotions. Any activity or exercise done outside increases your inhalation of fresh air, which also aids in cleansing the body of impurities.

One of the greatest things you can do outdoors is gardening. Getting your hands in the earth has a miraculous calming effect upon your whole being. Digging up weeds or planting flowers and vegetables is great therapy. You can do other things outside too—sweep off your front step, water your lawn, rake leaves, or wash windows. Anything that gets you outside for a few minutes every day is good for your emotional and physical health.

Of course, you need to be careful not to do these activities in extreme heat or cold, and you need to take precaution against exposure to UVB rays by using a good sun block on exposed skin. Then the benefits of natural sunlight get through without the damaging effects.

7. *Ask God to show you about getting enough rest.* You need to be able to achieve a deep, sound, completely refreshing sleep naturally, without drugs. During sleep food is transformed into tissue, the entire system is cleansed of poisons, and the body repairs itself and recuperates. Those things can only happen fully during sleep when the nervous system slows down. Sleeping pills, alcohol, or drugs interfere with those processes. Make it your goal to experience deep rejuvenating sleep without them.

If everything is working properly in your life, good sleep comes automatically. If it doesn't, it usually means that one or more of the other six areas of health care is out of order. Don't make any life-changing decisions when you're exhausted. A good night's sleep could change your mind—completely.

Don't look at the care of your health as an overwhelming and complex task. It's really not. It's the way God wants us to live and a point of obedience. The Bible says,

"Do you not know that your body is the temple of the Holy Spirit who is in you, whom you have from God, and you are not your own? For you were bought at a price; therefore glorify God in your body and in your spirit, which are God's." (1 Cor. 6:19–20)

Are you taking good care of God's temple?

■ ———————— *What the Bible Says About* ———————— ■
Taking Care of Your Body

I beseech you therefore, brethren, by the mercies of God, that you present your bodies a living sacrifice, holy, acceptable to God, which is your reasonable service.
Romans 12:1

Therefore, whether you eat or drink, or whatever you do, do all to the glory of God.
1 Corinthians 10:31

Your ears shall hear a word behind you, saying,
"This is the way, walk in it"
Whenever you turn to the right hand,
Or whenever you turn to the left.
Isaiah 30:21

A sound heart is life to the body.
Proverbs 14:30

Do you not know that you are the temple of God and that the Spirit of God dwells in you?
1 Corinthians 3:16

◼—————————————————————————◼

LIVE IN OBEDIENCE BY SPENDING TIME WITH OTHER BELIEVERS

While we were getting ready to go to someone's house for dinner, Michael and I had a heated argument. We had misinterpreted each other's intentions and said words that were hurtful and pain provoking. I was reduced to tears and he to silence.

Great! I thought. *The last thing I want to do is be with other people feeling like this.* I silently ran through a list of reasons we could possibly cancel, but they sounded too feeble so I resigned myself to the evening.

We sat in silence during the entire drive to our host's home, except for Michael's asking, "Are you going to not speak to me all night?" To which I cleverly replied, "Are you going to not speak to *me* all night?"

I started thinking about the couple we were going to visit. Bob and Sally Anderson were one of the first Christian couples Michael and I befriended after we were married. We had a lot in common, including our children. Their daughter, Kristen, and our son, Christopher, were born about the same time and had become good friends. We loved being with them because they were solid in their relationship as well as their faith, and we knew there weren't going to be any weird surprises in store for us.

From the moment we arrived at their home I felt the tension between Michael and me dissipate. Throughout the evening our hearts softened, and by the time we went home we were laughing. It was as if the goodness of the Lord in the Anderson family had rubbed off on us and we were strengthened by it.

This kind of thing happened so many times that when Pastor Jack exhorted us to "be in fellowship with other believers" and waved his hand across the congregation as if to get his sheep moving, I understood the need for it.

More Than Just Friendship

The word *fellowship* sounded strange and "churchy" when I first heard it. It reminded me of tea and cookies after a missionary meeting or a potluck dinner in the church basement. I've since discovered it's much more than just coffee hour. Its dictionary definition is "companionship, a friendly association, mutual sharing, a group of people with the same interests." In the biblical sense, it's even more than that.

"Fellowship has to do with a mutuality in all parts of your life," Pastor Jack taught us. "You bear one another's burdens and fulfill the law of Christ. You pray for one another, you love one another, you help one another when there is material need, you weep with those who weep and rejoice with those who rejoice. It's growing in an association with people who are moving in the same pathway you are and sharing with each other in your times of victory or need or your times of trial or triumph. It's growing in relationship."

Fellowship is instrumental in shaping us. The Bible says that we become like those we spend time with and good friends sharpen one another just as iron sharpens iron (Prov. 27:17). This is reason enough to spend time with other believers, but there is even more to it.

Inside the Church

First and most basic of all, it is very important that you find a church home and spend time with that body of believers in church. I have not seen the kind of restoration and healing I'm talking about in this book happen without it. I certainly understand if you have been hurt or burned out by a church, but please hear me out. No two churches are alike. Each has its own personality. Some are great, some good, and some not quite what you hoped they'd be. Somewhere there is a right church for you, and you need to ask God to help you find it.

Contrary to what some people think, the church doesn't have to have a fancy building. You can find a good church wherever a body of believers meet with a pastoral leader who is *also* submitted to *other* pastoral leadership. They must believe the Bible is the Word of God and offer good solid teaching from it.

The next important indication of a good church is that you sense the love of God there and you receive it in abundance from the people. Some churches make an outgoing display of love, yet others who are more reserved may be just as genuine. If you pick up feelings of pride, competition, selfishness, self-righteousness, or coldness, determine whether that is the overall atmosphere or an isolated case. Remember that in any church you could find someone to exemplify these traits. Ask yourself if you generally feel love and acceptance there. You also need to be aware that you can't go into a church and *demand* that people love and care for you. You can communicate your needs, but you can't dictate how others should relate to you.

If you go to a church that doesn't believe in being born again or being baptized, then you need to find a church that does. If the pastor can't bring himself to talk about the Holy Spirit working in power in your life and the members of the congregation don't praise and worship the Lord, then you haven't found the right place yet. God can't work as powerfully in a church that limits Him and doesn't practice certain basic steps of obedience. Continue to look until you've found a solid church you can call home. If you are in a church where you're miserable, then get out. It's hard to receive God's love and life from a church you detest. This is not license to "church hop" whenever the pressure to grow is on, but don't fall for the "Now we gotcha!" trap either. Leave any church that tries to control your every breath.

Ask God to lead you to the right place. When you find it, make a commitment to stay and watch yourself grow. Go as often as you can. If once a week feels like a major commitment, start there. If once a week is easy, then go to midweek services also. Once you accept Jesus, you have eternal life whether you ever go to church or not, but I'm talking about living in the fullness of all God has for you. I'm talking about expelling the pain from deep within and living in love, peace, and joy. Certain visitations of God's power happen only in the midst of such gatherings of believers. Make it a point to be a part of that.

Outside the Church

There is also strength in being with believers *outside* the church. When you make friends with people who follow the Lord, there is a strong bond of love that makes other relationships seem shallow.

Such friendships are the most fulfilling and healing. They can also be the most frustrating because we expect *Christians* to be perfect when in reality only *Christ* is perfect.

It's helpful to think of all fellowship with believers as beneficial: the pleasant encounters are *healing* and the unpleasant ones are *stretching*. When you run across believers who stretch you more than you feel you can handle, don't turn away from God. Remember He is still perfect and good even if some of His children aren't. God always loves and respects you, even if a few of His offspring don't. I know that nothing hurts worse than a wound inflicted by a brother or sister in the Lord. Having been wounded many times like that myself, I am forced to remember that we will be imperfect until we go to be with Jesus. So we need to be merciful to those who "stretch" us and forgive quickly. Besides, we are probably stretching others ourselves.

The Bible says we should "not be unequally yoked together with unbelievers" (2 Cor. 6:14), but this doesn't mean you have to avoid them. It just means that your closest relationships, the ones that deeply touch and change your life, need to be with believers. Ask yourself, *Am I a godly influence in the lives of my unbelieving friends?* If so, then consider the relationship good. However, if they influence you away from God and His ways, then cut off this relationship immediately.

If your spouse is not a Christian, don't let his or her negative response to Jesus keep you from receiving the Lord's restoration for you. Check around for a Christian prayer group, Bible study, or a group with similar interests. I know someone who joined a Christian arts and crafts group and found great healing while making some of the best Christmas ornaments I've seen.

Believe me, I understand if you are so depressed and crippled emotionally that you barely have the energy to get out of bed, let alone do anything social. I've been that way myself. But you've got to start somewhere. Make a phone call to another believer and ask for prayer. Meet someone for lunch and talk about what the Lord has done in your lives. Open up and extend yourself in some way. You may feel you don't have anything to share, but if you have the Lord, He's all you need. The point is to seek out and develop godly relationships with other believers. Emotional healing and growth can't be experienced fully without it.

Ask God to help you by praying, "Lord, I acknowledge my need for other people. I ask You to lead me to relationships whereby I might grow in You and Your will might be fulfilled in me. Show me what steps to take to see that come about."

If our first goal in any relationship is our own fulfillment, we will ultimately be let down or disappointed. As painful as it is, we have to give up that desire and lay it down at Jesus' feet. However, there may be times when we have done all we can do in a relationship and it is still filled with problems. As hard as we try to make things good, a certain person may always leave you feeling depressed, angry, insecure, frightened, or hurt. When that happens, it is best to let the friendship go and give it to God to restore or remove as He sees fit. In a marriage, seek godly counseling on how to resolve your conflicts.

Fellowship is a step of obedience that expands our hearts, bridges gaps, and breaks down walls. It encourages, fulfills, and balances our lives. All of this is necessary for total restoration.

■ ———————— *What the Bible Says About* ———————— ■

Spending Time with Other Believers

Let us consider one another in order to stir up love and good works, not forsaking the assembling of ourselves together, as is the manner of some, but exhorting one another.
Hebrews 10:24–25

Practice hospitality.
Romans 12:13 NIV

Do not be unequally yoked together with unbelievers.
2 Corinthians 6:14

But if we walk in the light as He is in the light, we have fellowship with one another, and the blood of Jesus Christ His Son cleanses us from all sin.
1 John 1:7

■ _____ ■

LIVE IN OBEDIENCE
BY WATCHING WHAT YOU SAY

God created the world by speaking it into existence. Since we are made in His likeness and His Spirit dwells in us, we have the power to speak our own worlds into existence too. When we speak negatively about ourselves or our circumstances, we cut off the possibility of things being any different.

I spoke many negatives like "I'm a failure." "I'm ugly." "Nothing ever goes right." "Nobody really cares about me," until one day the Holy Spirit spoke to my heart through Proverbs 18:21: "Death and life are in the power of the tongue." A quick inventory of the things I had said aloud and in my mind revealed that I had been speaking death. This thought was frightening.

One clear example of what this Scripture was saying to me had to do with my speech problems. I'd had them since childhood and was teased about them all through school. This may seem insignificant, but having something wrong with your speech is like having something wrong with your face. Everyone observes it and forms an immediate opinion and response to you because of it. As soon as I was old enough to work and afford professional help, I worked with a speech therapist every week. I practiced day after day, year after year, to gain what seemed to be only a little improvement. Together we worked on lines I had to perform on television until they were smooth.

Two years after Michael and I were married, we did a few music concerts together, and I was asked to speak on health care in weekly classes at church. In spite of all my hard work with the therapist, I still lost my voice about halfway through each engagement, due to the tension in my neck. I became deeply discouraged and felt like a failure.

"I'll never be able to speak right," I cried time and again in despair and frustration. But as I spoke those words one day, the Lord spoke to my heart saying, *You're bringing death to your situation because you're not speaking the truth about it.*

"What does that mean, Lord? Am I supposed to deny what's really happening to me?" I asked God.

Do not speak what you think to be truth or what seems to be truth, He replied to my heart, *but rather speak what you know to be the truth of my Word.*

"What does Your truth say about my speech impediment?" I questioned further. "Show me, Lord. Help me to see."

Over the next few days, certain Scriptures came to my attention. First I read Isaiah 32:4: "The stammering tongue will be fluent and clear" (NIV). Then Pastor Jack read Isaiah 51:16 during his Sunday sermon:

> I have put My words in your mouth;
> I have covered you with the shadow of My hand.

Later, when I told my prayer group about my struggle, one of the women shared Isaiah 50:4 with me:

> The LORD God has given Me
> The tongue of the learned,
> That I should know how to speak
> A word in season to him who is weary.

Okay, Lord, I get the point, I thought. *The truth of Your word is that I can speak with intelligence, fluency, and clarity because You have put Your words in my mouth.*

After that, each time I was tempted to give in to discouragement, I spoke those Scriptures to myself and said, "Thank You, Lord, for helping me to speak slowly and clearly. I can do all things through Christ who strengthens me. Praise You, Lord, that You will give me the words to say and anoint them to have life. Thank You for my instructed tongue. Because of You I *can* speak."

I purposely cleared out other negatives from my speech. I no longer said "I'm a failure" because God's Word says the opposite is true about me. I stopped saying "I'm hopeless" and started acknowledging God as the hope of my life.

Soon after, when I was asked to speak at a large women's meeting, I took all my fears about it to the Lord in prayer and didn't let my mouth say that I was going to fail. I spoke God's truth instead of voicing my own negative opinions. As a result, my talk went so well that an entire speaking ministry opened up to me. To this day, I say those Scriptures and praise God for them each time before I speak.

Look Who's Talking!

We often speak what we hear the devil saying to our minds, and think it's truth: "You're such a failure. You'd be better off dead." Or we repeat to ourselves what someone else said to us years ago: "You're worthless. You'll never amount to anything." The Bible says, "You are snared by the words of your own mouth" (Prov. 6:2). That includes our silent messages to ourselves as well as what we speak aloud. We can't be healed if we continually speak bondage upon ourselves and infect our own emotions. We need to learn exactly who's talking in our minds. Is it the voice of God, is it our flesh, or is it the devil?

When talking about yourself, speak words of hope, health, encouragement, life, and purpose—they are God's truth for you. Wipe words of hopelessness, doubt, and negativity from your vocabulary. I'm not talking about when you're in counseling or pouring out your heart to God or to a friend. By all means be honest about your feelings. Giving the impression that nothing is wrong when something *is* wrong is living a lie. But when you are speaking about the way you feel, speak God's truth along with it. Rather than say, "Life is the pits," say, "I feel sad today, but I know God is in charge of my life and will perfect all that concerns me" (Ps. 138:8). If you can't think anything positive, say, "Lord, show me Your truth about my situation."

What you speak may seem harmless to you, but it affects your body and soul. It promotes either health and life or sickness and death. The best way to monitor your speech is to monitor your heart because "out of the overflow of the heart the mouth speaks" (Matt. 12:34 NIV). Purity of heart will overflow into your speech.

Check to see how you have been speaking lately by asking yourself these questions:

____ Do I ever say anything negative about myself or others?

____ Do I ever speak words that bring death into my situations and relationships rather than life?

____ Is my first reaction to people and events influenced by dread, fear, anger, and hopelessness, rather than calm assurance that God is in charge?

If you answered yes to any of these questions, then let that be a sign to you that your heart needs to be filled with more of the Lord. Don't even take the time to feel condemned—go straight to God and say, "Lord, forgive me for speaking negatively. Help me to speak only words of truth and life. Give me a fresh filling of Your Holy Spirit and let it overflow through me."

Don't work against what God wants to do in you by allowing negative speech. And don't be hard on yourself. Treat yourself with respect and kindness. Say as David did, "I have resolved that my mouth will not sin" (Ps. 17:3 NIV).

Let the words of my mouth and the meditation of my heart
Be acceptable in Your sight,
O LORD, my strength and my redeemer. (Ps. 19:14)

Walk in obedience to the Lord by only speaking words that reflect the wholeness you desire.

■ ——————— *What the Bible Says About* ——————— ■
Watching What You Say

He who guards his mouth preserves his life,
But he who opens wide his lips shall have destruction.
Proverbs 13:3

But I say to you that for every idle word men may speak,
they will give account of it in the day of judgment.
Matthew 12:36

There is one who speaks like the piercings of a sword,
But the tongue of the wise promotes health.
Proverbs 12:18

A word fitly spoken is like apples of gold
In settings of silver.
Proverbs 25:11

The lips of the righteous know what is acceptable,
But the mouth of the wicked what is perverse.
Proverbs 10:32

■ ■

LIVE IN OBEDIENCE BY GIVING YOURSELF AWAY

When I was ten years old, I lay awake in the middle of a cold, pitch-black night because I was too hungry to sleep. The pangs in my stomach were magnified by the knowledge that there was no food in the house and no money to buy any. My mother was asleep in the only other bedroom, on the opposite side beyond the service porch, and I felt isolated, alone, and afraid.

"There's nothing to eat," I had said to her earlier that evening after I searched the tiny kitchen. All I saw in the refrigerator were half-empty bottles of ketchup and mayonnaise. She had thrown remnants of old leftovers on the table for dinner—none of which went together in any appealing way—and made no apology for the fact it wasn't enough to sustain either one of us.

"Stop your complaining—we don't have money for food," she snapped and went back to talking to herself the way she often did for hours at a time. She hated it when I intruded on her imaginary world.

Now, as I lay in bed, my mind reeled with fear about the future. I feared I could starve to death and no one would care. I felt old.

Going hungry was terribly frightening. Having to be totally dependent for life and sustenance upon someone I couldn't depend on bred deep insecurity. I'm sure now that my mother knew Dad would bring money when he came home, but she told me there was nothing at all to eat and no way to buy it and that was that. We had no friends and Mother always made it seem as if we had no family either, since she considered them all to be her enemies. I had *nowhere* to turn and *no one* to help. We had nothing to sell, and as far as I could see we had no prospects for making any money. I became desperately afraid for my future.

Once I was out of school and self-supporting, I handled money very carefully. I felt the weight of being entirely responsible for my life, and the horror of someday starving to death always bubbled just below the surface of my mind. After I came to know the Lord and started going to church, I put money in the collection plate according to what I had with me—a couple of dollars at first, then a five, a ten, and later a twenty. It was more like donating to a good cause or tipping the piano player than having any thought of actually giving to God. But when I heard Pastor Jack teach on what the Bible says about giving, I knew I had far more to learn about the subject than I ever dreamed.

I learned first of all that giving was actually giving *back* to God from out of what He had given me, and by doing so I would never lose anything. In fact, I would be enriched. I also learned that the Bible teaches we are to give a tithe (10 percent) of our income to the Lord. When I started doing that, I found that my financial blessings were greater and the drains on my finances were fewer. I found, too, that the more I gave, the less fear I had about not having enough. My future felt more secure. Because I experienced such a flow of God's blessing in my life, the thought of *not* giving became more frightening than giving.

Giving is a step of obedience that brings life, health, healing, and abundance. Not giving will stop up our lives and our bodies and eventually lead to emotional and physical sickness and poverty. The Bible says that a person who gives will have a secure heart and will triumph over his foes. Giving is linked to protection and deliverance. There are two types of giving that are important: giving *to the Lord* and giving *as unto the Lord*.

Giving to the Lord

Because we can't separate our money from our lives, God must be made Lord over our finances, and we must obey Him. God says in His Word that we need to give a tenth of our earnings back to Him for His purposes. When we realize that every cent we have comes from God in the first place, that's not such an unreasonable request. A good steward of money realizes he has nothing on his own, but only manages what he has been given.

If we tithe, the Bible promises we will receive a multiplied return of God's abundance and His power. The Lord asks us to try Him and see if He is not faithful to pour out more blessings than we can contain. When we cut ourselves off from this life principle, the devourer comes in to eat up everything we have. I see people who don't give and then lose what they could have given in medical bills, appliance and car repairs, and a general lack of power to change their lives. God still loves them, but they've stopped up the flow of His blessing to them. The only way the storehouse of God's abundance can be opened is for them to start the process by opening themselves up to giving.

We often feel we will lose something if we give. We think, *If I didn't have to give this, I would have more for myself.* But actually that attitude will cause us to lose. The Bible says that if we give to the Lord, we will have everything we need in our life. If we don't, we won't.

If you have a hard time with this, tell God. Say, "Lord, I want to do what's right, but 10 percent of my income seems like too much to me. I feel I won't have enough if I do that. Help me to learn how to give the way You want me to. I want to receive all You have for me and become all You made me to be." Then, give as you are able and watch God move you into His ways.

Giving as Unto the Lord

Besides giving *to* the Lord, we need to get into the habit of giving to others as *unto* the Lord. This means we are to bless others because it blesses God—without expecting something in return. What-will-I-get-back thinking sets us up for disappointment and unhappiness, but when we give and expect nothing, the Lord will reward us.

Giving is a principle of release: "Give, and it will be given to you: good measure, pressed down, shaken together, and running over will be put into your bosom. For with the same measure that you use, it will be measured back to you" (Luke 6:38). To receive things that last you must give from what you have. If you need release in any area, give something away of yourself, your possessions, or your life, and you will see things begin to open up to you.

There is much to give besides money or store-bought gifts. We can give food, clothing, services, time, prayer, assistance, a ride in our car, or any possessions or abilities that could help someone else. It's important, however, to ask God for wisdom and direction about giving. Once my husband and I gave money to a person in need and, instead of feeding his family and paying his rent, he spent it on drugs. We've never made that mistake again.

You may be so depleted that you feel you have nothing to give or so overwhelmed by circumstances that giving of yourself seems monumental. If so, say, "I don't have anything to give, Lord. Provide me with resources beyond myself." As long as you have the Lord in your life, you will always have at least one thing to give— His love. People need someone to love them, to listen, to encourage, and to pray for them. You might say to someone, "My gift to you is a promise to pray for you every day for a month." Who wouldn't love that gift? I know I would.

When we live in fear that we won't have enough, it's hard to give. But the truth is, the more we give to others, the more will be released to us. We will reap a spiritual as well as material harvest. While it's good to save and plan wisely for the future because extreme poverty is also emotionally crippling, giving to the Lord and to others must not be excluded. If we don't give as the Lord directs, we end up losing what we think we're saving anyway.

My mother never gave anything away, and I believe that was part of her mental and emotional illness. She hoarded everything out of fear that she would someday need it. Her closets, sheds, rooms, and garages were full of "stuff." The Bible says, "He who gathered much had nothing left over, and he who gathered little had no lack" (2 Cor. 8:15). The sheer volume of my mother's stuff rendered it unusable.

Whenever my life seems not to be moving in any direction, deliberately giving of myself always brings breakthrough. It's not a matter of giving to get but of taking this step of obedience to release the flow of all God has for you. It's not that you can't receive any of God's blessings unless you give but that you can't receive *all* of them and life becomes more of a struggle. A heart ready to give makes room for all God has.

■ ———————— *What the Bible Says About* ———————— ■
Giving Yourself Away

You shall surely give to him, and your heart should not be grieved when you give to him, because for this thing the LORD your God will bless you in all your works and in all to which you put your hand.
Deuteronomy 15:10

But this I say: He who sows sparingly will also reap sparingly, and he who sows bountifully will also reap bountifully. So let each one give as he purposes in his heart, not grudgingly or of necessity; for God loves a cheerful giver.
2 Corinthians 9:6–7

Blessed is he who considers the poor;
The LORD will deliver him in time of trouble.
The LORD will preserve him and keep him alive,
And he will be blessed on the earth;
You will not deliver him to the will of his enemies.
The LORD will strengthen him on his bed of illness;
You will sustain him on his sickbed.
Psalm 41:1–3

There is one who scatters, yet increases more;
And there is one who withholds more than is right,
But it leads to poverty.
The generous soul will be made rich,
And he who waters will also be watered himself.
Proverbs 11:24–25

LIVE IN OBEDIENCE BY FEASTING AT THE LORD'S TABLE

When I was thirteen, we left our rundown house behind the gas station where my father worked and found a home in a better neighborhood. Whenever we moved, my mother's mental condition improved somewhat, and for a short time she acted as if she had a new lease on life. Looking back, I believe she tried hard to pull herself together at those times, but her confusion was far too overpowering for her to withstand alone. Before long she lost the battle and retreated to her make-believe world again.

During this one brief reprieve, when our lives temporarily resembled normalcy, Mother took my baby sister, Suzy, and me to a nearby church. Although the Godhood of Christ was taught there, I don't remember any emphasis on a personal relationship with Jesus. I do remember that the Communion service was formal and beautiful and moved me to tears each time I heard about Jesus' suffering. I thought, *How cruel to have tortured and killed this good man,* as I closely related to His unjustified punishment.

That church experience didn't last very long because my mother soon fell back into her old reclusive ways. It was the last time any of us went to church until I came to the Church on the Way years later. There, two distinctly different aspects of the Communion service impressed me. First, it was called the *Lord's* Table. It was considered *His* table, not ours. *He* invited us, not the church. Second, Communion was a joyful celebration of what Jesus accomplished for us on the cross as opposed to a mournful commemoration of His suffering. Pastor Jack called it "a celebration of victory, a reminder of Jesus' complete victory over our adversary, the enemy." Pastor Jack's words resounded in my soul when he explained, "What Jesus says about the Lord's Table is 'I was broken for you, I bled and died for you, and I want you to never forget the deliverance and the victory and the triumph that it's intended to give you all the time. Because I did that, you don't have to be bound up in suffering and agony and hellishness. I want you to partake of that regularly and make it, every time, an annunciation of my triumph so that you're reminded of it.'" Each time I took Communion, it reminded me that whatever I needed in my life already had been provided on the cross. The battle I faced had already been won!

A Joyful Reminder

Communion is a step of obedience to Jesus who said "Do this in remembrance of Me" (Luke 22:19). If there were no other reason, that would be enough. But it also serves to remind us that Jesus forgives, heals, and delivers and that no power of sin, sickness, or Satan can prevail among those who lift up the power of Jesus' death in Communion. We partake of the Lord's Table to acknowledge joyfully what He accomplished for us personally on the cross so it will become a part of us. God knows we have short memories and need to be reminded frequently.

Just as there is no magic in the water of baptism, there is also nothing magical in the wine, grape juice, bread, or cracker of communion. The power lies in our participation. That's why it's good to take communion regularly—once a month if possible, or however many times the Lord prompts you. If you can't get to a Communion service in your church, then do it at home by yourself. All you need is a small amount of grape juice and a piece of bread or a cracker. (While it's true that Jesus and His disciples drank wine at the time of the Last Supper, many churches substitute grape juice for wine.)

As you eat the bread or cracker, remember it is symbolic of His body, which was broken so your life can be mended. You are taking into yourself His wholeness so you can be nourished to become the whole person He made you to be. You drink the wine or juice to remind you that His blood was shed so that you could be forgiven and not have to live in the consequences of sin.

Fortunately, the blessings of receiving Communion don't depend on our full comprehension of what it means. God says we will never understand His ways completely. As long as we do it without allowing it to dissolve into a religious ritual and as long as we ascribe the proper worth to what Jesus did on the cross, there is power in simply being obedient. Along with obedience comes complete restoration.

What the Bible Says About
Feasting at the Lord's Table

The Lord Jesus on the same night in which He was betrayed took bread; and when He had given thanks, He broke it and said, "Take, eat; this is My body which is broken for you; do this in remembrance of Me."

In the same manner He also took the cup after supper, saying, "This cup is the new covenant in My blood. This do, as often as you drink it, in remembrance of Me." For as often as you eat this bread and drink this cup, you proclaim the Lord's death till He comes.

Therefore whoever eats this bread or drinks this cup of the Lord in an unworthy manner will be guilty of the body and blood of the Lord. But let a man examine himself, and so let him eat of that bread and drink of that cup. For he who eats and drinks in an unworthy manner eats and drinks judgment to himself, not discerning the Lord's body. For this

reason many are weak and sick among you, and many sleep.
1 Corinthians 11:23–30

LIVE IN OBEDIENCE BY WALKING IN FAITH

What if this Jesus thing is all a hoax? I thought to myself in horror one day nearly two years after the deliverance counseling in Mary Anne's office. *What if none of it's true? What if the pastor suddenly says, "This is all a joke, and you fell for it! Jesus isn't real and you're not really saved!"*

That day a wall of doubt settled around me like steel bars separating me from my future. The possibility of a life of nothingness became a temporary reality, and I panicked. *What brought this on all of a sudden?* I wondered. I struggled with that flash of doubt for days, and the more I thought about it, the more unhappy I became. I knew I had to reevaluate everything.

"What was your life like before you met Jesus?" I asked myself.

"I was dying inside," I replied.

"How did you feel?" I questioned further.

"Full of pain, hopelessness, and fear," I answered.

"Are things better now?"

"Much."

"What's different?"

"I don't feel depressed, fearful, or hopeless."

"When did that change?"

"When I received Jesus, I started to feel better."

"What about counseling with Mary Anne? Did anything *really* happen there?"

"Yes. I went in depressed and fearful, and I came out hopeful and free of depression. I have never gone back to that former life. I felt something happen. I mean I physically felt something leave my body. And I know I didn't conjure it up because I've never even imagined anything like that."

"Your experience with the Lord was real?"

"Well, yes, I think so."

"Then what's your problem?"

"The problem is I can't *prove* that Jesus is real."

"Can you prove that He isn't?"

"No."

"Well, then it looks like the choice is up to you, doesn't it? To believe or not to believe. It's your decision."

"It's my decision."

"Yes!"

"Okay, then. Weighing the quality of my life before I met Jesus against the quality of my life since then, I choose to believe Him."

"Are you sure?"

"Yes. I have decided to follow Jesus. No turning back. No turning back."

This little scenario happened five or six times in the first ten years of my walk with the Lord. In retrospect, I believe it occurred in busy and stressful times when I had not spent enough time in the Word of God or had neglected being alone with the Lord in prayer and praise. Eventually I realized that sending a doubting spirit to torment us is one of the devil's favorite tactics.

Without a Doubt

Faith is a spiritual muscle that needs to be exercised in order to prevent atrophy, which makes our entire spiritual being weak. Faith is first a decision, then an exercise in obedience, then a gift from God as it is multiplied. Our first step of faith is taken when we decide we will receive Jesus. After that, every time we decide to trust the Lord for anything, we build that faith. Whenever we decide *not* to trust Him, we tear it down. Faith is our daily decision to trust God.

The Bible says, "Whatever is not from faith is sin" (Rom. 14:23). How much clearer can it be? Faith is obedience. Doubt is disobedience. Faith is a gift from God because He enables us to believe, but we have to obey by building on that faith. Scripture also says that a person who doubts is unstable in every way and cannot please God. If that's true, emotional restoration is not possible without faith.

Built on the Word

How do we start building faith? Once we have a little, how do we get more? The first step is to be totally open and honest about any doubt in God's ability or His faithfulness to provide for our every need. Oswald Chambers says, "Faith is unutterable trust in God, trust which never dreams He would not stand by us" (*My Utmost for His Highest,* 177). Doubt emanates from a lie of the enemy, which says God is not all-powerful. If you've listened to this lie, confess it as sin.

The next step is to fill your mind with the Word: "Faith comes from hearing the message, and the message is heard through the

Fifteen Characteristics of Faith

Faith is a choice.
Faith is a step of obedience.
Faith is a spiritual exercise.
Faith is taking God at His Word.
Faith is saying yes to God.
Faith is looking to Jesus for everything.
Faith is knowing you are never without hope.
Faith is what lifts you out of your circumstances.
Faith is not holding anything back from God.
Faith is being obedient even if we don't feel like it.
Faith is a gift from God as we read His Word.
Faith is knowing that everything will work out.
Faith is a way out of our limitations.
Faith is the mother of hope.
Faith is the road to peace.

word of Christ" (Rom. 10:17 NIV). Reading the Word daily, regularly submitting to Bible teaching, and speaking the Word aloud will build trust. Your mouth and heart have to be united in this. One can't be saying, "God can" while the other says, "God can't." Your mind will convince your heart as you read or speak God's Word.

Because your prayers will only be as strong as your faith in God, it's always good to read the Word *before* you pray. Ask God to give you faith every time you do and try to keep reading until you sense faith rising in your heart. Faith leads the way to answered prayer. Whenever I'm afraid or doubt that my life is secure, I read the Bible until I sense God's peace in me. The more I read, the more hope I have. Then, when I pray, I'm confident that God will answer my prayers. When you have hope enough to say with conviction, "I can believe for restoration in my life," then you can pray with conviction also.

Even if you are not given to fear and doubt, you can be attacked by a *spirit* of *doubt*, as I was. When that happens, don't carry it by yourself. Take it to the Lord immediately. Say, "I've made a decision to believe Jesus. I know God answers prayer even if I don't see the answer right now. No matter how it appears, I am certain that I am not without hope. Therefore, I'm glad that I'm conquering doubt through Jesus Christ who strengthens me." Ask a mature believer to pray with you if you need to.

Sensing your own limitations doesn't mean you don't have faith. Feeling that *God* has limitations is what indicates a lack of faith. When it has blossomed, faith gives birth to hope, and people who have been abused or emotionally injured often have lost hope to one degree or another. Hope says, "There is an end to this. I won't be in this situation forever. I won't always feel like this. I won't always hurt." Hope and faith together give you a vision for your life.

The Bible says of the people who could not go into the Promised Land, "They could not enter in because of unbelief" (Heb. 3:19). Don't let that happen to you. Choose to enter in to all that God has for you by taking this important step of obedience.

What the Bible Says About
Walking in Faith

Without faith it is impossible to please Him, for he who comes to God must believe that He is, and that He is a rewarder of those who diligently seek Him.
Hebrews 11:6

Let him ask in faith, with no doubting, for he who doubts is like a wave of the sea driven and tossed by the wind. For let not that man suppose that he will receive anything from the Lord; he is a double-minded man, unstable in all his ways.
James 1:6–8

But the message they heard was of no value to them, because those who heard did not combine it with faith.
Hebrews 4:2 NIV

Trust in the LORD with all your heart,
And lean not on your own understanding.
Proverbs 3:5

Count it all joy when you fall into various trials, knowing that the testing of your faith produces patience.
James 1:2–3

CHAPTER 5

Step Four:
Find Deliverance

Y
ou need deliverance," Mary Anne said the first time I met her in the counseling office. The words resounded in my head and immediately brought to mind red-eyed demons, green vomit, and whirlwinds. *Am I possessed?* I wondered.

Mary Anne assured me that deliverance was nothing to be afraid of, but was a process of becoming all God made us to be.

"Deliverance removes all past brokenness and bondage from a person's life so the real *you* can come forth," she explained. "I'm talking about oppression and not possession. There are spirits that attach themselves to you. They can come into anyone's life through the work of the devil, who has been allowed influence and access through our own sin."

"Will I become a different person?" I asked.

"Deliverance doesn't *change* you into a different person. It *releases* you to be who you really are," she explained.

If I need deliverance from demonic bondage, am I really saved? I wondered. But Pastor Jack answered that question when he spoke to the church the following Wednesday evening, "You can't get any more saved or forgiven than you are when you come under the covenant of the blood of the cross of Jesus. Deliverance has to do with possessing the full dimensions of what Christ has for us. It has nothing to do with being demon possessed, or being destined for hell, but it has to do with being rid of residual fragments of hell from your past. Residue from the past often manipulates us. Deliverance sets us free from that."

How I longed to be free from anything that kept me from becoming all that God made me to be. I grew more and more eager for that to happen and less intimidated by the mysteriousness that had formerly surrounded the word *deliverance*. I desired it more than I feared it. If Jesus wasn't the Deliverer, who would liberate me from the emotional pain I lived with daily, then death was the only other possibility of finally being free.

Fortunately, I *was* set free of depression, fear, torment, unforgiveness, bitterness, and a lifetime of other bondage as well. I know firsthand that Jesus is the Deliverer and that deliverance is real and available to anyone who seeks it.

Nothing To Fear

Don't let the word *deliverance* frighten you or put you off. It's not scary or strange. Explained as simply as possible, deliverance is the severing of anything that holds you other than God. It could be a spirit of fear, of anger, of lying, of depression, or of lust. It could be a behavior you've acquired for self-defense, like compulsive overeating or a habitual withdrawal from people. Being born again delivers us from death, but we need to be delivered from dead places in our lives as well.

People often fear the subject of deliverance because they think it's bizarre, but it was a primary ministry of Jesus. Preaching, teaching, healing the sick, and casting out devils were basic to Jesus' life on earth. The Bible says numerous times that Jesus is the Deliverer.

Jesus said, "If you can believe, all things are possible to him who believes" (Mark 9:23). This is true for anything in your life, but Jesus said it in direct reference to deliverance from evil spirits. He also said, "In My name they will cast out demons" (Mark 16:17). Jesus gives us the power and authority to drive out all that is not of God. We do it in His name. He also said not to dwell on the devil but rather to keep our minds focused on the Lord and His delivering power.

Pastor Jack Hayford says, "Jesus deals just as easily with the tormented areas of our lives as with problems in the body. It was a regular part of His ministry. When people needed to be physically healed, He healed them. When they were bound and tormented, He delivered them. If demons weren't real, Jesus would have told us so."

People fear the demons or what they think might happen to them if they are delivered. But we don't have to be afraid. As terrible as demons are, their power doesn't approach the power of God. The presence of Jesus dwelling in us cannot ever be shaken, so we don't have to fear losing control. Actually, when we're in bondage, we've already lost control to Satan. Deliverance assures that we are God-controlled.

People often don't seek deliverance because they're ignorant of what deliverance does. They fear it might change them so dramatically that they'll become unrecognizable and will forever lose themselves. Actually, the opposite is true. You will feel more like yourself than you ever have.

People also don't seek deliverance because they've been sucked into thinking their bondage is their fault. Never realizing that the real culprit is the devil, they become disappointed in or even loathe themselves. They feel they aren't eligible for deliverance or don't deserve to be free. Neither is true.

What Deliverance Really Is

All bondage comes from disobedience. Behind every sin, there is an evil spirit. When you sin, you give that spirit a foothold in your life. We can come under it through our own ignorance ("I didn't know that was wrong"), rebellion ("Even if it's wrong, I'm going to do it anyway"), irresponsibility ("I know I probably shouldn't be doing this, but it won't hurt just this once"), being victimized by the sins of others ("What he did to me was emotionally damaging and now that's why I do the things I do"), or inheriting the tendency from a parent ("I don't know why I do that—I must be just like my father").

Deliverance, then, is evicting the devil and refusing to be crippled by him. God doesn't force it on us; we have to desire it. We have to want to put away all the pain of the past, the bad habits, the negative emotions, the sin and the self-indulgence. We have to want to be free. God is committed to removing burdens from our lives, but the first step is up to us.

Although this subject makes most people think of *The Exorcist*, most deliverance is not like that. Much of it is a gradual stripping away, layer by layer, little by little. God delivers you a step at a time as you are able to allow Him. In one area, such as fear for example, you may be set free all at once. In another, such as anger, it may be done a little at a time. It can also happen in many ways. Sometimes you will find deliverance in the presence of the Lord alone. Sometimes you will experience deliverance when you're with others who counsel and pray for you. Always it is *His* way—and in *His* timing, not ours.

Can a Christian Be Demon Possessed?

If you've received Jesus as your Savior and are filled with the Holy Spirit, then you absolutely *cannot* be demon *possessed*. When you were born again, your spirit was covered by the blood of Jesus. Satan can't touch your spirit because "He who is in you is greater than he who is in the world" (1 John 4:4). *Jesus* is in you. Evil spirits are *not* in you. However, Satan can touch your soul, and you *can* be demon *oppressed*. The torment is very real and miserable, and God wants to release your soul from it.

You are body, soul, and spirit. Your spirit is the very core of your being. Your body is the outer layer. In between those two is the soul, which is made up of your mind (what you think), your emotions (what you feel), and your will (what you decide to do). Satan can oppress your mind and emotions, influence your will, and attack your body, but if you've been born again, he cannot touch your spirit.

The real question is, have you allowed an evil spirit to express itself through you by sinning? Are there any places in your life where another power other than God's is in control?

Even though you are filled with the Holy Spirit and cannot be demon possessed, you are still responsible for your life. Spirits can only possess what is given to them. God does not overrule human will. And you don't have to *choose* the will of hell for it to happen; it will happen if you are not actively choosing the will of God.

Through confession we are forgiven of our sins immediately, but we still have to throw off the bondage that came with them. The best way to do this is to give no place to the devil. Each morning say, "Lord, fill me afresh with Your Holy Spirit this day and crowd out anything that is not of You."

Being born again does not remove a person from the possibility of satanic attack. And if our defense is weak or we haven't dealt with residue from the past, Satan can establish points of manipulation. In deliverance, God frees us from any manipulation that obstructs, binds, torments, or hinders us.

How Can You Be Demon Oppressed?

You can be demon oppressed:

1. *Whenever there has been direct disobedience to God's laws.* We must live the Lord's way. We can't create our own rules. When we dabble in any disobedience, the devil gets a foothold. Lying, for example, starts with one small lie. If there is no repentance, it will happen again and again and eventually can't be stopped, even when the person wishes to stop, because a lying spirit has gained control. Yielding to a wrong action until it becomes a habit one can't break, brings bondage.

2. *When there are long-term negative emotions.* Negative emotions—unforgiveness, guilt, fear, anger, rage, bitterness, greed, self-pity, hatred, jealousy, or any other wrong attitude of heart—that go unconfessed and are entertained in your mind for any length of time will create bondage, and the spirits behind them will attach themselves to you. For example, allowing yourself to remain bitter will give place to a spirit of bitterness. If these negative emotions are allowed to linger, they can cause sickness and infirmity. The body is not designed to carry these emotions, and they will begin to break it down.

3. *During times of involvement in any occult practice.* The Bible makes it very clear we are not to be involved in any occult activities, no matter how harmless they may seem.

4. *During times of tragedy or trauma.* The traumatic death of a loved one, such as a parent when you were young, or a spouse or child when you are older, can open the way for spirits of fear, grief, bitterness, anxiety, or denial to gain points of control. It's one thing to grieve; it's another to be dominated by a *spirit* of grief that you can't rise above. Bad memories of the past can create a point of bondage in you because of the negative emotions they stir up. Bring bad memories before the Lord and give them to Him so He can release you.

5. *During times of great disappointment.* This can happen to anyone, but most easily to children—when a father comes home drunk and destroys a favorite toy, or when a parent deserts them.

6. *By hardening the heart against God.* You can have been raised in a Christian home and faithfully followed the Lord Jesus all your life, but the moment your heart becomes hardened to the things of the Lord, you open yourself up for Satan to get a hook in you. For example, becoming so impressed with your own accomplishments that you no longer acknowledge God's power as your source opens the way for pride. And pride opens the way for bondage.

7. *By inheriting spiritual bondage.* Psychologists call this "the multigenerational chain of dependency." The Bible calls it "visiting the iniquity of the fathers on the children to the third and fourth generation" (Num. 14:18). You can inherit spiritual bondage from your parents, grandparents, and even great-grandparents, just as you inherit eye color or the size of your nose. This bondage has to be broken by laying the spiritual ax of deliverance to the root of the family tree and declaring your birth into another family in which you inherit qualities from your heavenly Father. This chain of bondage is like a bullet wound that can't heal because the bullet is

buried deep inside. Deliverance removes the bullet so healing can happen.

The Flesh or the Devil?

There is a difference between bondage of the flesh and satanic bondage. Fleshly bondage has to do with my wanting to serve my own will, my own appetite, my own way, my own desires. Uncurbed fleshly bondage eventually leads to satanic bondage. Repeatedly giving in to flesh leads to the entry of the devil to establish a stronghold. We are the ones who open the door for the devil's rule in our lives. To determine whether you're dealing with fleshly bondage or satanic bondage, check to see if you're giving in to your flesh or if your flesh is being pulled against your will. We can't excuse our flesh and call it the devil. However, if Satan can dominate people's lives and make them think *they* are in control, he will.

If I am drawn to pornography, I am in fleshly bondage. I can give in to the flesh and look at pornography once or twice, and I still am in fleshly bondage. If I become unrepentant and repeat the offense until I am uncontrollably drawn to it, then I have given control to the devil and the bondage is satanic.

No matter what kind of bondage you suffer, ask God to show you where you need deliverance. Then ask Jesus, the Deliverer, to deliver you and to show you what you must do. You don't need to become preoccupied with the demon or the bondage, but only to seek the Deliverer. He'll take care of the rest.

How Do You Know If You Need Deliverance?

When I'm anxious or depressed, I take mental inventory of my life to see if I need deliverance. You can do that too; check the statements below that reflect your life at this moment:

_____"I have memories of past hurts and failures that never go away."

_____"I can't forgive some people who have hurt me, even though I've tried time and time again."

_____"I've been involved with the occult in some way."

_____"I am addicted to drugs or alcohol."

_____"I eat whenever I feel unhappy."

_____"I have trouble controlling my anger."

_____"I hit my spouse or children when I'm angry with them."

_____"I've had an adulterous affair or sex outside of marriage."

_____"I frequently tell lies."

____"I am doing everything I know to do in the Lord, and I'm still depressed."

____"I cannot forgive my parents enough to feel love and compassion for them."

____"I cannot sense God's presence in my prayer or worship time."

____"I feel empty and distant from God, even when I'm reading the Bible."

____"I don't feel I'm growing in my walk with Jesus, and I never sense a fresh flow of His Spirit when I ask for it."

____"I have trouble sustaining friendships."

____"I can't make decisions about minor matters, and the smallest task seems too difficult."

____"I have confessed my sins, forgiven those who have hurt me, and done everything I know to do, yet I never experience breakthrough with some problems."

If you checked any of these statements, ask God for deliverance in that area. Then read on to see what step to take next.

Remember, deliverance doesn't change you; it frees the real you to emerge. You will not become super spiritual, mystical, or mysterious; you will actually be more human, more transparent and real. When the real you is covered up in bondage and distorted by brokenness, you can't see who you really are. Some people say, "What if I don't like the real me?" Believe me, you will like the real you that God created. The real you is wonderful, witty, considerate, pure, peaceful, attractive, dynamic, positive, fulfilled and full of purpose. I guarantee that when God is finished putting you together, you're going to like what you see. After all, you're going to be seeing His reflection.

■ ———————— *What the Bible Says About* ———————— ■
Finding Deliverance

We had the sentence of death in ourselves, that we should not trust in ourselves but in God who raises the dead, who delivered us from so great a death, and does deliver us; in whom we trust that He will still deliver us.
2 Corinthians 1:9–10

And the Lord will deliver me from every evil work and preserve me for His heavenly kingdom.
  2 Timothy 4:18

And the LORD said: "I have surely seen the oppression of My people who are in Egypt, and have heard their cry because of their taskmasters, for I know their sorrows. So I have come down to deliver them out of the hand of the Egyptians."
  Exodus 3:7–8

He shall call upon Me, and I will answer him;
I will be with him in trouble;
I will deliver him and honor him.
With long life I will satisfy him,
And show him My salvation.
  Psalm 91:15–16

FIND DELIVERANCE IN HIS COUNSEL

"I'd like to make an appointment with the doctor," I said to his stern assistant over the phone. It was my first attempt to seek professional help since I left college a few years before.

"What is the nature of the problem?" she asked matter-of-factly.

"Well, I'd rather talk about it with the doctor," I said meekly, not sure how to verbalize the complexities of my situation.

"I preview all cases before the doctor sees them," she said tersely. "I can't make an appointment for you unless I know the nature of your problem."

"I see. Okay. Well, I was raised by an abusive mother. Her hatred expressed toward me has caused me to be extremely depressed and unable to function well and . . ."

"It is our policy that we do not accept the story of child abuse," she interrupted in her businesslike voice. "We believe it is all in the mind of the child, and it is our job to help you adjust your thinking to what is reality."

I was stunned and speechless as if I had been slapped in the face. After finally mustering up enough courage to call this highly recommended psychologist, I was being told that everything that had happened to me was all in my mind.

"You're saying that I imagined these things?" I said carefully so as not to reveal my inner anger.

"Let's just say you think you've been abused. We can help you straighten out your thinking."

"Oh, I see. Thank you. That's all I need to know," I said, and I hung up the phone before she had a chance to say any more. Devastated, I sat for a few moments and then felt the all too familiar tight constriction in my throat. I had always feared if I were to let go and cry to the depth of my feelings, I would die from it. So I held it all back in my throat.

I fell over onto my bed and doubled up with the pain. I'd spent the entire morning mustering up the nerve to make this call, and now I wished I'd never heard of this doctor. Several of my friends had recommended him after I made slight reference to my relationship with my mother. Even though I'd been out of the house for years and traveled all over the world, I couldn't get far enough away from her to eliminate her influence from my life. It looked as if the past would follow me forever unless I found some way to disconnect myself from it.

Now I felt even more hopeless. There was nowhere to turn. I believed that this must be the policy of all counselors, and I resolved to never seek counseling again. I had been to numerous psychiatrists and psychologists before, but I had not told them about my mother's abusive behavior. Feeling closed off to further help, I was left with the sense that suicide was the only option. I never again tried to talk to anyone about my childhood until I began counseling with Mary Anne.

After Michael and I were married and I shared with him about my early home life, he was the one who insisted that I see the counselors at the church, assuring me they could be trusted. Each counselor I saw there only talked and prayed with me about the way I was feeling at the time. We didn't talk about the past. If they didn't ask, I didn't volunteer anything about my abusive childhood—they might think I was crazy. Even though they never reached the core of my problem, each one was instrumental in beginning to crack the wall and open me up to the massive deliverance I would experience with Mary Anne.

Counselors for His People

When all the praying and seeking God for deliverance is to no avail and nothing changes, when you can't move out of your situation no matter how hard you try, when you are so overcome with guilt, torment, feelings of worthlessness, and other negative emotions that you can't handle your life anymore, when you can't see clearly what your problem is, that's when you need to seek counseling. A counselor who has discernment or revelation from God can identify the source of your problem and give you the truth of God that will set you free:

> Where there is no counsel, the people fall;
> But in the multitude of counselors there is safety. (Prov. 11:14)

This is not only a case for counseling, but also for seeing more than one in your lifetime. But God wants you to seek *His* counselors because He wants you to know *His* counsel. Psalm 1:1 says,

> Blessed is the man
> Who walks not in the counsel of the ungodly.

Your counselor must be lined up with the Word and law of God.

A counselor who has been born into the kingdom of God through Jesus and who is counseled by the Holy Spirit can help you find total restoration, since Jesus is the only one who can set you *free* of it. I'm not critical of unbelieving doctors and psychiatrists; I thank God for all the good they do. But I know that even *they* become frustrated. Mental hospitals and jails are full of the testimony of that frustration.

The Holy Spirit is the greatest psychiatrist you will ever find. Jesus said, "And I will ask the Father, and he will give you another Counselor to be with you forever—the Spirit of truth" (John 14:16–17 NIV). Spiritual problems will not subside until they are addressed in the spirit realm. Only counselors who know *the* Counselor can help you do that.

Even Christian counselors need to be qualified and highly recommended. I have seen terrible damage, discouragement, and defeat from bad counseling. Girls who were sexually molested by their fathers as children have been told by counselors that they were at fault: "You were raped because you wanted to be. You let your dad do it because you enjoyed it. You need to take responsibility for your actions." Such counsel, which really makes the child responsible for parental actions, is devastating.

I also have heard of far too many incidents in which a woman in counseling has been seduced by the counselor. That self-serving men who call themselves counselors abuse the vulnerability of emotionally damaged women is deplorable. That's why I am adamant that a Christian counselor must be submitted to a church body and must strictly follow biblical principles. You need to be shown how to walk in the ways of God and stand strong in the freedom Christ gives you. This is not likely to happen when you are receiving counsel from someone who is not able to do those things himself.

A good Christian counselor will also have discernment. Often we need someone with a discerning spirit who will recognize the bondage that we are unable to see. It takes no particular gift to be able to point out what's wrong with someone, but it does take a real gift to discern the *root* of the problem and know how to put a spiritual ax to it. It's easy to say to an alcoholic, "You need to stop drinking," but God will reveal to a person with a discerning spirit that the root of the problem is a spirit of rejection, rooted in an abusive childhood. The drinking is only the symptom.

Very shortly after Michael and I were married, we went to marriage counselors (a husband and wife team) for help. We had been struggling with negative emotions from our individual pasts, and our undeveloped coping skills made our relationship shaky. Though not Christians, the counselors had been highly recommended by some acquaintances who were. These doctors ultimately advised us to get out of the marriage. We knew this was not God's will for us, so we came home and asked our church to recommend a Christian psychologist who specialized in marriage counseling.

This Christian counselor showed us that our problem was not our relationship with each other, but our own bondage. It took a Christian counselor to show Michael that his depression came from spirits with which he had unwittingly aligned himself. It took a Christian counselor to show me my authority in Jesus over the powers of darkness I had given place to. We might have grown into recognizing these things ourselves, but I'm sure it happened much more quickly with the help of qualified Christian counselors.

The Reluctance to Seek Counseling

Counseling doesn't carry the stigma that it used to have. It's no longer for the mentally ill, the emotionally weak, or people who are messed up. It's not an admission of failure or an acknowledgment that you are unstable. It's for anyone who is caught in the stressful, complex web of human interaction called life and who wants to grow into a new level of completeness. Most of us can use some good counsel at one time or another.

Some people have hurts so deep within that only God knows for sure what they are. These hidden hurts grow, and the pain gets worse, not better, as we get older. When you have a cut, a Band-Aid™ provides a protective covering, but a wound needs light to heal totally. When you are emotionally wounded, you need more than a mental Band-Aid;™ you need the light of God's Word penetrating like a laser beam to that hurt area. A Christian counselor can help that to happen.

Many of us are still afraid of what others would think if they found out we were in counseling, but people respond to the type of person you are and the fruit of your life, not how many counselors you've seen. Be released in the knowledge that seeking good Christian counseling is not only good but it is scripturally right. Proverbs 19:20–21 tells us,

> Listen to counsel and receive instruction,
> That you may be wise in your latter days.
> There are many plans in a man's heart,
> Nevertheless the LORD's counsel—that will stand.

Some people don't seek counseling because they feel it would take a miracle to change things and they're sure that God doesn't do miracles today. For those people He doesn't—He doesn't do miracles where faith is absent. But God says He doesn't change. He is the same yesterday, today, and tomorrow. Why would He have done miracles for thousands of years and stop now? He *can* do a miracle in your life.

Call on God First

Always call on God *before* calling a counselor. In fact, before you make an appointment with any counselor, try spending one hour each day for a week alone with God, and then see if you still need the counseling. You may be surprised at what that accomplishes. It certainly will better prepare you to receive what the Lord and a counselor have to say to you.

And always weigh what the counselor says against the Word of God; if it holds up, then follow his instructions. If you are asked to come to church, read the Bible an hour a day, and stop seeing that married man, then do those things. The Bible describes people who wouldn't listen to God's counsel as

> Those who sat in darkness and in the shadow of death,
> Bound in affliction and irons—
> Because they rebelled against the words of God,
> And despised the counsel of the Most High. (Ps. 107:10–11)

Hearing His counsel and refusing to abide by it is a serious offense.

However, if your counselor recommends actions that violate God's Word, then you have the wrong person. Leave him immediately and keep searching for the right one.

If you call on God first as *the* Counselor and let Him guide you to *His* counselors, then deliverance in *His counsel* is sure.

■ ——————— *What the Bible Says About* ——————— ■

Finding Deliverance in His Counsel

The Counselor, the Holy Spirit, whom the Father will send in my name, will teach you all things and will remind you of everything I have said to you.
John 14:26 NIV

"Woe to the rebellious children," says the LORD,
"Who take counsel, but not of Me,
And who devise plans, but not of My Spirit,
That they may add sin to sin."
Isaiah 30:1

Every purpose is established by counsel.
Proverbs 20:18

Counsel and sound judgment are mine.
Proverbs 8:14 NIV

I have not obeyed the voice of my teachers,
Nor inclined my ear to those who instructed me!
I was on the verge of total ruin.
Proverbs 5:13–14

■   ■

FIND DELIVERANCE IN HIS PRESENCE

I was elated over the birth of our first child, and I was determined to be the perfect mom. Surely that meant doing everything exactly opposite of my mother.

One night, just a few months after Christopher was born, he was crying hysterically, and nothing I did for him made him stop. In fact, the harder I tried, the more he cried until something snapped in me. Hearing rejection of me in his crying, I slapped him on the back, the shoulder, and the head. My heart pounded, my face burned, and I could hardly breathe. I knew if I didn't get away from him, I could hurt him badly.

I gathered every bit of control I could pull together and laid the baby in his crib. Then I went to my room and fell before the Lord while he cried himself to sleep.

God, help me, I sobbed as I fell on my knees and buried my face in the bedspread. *There's a horrible monster inside me. You've got to take it away, God. I don't know what it is; I don't understand it. How can a mother hurt a child she loves? Please, God, whatever is wrong with me, take it away.* I stayed before the Lord for nearly an hour and pulled myself together. Michael came home, the baby woke up, and except for my intense feelings of guilt, no damage seemed to have been done.

I was on the way to chalking it up to a one-time moment of weakness when several days later it happened again. The baby cried so long that I sensed the feelings of rejection and rage rising up in me. I started to hit him, then realized what was happening and put him back in his crib. I left the room and went into my bedroom and fell on my knees, crying to the Lord for help.

After a few of these incidents, I finally confessed what was happening to my husband and Mary Anne. Both of them took it calmly, probably because no harm had come to the baby. I'd had enough healing and deliverance to be able to remove myself from the baby when I lost control, so they felt he was safe.

"This isn't going to be solved through instant deliverance this time, Stormie," Mary Anne told me. "It will be a step-by-step process. God wants to teach you something about Himself."

Over the next few months I learned that I was a potential child abuser because of my mother's violent abuse of me. The only way I could cope with this frightening revelation was to be in the Lord's presence. Each time I fell before Him in utter guilt and failure, His love came like a healing balm. Each time I cried out to Him for deliverance, He faithfully set me free. Eventually I was completely freed from my anger and rejection, and I learned how powerful, how merciful, how tender, and how complete His presence is. I finally came to understand the depth of God's love toward me.

Is It Possible to Find Deliverance Without a Counselor?

God would not be so unfair as to say, "There is deliverance for you, but you have to find yourself a good deliverance counselor in order to get free." First of all, there aren't nearly enough deliverance counselors for all the bondage in the world, and even if there were, not everyone could get to them. God has provided a way to be free by seeking the presence of Jesus, the Deliverer. If you are isolated on an island, out in the woods, or in solitary confinement, Jesus is there if you seek His presence and cry out to Him for deliverance: "Where the Spirit of the Lord is, there is liberty" (2 Cor. 3:17); and "From the LORD comes deliverance" (Ps. 3:8 NIV). In these two promises alone, God gives you reason to know there is deliverance for you whether you find a deliverance counselor or not.

Finding deliverance by being in the Lord's presence doesn't mean seeking His presence for five minutes and then doing your own thing. It means remaining in His presence *all* the time. It means deciding you will walk in the spirit and not in the flesh.

Walking in the spirit means saying with conviction, "I don't want what the devil wants; I want what God wants." It means facing the hell in your life and knowing every part of *you* wants nothing to do with *it* because "those who live according to the flesh set their minds on the things of the flesh, but those who live according to the Spirit, the things of the Spirit" (Rom. 8:5). Walking in the Spirit means focusing on Jesus and choosing to live God's way. When you do that, ongoing deliverance is yours.

How to Find Deliverance in His Presence

Anything you do to move closer to the Lord can also be a means of deliverance. Here are some of the most important ways:

1. *By establishing the lordship of Jesus.* Sometimes the simple act of inviting Jesus to be Lord in a certain part of your life will be enough to set you free from that bondage. It depends on how entrenched the bondage is.

2. *By hearing the Word.* Reading or hearing the Word of God and

letting it penetrate your heart will increase your knowledge of the truth that can liberate you: "You shall know the truth, and the truth shall make you free" (John 8:32).

The Bible also says, "Through knowledge the righteous will be delivered" (Prov. 11:9). Knowledge of the Lord's truth brings deliverance. It is not enough to know why your father beat you; you must know that God has a plan to redeem all that happened to you and make it count for something good. *That* is liberating!

3. *By crying out to God in prayer.* Deliverance can happen just by praying for it and calling out to God from the depths of your being—just you and the Lord, or with one or more believers praying with you. Sometimes simply crying in the presence of the Lord brings deliverance. Psalm 34:17 says,

> The righteous cry out, and the LORD hears,
> And delivers them out of all their troubles.

4. *By singing or speaking praises to the Lord.* Worship invites God's presence, and that's where deliverance happens. Two men in prison were singing praises to God when suddenly the prison doors flew open and their chains fell off (Acts 16:26). In the spirit realm when we praise the Lord, the prison doors of our lives are opened, our bonds are broken, and we are set free. Praising God opens you to experience His love, and it will liberate you.

5. *By walking in obedience.* Deliverance comes when we take steps of obedience in response to the Holy Spirit's commands. When you are living a life of purity and there is no unconfessed, stubborn, or rebellious sin in you, then hell can't penetrate or hold you. When we hear the counsel of the Lord and do what we are instructed to do, deliverance happens.

6. *By fasting.* Certain deliverance happens only in a time of fasting and prayer. When the disciples couldn't cast out a demon, Jesus said, "This kind does not go out except by prayer and fasting" (Matt. 17:21). Sometimes the deliverance happens *during* the fast, sometimes afterwards.

7. *By speaking words of deliverance.* You have power in your mouth to loosen hell upon yourself, (curse), and you have the power to loosen God's grace and open the way for deliverance (bless). The Bible says, "Bless and do not curse" (Rom. 12:14). Make your tongue line up with the Word of God and speak words of deliverance. Repeatedly saying, "In Jesus' name, I have been set free of depression," can deliver you.

Many people don't need a counseling appointment; they just need more of the Lord. If we continually give place to Jesus *in* us, the power of the Holy Spirit flowing *through* us, and the presence of God *with* us, we will eventually find our personalities purged of negatives and imbalances. God wants us to reach out and touch Him so that He can touch us with His wholeness in every part of our being.

What the Bible Says About
Finding Deliverance in His Presence

For He will deliver the needy when he cries,
The poor also, and him who has no helper.
　　Psalm 72:12

In my anguish I cried to the LORD,
and he answered by setting me free.
　　Psalm 118:5 NIV

All who touched him were healed.
　　Matthew 14:36 NIV

But those who seek the LORD shall not lack any good thing.
　　Psalm 34:10

You are my help and my deliverer.
　　Psalm 70:5

FIND DELIVERANCE IN HIS WAY

No two of my deliverances have been alike except for the fact that Jesus the Deliverer has attended every one. They have been similar in some ways, but never exactly the same. My first major deliverance (from depression) came in a counseling office after three days of fasting and prayer. My next experience with major deliverance (from child abuse) happened over a period of time as I sought the presence of God. I found deliverance from a spirit of fear as I took simple steps of obedience. I was delivered from self-sufficiency as I sat in church listening to the teaching of God's

Word on grace. I experienced deliverance from a hardness of heart as I worshiped God with other believers in church. I received deliverance from emotional torment as I cried out to God in my prayer closet all alone in the middle of the night. Layer after layer of bondage has been stripped away, with no two instances identical.

I've learned not even to try to second-guess God. His ways are far above ours, and He is much too creative for our limited minds to comprehend His thoughts and actions. Even though we glimpse His ways in times spent in His presence, we can never predict how He will accomplish deliverance next. The only thing we can know for sure is that as long as we want Him to, He will continue to work deliverance in us until we go to be with Him.

Five Basic Steps to Deliverance

No matter when, where, or how deliverance occurs, five steps *are* common. Not to pay attention to them may short-circuit the flow of deliverance in your life.

1. *Confessing.* The devil has a hook in you wherever there is unconfessed sin. Repeated returns to the same sin are no excuse for not confessing. You must keep your life totally confessed before the Lord so as not to block the deliverance process.

If God shows you the work of an evil spirit in your life, repent of anything you may have done to give that spirit control. Say, "Lord, I confess that I have aligned myself with a lying spirit by not being honest. Forgive me for lying. I repent of it and ask You to help me not to do it anymore."

2. *Renouncing.* You can't be delivered from something you have not put out of your life. Confessing is speaking the whole truth about your sin. Renouncing is taking a firm stand against it and removing its right to stay. It's possible to renounce without confessing, and many people confess without renouncing. You have to separate yourself from all that is not of God so that you can be aligned with all that *is* of God. Certain keys to deliverance won't be revealed to you unless you renounce whatever is not of God.

The first step in renouncing sin is to ask God from what exactly you need to be delivered. If you're dealing with evil spirits, ask Him to show you which ones. Say, "God give me revelation. Show me if an evil spirit is causing my fear." Then speak a Scripture from the Word of God that backs up your authority to cast out this spirit. Choose a Scripture that applies to your own life. For example, say, "God has not given *me* a spirit of fear, but He has given *me* a spirit of power and of love and of a sound mind." Then cast out the spirit.

Speak directly to the evil spirit with confidence and boldness and the full knowledge that Jesus has given you authority to do so in His name. Be specific. Say, "I address you spirit of fear. I renounce you and remove your right to stay. I say you have no power over me. I bind you in the name of Jesus Christ and in the authority He has given me. I cast you out of my life and command you to be gone."

Because the Bible says, "The yoke will be destroyed because of the anointing oil" (Isa. 10:27), it's good to have a pastor, elder, or strong believer anoint you with oil, lay hands on you, and pray for you. If you are alone and there is absolutely no one you can call, then do it yourself. Place your hand on your heart and say, "Jesus, because You dwell in me and all of me belongs to You, You have made my hands holy." Now put a drop of oil on your finger and touch it to your forehead. Say, "Lord, I anoint myself with oil and ask You to deliver me," and name the specific area in which you want deliverance. Then praise the Lord who gives you power over the devil. Worship seals the deliverance against undermining. Every time you feel that spirit creeping up on you again, praise God that He has set you free of it. Evil spirits cannot tolerate praise to God.

3. *Forgiving.* Unforgiveness of any kind will be a hindrance to deliverance. We have to be ongoingly forgiving whenever and wherever forgiveness is needed. Ask God to help you remember anyone or any incident that needs to be forgiven, even if it has nothing directly to do with the deliverance you seek. Openly face any memory that comes to mind, no matter how repulsive or painful, and bring it before the Lord so you can be released from it. Where there is *no* memory, ask God to make you aware of any repressed memory that needs forgiveness.

4. *Speaking.* Jesus commanded a man who had been delivered to "Return to your own house, and tell what great things God has done for you" (Luke 8:39). We can do no less. When we have been delivered from anything, our joyful proclamation for everyone who will listen cements in our minds what God has done in our souls:

> Let the redeemed of the LORD say so,
> Whom He has redeemed from the hand of the enemy.
>   (Ps. 107:2)

This keeps the enemy from trying to steal away what God has done. If the devil is tormenting you, speak to him aloud saying, "Jesus has delivered me from a spirit of fear and I refuse to give place to it anymore. What Jesus did on the cross was enough for my absolute freedom from your hand."

5. *Walking.* If you've been delivered, you have to walk like it. Refuse to be drawn back into the same error. Deliverance means severing bad habits and establishing new ones, so set your will to not be tempted back into the old ways of thinking and doing. Resolve not to do anything to promote bondage.

The devil will always try to kill the work done in you and destroy your hope for life ever being any different, so be ready to combat that attack by deliberately and carefully walking God's way. If you've been delivered from a spirit of lust, refuse to succumb to it again. Say, "I will not be tempted by you, Satan, for I have been delivered through Jesus Christ the Deliverer. You may have controlled me before, but now that spirit has been broken in my life and I have the power to withstand it. I praise God for His delivering power."

And God doesn't give up on us when we fail to walk in the deliverance He has given us. We suffer because our wholeness is delayed, but He doesn't withdraw His power toward us.

> Many times He delivered them;
> But they rebelled against Him by their counsel,
> And were brought low for their iniquity.
> Nevertheless He regarded their affliction,
> When He heard their cry;
> And for their sake He remembered His covenant.
> (Ps. 106:43–45)

Try to walk in deliverance to the best you are able.

Sometimes deliverance is painless—you are simply released and set free. Other times, however, you find deliverance only through the pain of remembering and facing the point in your past where you received the bondage. Pain is part of growth and healing, so don't be surprised, discouraged, or frightened by it. Deliverance is often emotionally painful, and one of people's biggest fears is that it will be more painful than they can bear. But God has promised to never give you more than you can handle. You are safe with Him.

We can do all we know to prepare for being free, but the bottom line is that it is the Lord's battle and it is His deliverance that will accomplish it. Just be sure you are looking to Him to deliver you in *His* way.

■ ——————————— *What the Bible Says About* ——————————— ■
Deliverance in His Way

Many are the afflictions of the righteous,
But the LORD delivers him out of them all.
    Psalm 34:19

For great is your love toward me;
you have delivered my soul from the depths of the grave.
    Psalm 86:13 NIV

The horse is prepared for the day of battle,
But deliverance is of the LORD.
    Proverbs 21:31

For He looked down from the height of His sanctuary;
From heaven the LORD viewed the earth,
To hear the groaning of the prisoner,
To loose those appointed to death.
    Psalm 102:19–20

He who trusts in his own heart is a fool,
But whoever walks wisely will be delivered.
    Proverbs 28:26

■ ——————————————————————————————————————— ■

FIND DELIVERANCE IN HIS TIME

If you sat in a dark closet all your life and suddenly hundreds of high wattage floodlights were turned on you, you would be blinded. It's the same with deliverance. Too much light all at once would be too difficult to manage. That's why deliverance must take place a layer at a time to match your growth in the Lord.

You don't have to be a spiritual powerhouse to be delivered. If that were so, few people would be. But you can't be delivered from a problem you aren't ready to let go of, nor can deliverance be forced on you if you don't fully desire it. Also, learning to walk in the freedom you've been given takes time, and if God freed you of everything at once, you couldn't do it. Continued deliverance comes after you have lived in what you've received already.

Deliverance can come all at once or slowly, a step at a time. One is not more holy than the other, so don't be hard on yourself if there is no sign of immediate healing. It took fourteen years for me to be free of emotional pain, but I didn't pray for healing in 1970 and have it suddenly happen in 1984. It was being stripped away, layer by layer, the whole time. I wasn't delivered any sooner because I needed to have enough faith, knowledge of God's power, and grounding in His Word to be able to sustain the deliverance. The only way we can speed up the deliverance process is to immerse ourselves totally and without reservation in the life of the Lord, holding nothing back from Him.

You may feel too much of life has passed you by and it's too late for you to find deliverance and wholeness now. But this is not true. It's never too late for God's presence to make a difference. Seventy-year-old women have told me that my book *Stormie* helped them find healing and deliverance from the emotional pain of sixty years earlier.

If you have ever felt deserted in your past—especially by a parent—you may fear that God will not come through for you now. But that's not true either. He assures us that "those who hope in me will not be disappointed" (Isa. 49:23 NIV). The Deliverer waits for you to cry out to Him so He can change your life.

In the movie, *Back to the Future*, one small incident affected everyone's future. It's like that with deliverance. The deliverance and freedom in the Lord that you gain right now will affect your entire life and the lives of your children and their children, whether you or they realize it or not. The Bible says,

> The righteous man walks in his integrity;
> His children are blessed after him. (Prov. 20:7)

Every deliverance, no matter how small it may seem, has effects far beyond what you can imagine.

New Levels of Deliverance or Same Old Bondage?

Once we've been delivered of something, we tend to think that we will never have to wrestle with that particular problem again. This is often the case, but other times our bondage in a specific area is so deep that we have to be set free a layer at a time. On occasion, after you've been delivered of a particular thing, it may seem as if the same old problem is coming back. You may feel as depressed and emotionally hurt as you ever did, if not worse, and you'll fear you're going backward. But if you've been walking with the Lord and obeying Him to the best of your ability, then you can trust that God is wanting to bring you to a deeper level of deliverance than ever before. This process may feel just as painful, if not more so, than it ever did, but the new level of freedom will be far greater than you've ever experienced.

Being born again doesn't remove you from spiritual oppression, satanic attack, and emotional conflict. And being delivered once doesn't mean you never need deliverance again. In fact, if the devil can gain back a point of control in your life, he will. You can count on that.

Because deliverance is ongoing and done in layers, total deliverance never happens overnight. God is the only one who knows which layer should come off first and when it should happen. In other words, a person may not find total deliverance from a painful eating disorder today, but might be delivered from unforgiveness toward a parent. God always wants you to be delivered from *something* right now. No matter how He does it or how long it takes, you must trust that His timing is perfect. He knows when you're ready for the next step. It may not be exactly the way you want it at the moment, but there is always deliverance available to *us* anytime we make ourselves available to *it*. We must sustain a spirit of grateful dependence upon Him and be willing to say as David did,

> You are my God.
> My times are in Your hand;
> Deliver me from the hand of my enemies. (Ps. 31:14–15)

When you find yourself frustrated, check to see that you are not holding back the process because of a faulty foundation (check Step 2: Lay a Foundation). Also be certain you are not walking in disobedience. If you are clear on both points and you are seeking God for an end to your problem, then something *is* happening. It may be happening in the spirit realm and has not yet manifested itself in the physical.

God sometimes nudges us into a time of deliverance when we feel we're not ready. We like the way things have been going and we don't want any changes. We're comfortable where we are, misery and all. But God says, "No, I love you too much to let you stay the way you are. We're moving on. You're going to grow up now and put aside childish things. I'm bringing you to a time of deliverance in this specific area of your life." When that happens, resisting His working in your life will only prolong the agony. You will delay the process, but your misery will increase. You'll keep coming up against the same old thing, and you'll be slow to move on from where you are.

Every deliverance God works in your life will set up your healing and deliverance in the future. One builds upon another until freedom and wholeness become a way of life. Continue to look to the Lord for deliverance, wait for Him, and do not give up—and you *will* see it happen in *His* time.

■ ——————— *What the Bible Says About* ——————— ■
Deliverance in His Time

We had the sentence of death in ourselves, that we should not trust in ourselves but in God who raises the dead, who delivered us from so great a death, and does deliver us; in whom we trust that He will still deliver us.
2 Corinthians 1:9–10

For Jerusalem's sake I will not rest,
Until her righteousness goes forth as brightness.
Isaiah 62:1

Sustain me according to your promise, and I will live;
do not let my hopes be dashed.
Uphold me, and I will be delivered.
Psalm 119:116–117 NIV

I will make darkness light before them,
And crooked places straight.
These things I will do for them,
And not forsake them.
Isaiah 42:16

And the Lord will deliver me from every evil work and preserve me for His heavenly kingdom.
2 Timothy 4:18

CHAPTER 6

Step Five:
Receive God's Gifts

One year I gave my young daughter, Amanda, a little jewelry box with a tiny ballerina that danced when the lid was open. I put a small piece of jewelry that she had been requesting for a long time inside the box.

When she opened the gift and saw the jewelry box, she squealed and remarked on every detail. "Oh Mommy, this is so beautiful! Look at the pink roses and the painted ribbons, and see how tiny the gold lock is. This is the prettiest box I've ever seen."

Eager for her to see all I had for her and unable to wait any longer, I said, "Amanda, open it up."

She opened the box and saw the ballerina twirling to the delicate music. "Oh, the dancer is so pretty!" she exclaimed as her fingers went over every part of the figurine. "Look at her little skirt and her tiny hands. Feel the pink satin. It's so smooth!"

She was about to put the box away in her room when I said, "Amanda, do you see there's something in there?"

"Where is it?" She discovered a tiny drawer and pulled it out carefully. "The pearl earrings I wanted! Oh, thank you, Mommy!" she squealed as she ran off to put them on.

I sat there thinking, *She would have been happy with just the pretty box*. And then I thought of how our heavenly Father gives us gifts, and often we don't unwrap them or possess all He has for us because we don't see or understand there is a gift or we don't realize that it's there for *us*.

The Opening Act

Imagine someone giving you a present wrapped in shiny paper with an exquisite bow on top. You say, "Thank you so much for the gift. The paper is beautiful, the bow is breathtaking, and I will cherish it forever." Then you put the gift on the table and let it sit unopened. How sad the giver would be after spending time, effort, and resources to give it to you.

When Michael and I were married, I became financially secure for the first time. Even though my dad had worked hard all his life, he never made much money and we always lived on the bare threads of existence. When he retired and moved to a farm in central California with my mother, his retirement didn't even cover the basic essentials. Michael and I tried to give them money periodically, but Mother wouldn't hear of it. One especially cold winter day I called them and found out they were both sick with serious chest colds. They had been freezing for the past month because they didn't have enough money to buy fuel for the heater. Here I was, with more than enough money to help, and they were suffering needlessly. I immediately made arrangements for fuel delivery, and I realized how much our heavenly Father must be grieved at our needless suffering. I, too, forget that some things are my inheritance and my birthright because of Jesus, but I don't forget for very long anymore because I know what the gifts are and that they are there for me. I want you to know too.

God gives us first the gift of His Son Jesus (John 4:10) and the gift of His Holy Spirit (Acts 2:38). From those two gifts all other gifts flow—righteousness (Rom. 5:17), eternal life (Rom. 6:23), prophecy (1 Cor. 13:2), and peace (John 14:27). And these are just a few, for all good things are given to us from God.

Of the many gifts God has for us, four in particular are crucial to your emotional healing, restoration, and continued wholeness: the gift of His love, the gift of His grace, the gift of His power, and the gift of His rest. We can't receive these gifts on our own.

■ —————— *What the Bible Says About* —————— ■
Receiving God's Gifts

Every good gift and every perfect gift is from above, and comes down from the Father of lights, with whom there is no variation or shadow of turning.
James 1:17

If you then, being evil, know how to give good gifts to your children, how much more will your Father who is in heaven give good things to those who ask Him!
Matthew 7:11

As each one has received a gift, minister it to one another, as good stewards of the manifold grace of God.
1 Peter 4:10

But to each one of us grace was given according to the measure of Christ's gift.
Ephesians 4:7

Earnestly desire the best gifts.
1 Corinthians 12:31

■ ■

RECEIVE GOD'S GIFT OF LOVE

A few years ago I was invited to speak to a large group of inmates at a women's prison. Afterward, I was allowed to talk privately with any of the women who wished to talk. Because I had told my life story transparently, each one was quite open with me. One timid, fragile-looking young woman, whom I will call Tracy, confessed what she had done to put her behind bars. I say confessed because, although she had already been convicted of the crime, she was not required to reveal this, and I was strictly forbidden to ask why any inmate was there.

Tracy told me about being born to a mother who didn't want her, didn't like her, and frequently told her so. Her stepfather repeatedly and violently beat and raped her, holding her in contempt. She grew up desperate for love.

At fifteen she became pregnant by a teenage boy, and her enraged mother threw Tracy out of the home. The boyfriend deserted her too, and she had no other family members or friends to turn to. With state aid, she stayed alone in a tiny, one-room apartment and had her baby.

"I kept the baby because I wanted someone to love," she said with heartbreaking sincerity. But she was inexperienced and frightened and barely more than a baby herself, so she couldn't cope with her daughter's incessant crying. One night, when she couldn't deal with it any longer, the failure and rejection of a lifetime rose up in her with such force that she lost control. Grabbing a pillow, she held it over the baby's face until the crying stopped. The baby was dead.

Even though Tracy was full of remorse and despair, she enjoyed the profuse news media coverage of her crime. "When I was arrested and my picture appeared on the front page of the newspaper," she told me, "I felt proud because I thought, 'Now I am somebody. People notice me.'"

This chilling statement appalled and shocked me, but my heart broke for Tracy as well as the baby. I knew that anyone deprived of love as a child will desperately seek it anywhere, no matter how bizarre or irrational the method. The more extreme the conditions of abuse, the more extreme the acts of desperation. When you don't feel loved, you feel you don't exist. It's indescribably frightening, and you're always desperately searching for confirmation of your existence, even if it's a negative one.

Food for the Soul

Just as food helps us grow physically and education helps us grow mentally, it takes love for us to grow emotionally. If we aren't nurtured with love, our emotions stay immature, and we are always searching for the love we never had. But how do you ever get that love when the ones who are supposed to love you don't or have not been able to communicate it to you?

In the flesh you try anything. At a certain level of need, any kind of attention—even negative news coverage—is better than no attention at all. We do and say things we shouldn't to gain attention, acceptance, and love from others. But in the spirit, there is another way: receiving the love of God.

I explained to Tracy that the Lord had plans for her before she was born. Her parents' sins, however, were Satan's plans.

"Tracy," I said, looking directly at her, "I'm here to tell you that in the eyes of Jesus you have *always* been somebody. You've always been important to Him. He knows all your suffering. He has seen all that's happened to you, and His Spirit grieves with yours. He never wanted all this for you, and He desires to give you back everything that has been lost."

She started to cry, and I hugged her tightly. With deep despair in her eyes she sobbed, "But how can God accept me after what I've done? Isn't it too late for me now?"

"Tracy," I said, "God loves and accepts us the way we are, but He doesn't leave us that way. That's why it's never too late. No matter what we have become, when we allow Him into our lives and receive Jesus, He begins immediately to change us from the inside out. He'll take all the pieces of your life and put them together and make them count for something good. He'll free you to be the somebody He created you to be."

God's Love Shows No Favoritism

After I received Jesus I could sense the strong presence of God's love and I had no trouble believing He loved everyone. Everyone *else*, that is. I had a hard time believing He loved *me*. I could tell other people about God's love, but I couldn't receive it for myself. It took some time of walking with Him, learning about His nature, getting to know Him, allowing Him time to answer my prayers, seeing that His Word was truth, and receiving His deliverance, before God's love really sank into my being.

Man's love is conditional. It will always be limited. God's love is *un*conditional and *un*limited. Human love helps us to grow, but *God's love transforms us*. It burns away self-doubt, limitations, insecurity, and fear. Human love gives us a sense of comfort and belonging when we're around the person who loves us. God's love gives us a sense of belonging no matter who we're around. If you think God couldn't love you because you're not worth loving, you have to understand that He loves differently from us. You can do nothing to make Him love you more—and nothing to make Him love you less.

The Bible says, "The same Lord over all is rich to *all* who call upon Him" (Rom. 10:12, emphasis added). He loves you as much as He loves me or anybody. All the Lord's goodness shown toward Billy Graham is there for you and me, too. Mr. Graham probably committed and submitted himself to Jesus far earlier and more completely than you or I did, and he chose to live God's way and in His love sooner and more thoroughly than we have.

I explained to Tracy, "God will meet you right here and now, and, if you let Him, He will turn your whole life around."

Because Tracy sensed the love of God, she received Jesus as her Savior that morning. Several inmates and two of the guards told me later that they had never seen her cry or talk to anyone the entire three years she had been there. Something definitely touched her, and it wasn't me. Humans don't have that kind of power. Only the love of God can transform lives. I never saw Tracy again after that weekend, but I pray for her often. She was a prime example of the way a lifetime of being unnoticed and unloved takes its toll. Only the all-encompassing unconditional love of God can heal wounds of that magnitude.

Believing Is Receiving

The key to receiving God's love is deciding to believe that it is there for you, and choosing to open up to it. Nothing can separate us from God's love except our own inability to receive it.

The Bible says, "The LORD's unfailing love surrounds the man who trusts in him" (Ps. 32:10 NIV). The more you say, "Okay, God, I'm going to trust Your promises and all You say about me and my circumstances and choose to believe You," the more you will experience God's love.

Receiving the gift of God's love means that we don't have to do desperate things for approval. Nor do we have to be depressed when we don't receive love from other people exactly the way we feel we need it. When we sense God's love, it takes the pressure off relationships and frees us to be who we were made to be.

If you have doubts about God's love for you, ask Him to show it to you. Read what the Bible says about His love (see pages 159–60) and choose to believe Him. The love of God is not just a feeling; it's God's Spirit. Because He *is* love, just spending time in His presence in prayer and praise causes His love to permeate your being.

If no matter what you do you still don't feel God loves you, you probably need deliverance from some bondage. Ask Him to show you what it is and if you should seek counseling. It's too important a part of your healing and restoration to neglect.

Opening up and receiving God's love makes you more able to love others, even people for whom you have no natural affinity. Radiating love toward others is part of perfecting God's love in you. It also causes people to love *you* more. People who have the fullness of God's love flowing through them are always beautiful and attractive to those around them.

God's love is always more than we expect. That's why we are brought to tears so often in His presence. They are tears of gratitude for love beyond our imagination.

■ ——————— *What the Bible Says About* ——————— ■
Receiving God's Gift of Love

Yes, I have loved you with an everlasting love;
Therefore with lovingkindness I have drawn you.
Again I will build you, and you shall be rebuilt.
  Jeremiah 31:3–4

If anyone loves Me, he will keep My word; and My Father will love him, and We will come to him and make Our home with him.
John 14:23

Who shall separate us from the love of Christ? Shall tribulation, or distress, or persecution, or famine, or nakedness, or peril, or sword?
Romans 8:35

For I am persuaded that neither death nor life, nor angels nor principalities nor powers, nor things present nor things to come, nor height nor depth, nor any other created thing, shall be able to separate us from the love of God which is in Christ Jesus our Lord.
Romans 8:38–39

May your unfailing love be my comfort.
Psalm 119:76 NIV

RECEIVE GOD'S GIFT OF GRACE

"Quick, hop in the car," I instructed Amanda, who was three at the time. "The driver in back of us wants our parking place." I tossed our bag of purchases into the back seat, shut the passenger door, and hurried to the driver's side in response to impatient honking.

Why is everyone in such a hurry today? I asked myself as I slipped behind the wheel and fastened my seat belt. I pulled out of the parking space, crossed the lot, and turned right to go through the narrow, single-lane, one-way exit. Just as I was about to round the blind corner that led to the street, a car came speeding toward us. The driver had mistakenly entered the poorly marked "Exit" lane instead of the one marked "Entrance." I slammed on my brakes, as did the oncoming car. Only a fraction of an inch separated us from a head-on collision. Amanda went flying into the windshield.

"Oh, my God!" I cried. In my haste I had neglected to fasten Amanda's seat belt. "Oh, God, forgive me for being so negligent. Please let Amanda be okay. Please, God, let there be no damage to her. Please heal her, Lord," I prayed as I used tissues to mop up the blood coming from her mouth and nose. I feared her teeth and nose were broken, or worse, her neck and skull.

As it turned out there were no scratches or bruises and no damaged teeth, just a bloody nose and a cut on the inside of her mouth. I was totally aware of the miraculous hand of the Lord upon us and that what I deserved was not what I had received. I deserved the judgment of my failure, which is destruction. What I received instead was God's grace.

Not as We Deserve

I've spent fifteen years learning to understand what was accomplished on the cross, and it simply means that *Jesus took all that I have coming to me—pain, sickness, failure, confusion, hatred, rejection, and death—and gave me all that He had coming to Him—all His wholeness, healing, love, acceptance, peace, joy, and life.* Because of God's grace, all we have to do is say, "Jesus, come live in me and be Lord over my life."

In my early twenties my lifestyle was motivated by a desperate need for love. One disastrous by-product of this lifestyle was two abortions in less than two years. Both were ugly, frightening, and physically and emotionally traumatic (not to mention illegal at the time), yet I felt relief more than remorse about them. Only years later after I began to walk with the Lord and learn of His ways, did I see what I had done.

When Michael and I decided to have a baby, month after month went by and I didn't get pregnant. I, who had gotten pregnant so easily before, thought surely I was being punished for the abortions.

"God, I know I don't deserve to give birth to new life after twice destroying life within me," I prayed. "I deserve to be childless. But please have mercy and help me to conceive."

He answered that prayer, and my two children have been the greatest example of God's mercy and grace to me. *He gave me exactly what I did not deserve.*

God's grace is for those who live in His kingdom and whose kingdom lives in them. We can't receive His grace unless we receive *Him*. It's a gift that is with Him in His hand.

Grace and Mercy

Grace and mercy are much alike. *Grace happens when God refrains from punishing a person who is guilty. Mercy is God's compassion for our misery beyond what may be expected.* We need both.

If it weren't for God's grace *and* mercy, we wouldn't even be saved for the Bible tells us, "by *grace* you have been saved" (Eph. 2:8) and "according to His mercy He saved us" (Titus 3:5). Before we met Jesus we were "guilty" and "miserable," but His "grace" and "mercy" have saved us.

Grace has to do with it all being *Him. He* does it. Not us. Grace is always a surprise. You think it's not going to happen, and it does. Pastor Jack Hayford teaches about grace that "When the humble say, 'I don't have it and I can't get it on my own,' God says, 'I've got it and I'm going to give it to you.' That's God's grace."

Receiving the Gift

People who have been abused, rejected or emotionally damaged are often hard on themselves. If they don't achieve perfection, they reject their own flesh. It is harder to receive God's grace and mercy if we are merciless on ourselves. We also have a harder time showing mercy to someone else. And one of the stipulations for *receiving* mercy is *showing* it to others:

> The merciful man does good for his own soul,
> But he who is cruel troubles his own flesh. (Prov. 11:17)

We receive His grace and mercy when we are born again, but we must extend them too, for that brings emotional health. The Lord's mercies are "new every morning" (Lam. 3:23), and so should ours be also.

Another stipulation for receiving God's grace and mercy is humility, confession, and repentance:

> He who covers his sins will not prosper,
> But whoever confesses and forsakes them will have mercy.
>   (Prov. 28:13)

There is also mercy for anyone who sins in ignorance. If there weren't, we'd all be dead. The apostle Paul said, "I obtained mercy because I did it ignorantly in unbelief" (1 Tim. 1:13).

The difficult part of receiving God's grace and mercy is maintaining a balance between thinking *I can do whatever I feel like doing because God's grace will cover it all* and feeling on the other hand that *everything in my life—my success, my marriage, how my kids turn out, how whole I become—depends totally on what I do.* Neither extreme exemplifies grace and mercy.

Our success depends on God, not on what we do. But we have to act on God's Word as He reveals it to us, to show our love for Him through obedience. This allows Him to enable us to do things we otherwise could not, and it frees Him to bless us in any way He desires. That's why we don't have to worry about how to accomplish anything in our lives. We are to just seek *Him* and *He* will accomplish it. Psalm 147:11 says,

> The LORD takes pleasure in those who fear Him,
> In those who hope in His mercy.

Open up to His gift of grace, for that pleases your heavenly Father.

What the Bible Says About
Receiving God's Gift of Grace

For by grace you have been saved through faith, and that not of yourselves; it is the gift of God.
Ephesians 2:8

My grace is sufficient for you, for My strength is made perfect in weakness.
2 Corinthians 12:9

It does not, therefore, depend on man's desire or effort, but on God's mercy.
Romans 9:16 NIV

He scorns the scornful,
But gives grace to the humble.
Proverbs 3:34

Blessed are the merciful,
For they shall obtain mercy.
Matthew 5:7

RECEIVE GOD'S GIFT OF POWER

Late one evening shortly after our son was a year old, I had to go to the drugstore to pick up prescription medicine for his cough. I left him at home with my husband and rushed out, barely making it to the store before it closed. In fact, only a couple of cars were left in the usually full parking lot. I rushed in, made the purchase, and left the store just as they were turning out the lights. The parking lot was now empty and dim, and I felt nervous walking to my car alone. About a third of the way there, I saw a dark figure move from the shadows at the side of the building. It appeared to be a man on a bicycle and, although the bicycle lent an air of harmlessness, I quickened my pace, started praying, and readied my keys for unlocking the car door.

Jesus, help me! God protect me! I prayed silently as I continued walking deliberately. The quiet sound of the bicycle came steadily closer. Just as I was approaching the car, but not quite near enough to get into it, the figure jumped off the bicycle and grabbed me from behind. In that instant my do-or-die instinct summoned all my energy and fervently drew upon the only source of power I knew I had.

As he grabbed me, I whirled around and said with power and authority that I have never before or since been able to duplicate, "Don't touch me or, in the name of Jesus, you're a dead man!" What amazed me was that I said it not as a fearful victim but as the aggressive, dominant one.

It was a *young* man—possibly eighteen or nineteen—but large and strong enough to overpower me. I turned on him so fast I was able to see his expression change from aggressive to stunned. I drew from a source of power and authority that he had not anticipated. My eyes met his dead-on and nothing in me backed down.

"Someone is watching us and He will never let you get away with touching me," I said with powerful authority as I quickly unlocked the door and opened it without breaking eye contact.

The young man stood motionless as I got in the car, shut the door, locked it, started the engine, and pulled away.

"Thank you, Jesus! Thank you, Jesus," I said as I drove home, trying to fasten my seat belt with shaking hands. I quivered all over in amazement at two things: first, my totally vulnerable and dangerous position in a large, dimly lit parking lot late at night with a male molester; and second, my frightening him away by the power and authority God had given me. This was the first time I had ever tested it so visibly. I could hardly believe what had happened.

Needless to say, I never tested God by going into dark parking lots alone after that, but I believe His power manifested at that moment as a gift. And I do believe if that young man had carried out what he intended, it certainly would have brought death and destruction into *his* life as well as mine, so what I spoke to him was a word from God.

Receiving God's Miracle Power

God's power is a gift for us to use, among other things, for the healing of our souls, and anyone wanting emotional health and restoration must have access to it. God wants you to know the "exceeding greatness of His power toward us who believe" (Eph. 1:19), so He can "strengthen you with power through his Spirit in your inner being" (Eph. 3:16 NIV). To receive His power you first have to receive Him and know who He is. You also have to know who your enemy is and be convinced that God's power is greater. Then you have to use the keys that Jesus gave us to gain access to that power. Jesus said, "I will give you the keys of the kingdom of heaven, and whatever you bind on earth will be bound in heaven, and whatever you loose on earth will be loosed in heaven" (Matt. 16:19).

The Keys of the Kingdom

Pastor Jack described the keys of the kingdom as being similar to the keys to his car. "There is very little power in the key that fits my car," he explained, "but that engine with all its power does not come to life without my key being put in the ignition. I don't have the power to go outside and get myself going sixty miles an hour, but I have access to a resource that can get me going that speed. Jesus said, 'I will give you the keys of the kingdom of God.' Keys mean the authority, the privilege, the access. Some things will not be turned on unless *you* turn them on. Some things will not be turned loose unless *you* turn them loose. Some things will not be set free unless *you* set them free. The key doesn't *make* the power of the engine, it *releases* the power of the engine."

Pastor Jack made the distinction that the kingdom of God means the realm of *His* rule. Our will must be submitted to His until we are completely dependent upon *His* power. As Pastor Jack says, "His keys don't fit our private kingdom. His power is unleashed upon command but not for our own personal gain."

Opening Up to God's Power

Because I know Jesus and live in obedience and submission to Him, I have access to His power through what He accomplished on the cross. Because of Him, my prayers have power. When I live His way and am submitted to Him, I have access to the keys of His kingdom. This power saved me in that dark parking lot.

You can't conjure up, take, or demand God's power; you can only receive it from Him. Oswald Chambers says that God's purpose for me is "that I depend on Him and His power now" (*My Utmost for His Highest*, 152). By depending on God's power instead of your own, you are fulfilling God's purpose for your life.

If you feel powerless and weak in the face of your circumstances, then thank God that even though *you* are weak, *He* is not. He says, "My strength is made perfect in weakness" (2 Cor. 12:9). Just as Jesus was crucified in weakness and lives in all power now, the same is true for us if we come to Him in weakness. Our power comes from the Holy Spirit working in us. Jesus told His disciples, "Wait for the Promise of the Father. . . . You shall receive power when the Holy Spirit has come upon you" (Acts 1:4, 8). To deny the Holy Spirit a place in your heart is to limit the power of God in your life.

Because human nature inevitably works itself back into bondage, we are always in need of a fresh flow of the Holy Spirit. Ask for one daily. Every morning say, "God, I need a fresh flow of Your Holy Spirit power working in me this day. I am weak, but You are all-powerful. Be strong in me this day." This is a power-full prayer.

Achieving total restoration is a battle. The devil wants you destroyed. God wants you restored. The Holy Spirit's presence in us guarantees no power can successfully put us in bondage: "The weapons of our warfare are not carnal but mighty in God for pulling down strongholds" (2 Cor. 10:4).

The Bible warns that in the last days some people will be lovers of themselves, lovers of money, boastful, proud, and on and on in a list that ends by describing them as "having a form of godliness but denying its power" (2 Tim. 3:5). Don't let yourself deny the power of God and turn away the gift God has given you.

Don't be a victim of your circumstances. Don't allow yourself to be tormented. Don't sit back when life seems to be falling apart. Don't live your life in terms of human energy. Let the power of God enable you to rise above the limits of your life. Use the authority that has been given you over your world, keeping in mind that the devil will always challenge that authority. Don't let him get away with it.

What good are God's keys to us if we never use them to unlock any doors to life? What good is God's power to you if you never receive and use it? Open the gift of power He has given you. Your life depends on it.

■ ——————— *What the Bible Says About* ——————— ■

Receiving God's Gift of Power

He gives power to the weak,
And to those who have no might He increases strength.
   Isaiah 40:29

For though He was crucified in weakness, yet He lives by the power of God. For we also are weak in Him, but we shall live with Him by the power of God toward you.
   2 Corinthians 13:4

He who is in you is greater than he who is in the world.
   1 John 4:4

For God has not given us a spirit of fear, but of power and love and of a sound mind.
   2 Timothy 1:7

I give you the authority to trample on serpents and scorpions, and over all the power of the enemy, and nothing shall by any means hurt you.
   Luke 10:19

■ ————————————————————————————————— ■

RECEIVE GOD'S GIFT OF REST

In my own personality, it was often hard to discern between what was the way God made me and what was bondage. I naturally was a fast-moving person. Favorably described, I was energetic, motivated, upbeat, active, and full of life. The negative version of that was hyper, intense, nervous, and restless.

"There is unrest in your spirit, Stormie," Mary Anne said to me one day. "I see it surface occasionally."

Even though she had been right about me so often, I was not convinced. After all, I'd had thirteen years of healing, deliverance, and growth and had been teaching others about the hope of deliverance and freedom in the Lord. Surely that must count for something. At first I thought maybe Mary Anne was annoyed with my fast-lane personality, especially in contrast with her own laid-back pace. Perhaps I was losing her total encouragement and support.

Lord show me if this is true. Is there something causing unrest in me? I prayed when I was alone.

Later that week, Mary Anne phoned early one morning to tell me about a dream she had in which she felt God revealed to her that my unrest was because of unforgiveness toward my father (see Step 2, "Ongoing Forgiveness"). I rejected that idea immediately. Obviously she didn't know my father. He had never done anything bad to me.

After she hung up I pondered what she said and asked the Lord if there was any truth to it. When I did, a tidal wave of pain, rage, resentment, and unforgiveness toward my father poured forth. I confessed that sin before God, and tears that had not been cried for a lifetime flooded out, cleansing every part of my being.

This hidden unforgiveness had kept me from trusting all male authority figures, including God. I felt I needed to take care of things myself. It was a subtle subconscious thing that didn't manifest in me as rebellion, but rather as unrest. *I* had to be the one to make things happen or keep them *from* happening.

However, after this time of deliverance I entered into a deep place of rest in the Lord such as I had never known before. It was a place that God had provided for me, but because of my own hidden sin I had not been able to receive it.

Resting in Him

Rest is an "anchor of the soul" (Heb. 6:19), which keeps us from being tossed around on the sea of circumstance. It's not just the feeling of ease we get from a vacation or the relaxation of a sound sleep at night; true rest is a place inside ourselves where we can be still and know that He is God, no matter what appears to be happening around us.

Jesus says, "Come to Me, all you who labor and are heavy laden, and I will give you rest" (Matt. 11:28). He instructs us to not allow our hearts to be troubled, but resist it by deciding to rest in Him. We must say, "God, I choose this day to enter into the rest You have for me. Show me how."

When we do that, God reveals all that stands in our way. Resting is "casting all your care upon Him, for He cares for you" (1 Pet.

5:7) and learning to be content no matter what the circumstances (Phil. 4:11)—not necessarily being delighted *with* the circumstances but being able to say, "God is in charge, I have prayed about it, He knows my need, I am obeying to the best of my knowledge. I can rest."

Sabotaging Your Own Rest

Why, then, do we have so much trouble being able to rest? Why do we feel anxious all day? Why do we resort to tranquilizers, sleeping pills, alcohol, drugs, television or anything else to numb our minds and stop our thought processes? The Bible illustrates rest being disturbed by sin, rebellion, and anxiety.

1. *Sin.* Sin separates us from *all* God has for us, including His rest.

> But the wicked are like the troubled sea,
> When it cannot rest. . . .
> "There is no peace,"
> Says my God, "for the wicked." (Isa. 57:20–21)

We are not the wicked He is talking about, but we do commit sins. We worry, we doubt, we have bitterness and unforgiveness, we don't cast our cares on the Lord, and we don't always observe times of rest.

2. *Rebellion.* We are rebellious if we refuse to fast when God calls us to fast, if we refuse to give when God tells us to give, if we refuse to exercise when God speaks to us about the care of our bodies, if we refuse to forgive others, and if we keep going when He tells us it's time to rest. We are stubborn people:

> They always go astray in their heart,
> And they have not known My ways.
> So I swore in my wrath, "They shall not enter My rest."
> (Heb. 3:10–11)

When our hearts turn from what we know of living the way God intended us to live, we lose our place of rest.

3. *Anxiety.* David says in Psalm 55:4–6,

> My heart is severely pained within me. . . .
> Fearfulness and trembling have come upon me,
> And horror has overwhelmed me.

> And I said, "Oh, that I had wings like a dove!
> For then I would fly away and be at rest."

How many times have we felt that way? We are pressed in on all sides by anguish, trouble, pain, worry, fear, and horror, and we feel that the only way to find rest is to escape. But God commands us to pray and deliberately take time to rest in Him.

God's gift is that we should have one full day of rest during every week, and not lose anything by doing so. This means rest for the soul as well as rest for the body—a day of vacation from our concerns, problems, deadlines, needs, obligations, or future decisions. If God Himself observed a day of rest, how can we survive without it? Ask Him to remove anything that stands in the way of the gift of rest He has for you.

What the Bible Says About
Receiving God's Gift of Rest

There remains therefore a rest for the people of God.
Hebrews 4:9

My soul finds rest in God alone.
Psalm 62:1 NIV

Come aside by yourselves to a deserted place and rest a while.
Mark 6:31

He said, "This is the rest with which
You may cause the weary to rest,"
And, "This is the refreshing";
Yet they would not hear.
Isaiah 28:12

The LORD has given you the Sabbath.
Exodus 16:29

CHAPTER 7

Step Six:
Reject the Pitfalls

A lie is an inaccurate or untrue statement that only has power if we believe it. Then it becomes a deception. Deception is walking, thinking, acting, or feeling in opposition to God's way and believing it's okay to do so. It's also believing that things are a certain way when they really aren't that way at all. Satan is the deceiver, and we are deceived when we line ourselves up with him. Deception allows a lie to enter into our actions.

I believed the lie, "It's not a human being; it's just a mass of cells. The baby's soul and spirit enter his body at birth. Besides, it's my life, and I have my rights." Deceived, I had little conscious guilt about taking the life of another person through abortion. But that didn't make it any less wrong or the consequences any less shattering.

We must hold everything in our lives up to the light of God's Word to find the truth. We can't go by what the world accepts or rejects because that puts us on shaky ground. The deception of abortion is thinking that because it's legally accepted, there is nothing wrong with it. But when the very existence of another person is in the balance, it can no longer be just a matter of *my* life and *my* rights. There is someone else to consider and not to recognize that is to be deceived indeed. Since I was desperate at the time of the abortions, I attributed my ill feelings about them to embarrassment. I didn't have any concept of its being immoral until after I was born again and read the following Scriptures:

> Before I formed you in the womb I knew you;
> Before you were born I sanctified you. (Jer. 1:5)

> For You have formed my inward parts;
> You have covered me in my mother's womb. (Ps. 139:13)

I also read medical accounts of babies surviving outside the womb as early as the fifth month of pregnancy and of babies inside the uterus perceiving light and sound stimuli. "Babies in the womb may be able to see, hear, taste, and *feel* emotions," said John Grossman in "Born Smart" (*Health Magazine*, March 1985). I had to admit that I'd destroyed someone God had created with abilities and gifts, calling and purpose. I wept. No, I mourned. Abortion is a deception, and a pitfall awaits us when we go along with it.

Of course, God's grace means we don't pay for things as we deserve, but the effects are still there. I never heard anyone who had an abortion say, "I feel totally fulfilled and thrilled about what I've done, and I know I'm an enriched and better person because of it." Life was never the same again for me. I had added another dark secret to my already burgeoning collection, and I could not feel completely good about myself.

All evil happens by deception. The devil entices us to accept things that are in opposition to God's ways. He appeals to our flesh and clouds issues to make them appear various shades of gray. We accept the gray as just a different shade of white instead of the alteration of black it really is.

Stepping Over the Line

There is a definite dividing line between God's kingdom and Satan's, and there are people on the fringes of each. It doesn't take much to put people over the edge into Satan's territory and allow him to control a piece of their heart in the process. All it takes is accepting a little lie like "It's my body," "It's my life," or "I have my rights." Such lies lead to a little lust, a little adultery, a little stealing, and a little murder. Yet an act is either stealing, murder, adultery, lust, and lying, or it isn't. You are either lined up with God's kingdom or with Satan's. Black is black and white is white.

The evil behind the deception of abortion is a spirit of murder. This didn't mean I was going to go around murdering people because I had aligned myself with that spirit. It *did* mean that in my soul I would pay the price for my disregard for life as God made it. I would not experience life at its fullest because a death process was at work in me. And many of my actions—like taking drugs and excessive drinking—were indirect suicide attempts.

The good news is: *We don't have to listen to lies.* We may think we must give serious credence to everything that comes into our minds, but we don't. We only have to examine our thoughts in the light of the Word of God and see if they line up properly.

An evil spirit is always behind deception. This means that every deception brings bondage, which can only be removed by replacing it with God's truth and living accordingly. Without the Word filling your mind with truth, you can't identify the lies. And without daily praying, "Lord, keep me undeceived," you can't ward off the deceiver. Everything you don't know about God will be used against you by the devil.

One of the first steps of obedience is to take charge of your mind. Without praise and worship, which allow God's presence to fill and rule your mind, the deceiver creeps in to manipulate you for his purpose. Unless you control your thoughts and align them with God's truth, you will fall into the pit the tormentor has designed for you.

God wants us to be free of the death grip of sin, whether we've acted in ignorance or with full knowledge and whether we feel guilty or not. When you find you've been deceived, immediately confess and repent. If you've fallen into the abortion deception, for example, say, "Lord, I confess my abortion. I won't try to make excuses for what I've done because You know my circumstances and my heart. I realize from Your Word that You know each of us— even in the womb. Your plans and purposes for that person will never be realized. I regret my part in that and I repent of my actions. Help me, Lord, to live Your way and make choices for life. Pour Your mercy out upon me and release me from the death penalty of this sin. In Jesus' name I pray."

After you confess and pray, don't let the devil continue to accuse you. You have cleaned the slate with God, so be released to live in the fullness of all God has for you.

In this chapter we will consider twenty popular deceptions in alphabetical order so that you can review them when you feel tempted to fall into one of them. As you read, you may think, "Obviously these are pitfalls!" But don't be fooled. It's possible to be sucked into them so subtly that you don't see it happening. Personally, I've been snared, or at least tempted at one time or another, by every one on the list, but I now am able to recognize the deception that blinded my eyes.

At the beginning of each deception listed, I will state the main lie that has to be believed. If you are able to recognize these subtle lies when they are first spoken, then you can immediately reject them. Don't allow any part of your being to buy into any part of a lie.

◼ ———————— *What* the Bible Says About ———————— ◼
Rejecting the Pitfalls

There is a way which seems right to a man.
But its end is the way of death.
  Proverbs 14:12

For they have dug a pit to take me,
And hidden snares for my feet.
  Jeremiah 18:22

And he who comes up from the midst of the pit
Shall be caught in the snare.
  Isaiah 24:18

All the ways of a man are pure in his own eyes,
But the LORD weighs the spirits.
  Proverbs 16:2

But You have lovingly delivered my soul from the pit of corruption.
  Isaiah 38:17

◼ ———————————————————————————— ◼

REJECT THE PITFALL OF ANGER

The lie we believe when we have frequent outbursts of anger is "*My* rights are most important and if I see them as being violated, I am fully justified in my anger." The deception of anger is believing we have a right to be angry at anyone but the devil. People and situations that make us angry are actually pawns Satan uses against us.

After I was healed of deep-rooted unforgiveness toward my mother, I still had to deal with recurring anger toward her because of her verbal abuse of me every time I was with her.

"The devil is using your mother to attack you, Stormie," Mary Anne explained when I went to her office for help. "She is a willing vessel because she is controlled by those spirits. Your war is with Satan, not her."

Learning to be angry with the devil and not my mother was extremely difficult, especially when I was with her. I constantly had to remind myself who my enemy *really* was, and the lines of distinction became quickly blurred. Eventually I was able to master my anger when I wasn't around her, but she died before I could do it perfectly when we were together. At those times, I confessed my anger to God and asked Him to help me.

Dealing with Our Anger

The Bible doesn't say we are never to get angry; it just sets two limits on our anger. First of all, we mustn't hurt someone verbally or physically. Secondly, we are to master our anger quickly and not carry it around inside us so that we sin.

One way we master our anger quickly is to examine the devil's part in it and deliberately direct anger at him by rebuking him, denouncing him, and casting him down in the name of Jesus. Taking anger out on others—a husband, a wife, a child, a friend, an authority figure, a stranger, or ourselves—is misdirecting it. We have to refuse to give Satan the opportunity to manipulate us, and this must be decided *before* the anger arises.

My husband and I agreed with Mary Anne that I should avoid being alone with my mother. When we visited my parents, we went as a family. Before we went, we prayed and bound the spirits in my mother, stopping their power to attack me. I asked God to fill me with His love for her and remind me to direct my anger at Satan. This helped immensely. I can't say I always succeeded, but I was able to turn the other cheek to some of her barbs.

If anger is not dealt with properly before the Lord, it will become a *spirit* of anger, which will control your life. If you are susceptible to sudden angry outbursts or if your anger level outweighs the offense and is repeated and uncontrollable, then you may have a spirit of anger. It can be inherited from a parent or picked up from observing parental outbursts when you were a child. Or if you were the victim of someone else's anger, your own unforgiveness or inability to release that memory can cause you to react violently now. Anger usually has more to do with people's hurt than it does their hate.

The Bible says, "Let all bitterness, wrath, anger, clamor, and evil speaking be put away from you, with all malice. And be kind to one another, tenderhearted, forgiving one another, just as God in Christ also forgave you" (Eph. 4:31–32). It also says if we don't do that, we grieve the Holy Spirit.

You will never find peace, restoration, and wholeness if you nurture a spirit of anger. Every single angry outburst will be a step backward from where you want to go or be, and it will keep your prayers from being answered.

If you feel you've succumbed to the pitfall of anger, speak to the devil in a loud voice of authority saying, "Spirit of anger, I identify your presence, and I rebuke your control in the name of Jesus. I proclaim that you have no power over me and the only one I will be angry with is you. I refuse to let you take life away from me by my angry outbursts. I proclaim that Jesus is Lord over my life, and He rules my mind, soul, and spirit. Anger be gone from me in the name of Jesus." Then praise God out loud and thank Him that He is far more powerful than all evil spirits combined.

Either we vent our anger toward others, which leads to destruction, or we keep it inside, making ourselves physically sick and depressed, or we direct it rightfully at the devil. The choice is clearly ours. Avoid this pitfall by making the right one.

■ ———————— *What the Bible Says About* ———————— ■

Anger

"Be angry, and do not sin": do not let the sun go down on your wrath, nor give place to the devil.
Ephesians 4:26–27

Make no friendship with an angry man,
And with a furious man do not go,
Lest you learn his ways,
And set a snare for your soul.
Proverbs 22:24–25

An angry man stirs up strife,
And a furious man abounds in transgression.
Proverbs 29:22

Whoever is angry with his brother without a cause shall be in danger of the judgment.
Matthew 5:22

Do not hasten in your spirit to be angry,
For anger rests in the bosom of fools.
Ecclesiastes 7:9

■ ■

REJECT THE PITFALL OF
BELIEVING LIES ABOUT YOURSELF

The ultimate lie we believe when accepting lies about ourselves is "I don't have what it takes and there is no way I can get it." It's fine to recognize where we are weak or lacking, but we must do it before the Lord, acknowledging that *He* supplies all we need.

We fall into this deception by judging our worth according to the world's standards rather than God's. The world's system of competition and comparison is destructive and brings feelings of intimidation and inadequacy as it pits one person's God-given gifts and potential against that of another. God says we are all unique and valuable. *The pitfall is in trying to live up to what we think we should be and not be what the Lord says we are.*

Negative reinforcement from parents or those close to us makes it more difficult to recognize negative thoughts about ourselves as lies. We've heard them too long to doubt their accuracy.

"You're worthless! You're nothing! You're stupid! You're a failure! You're never going to amount to anything!" were words my mother used to say to me over and over again. They were reinforced by her lack of affection and inability to nurture. Because we lived on a ranch miles from anyone, I didn't have the positive reinforcement of friends or relatives, which could have lessened the impact of my mother's neglect. Every day I heard the same words, and I grew up believing those lies. This negative programming colored all my actions and decisions.

Since I believed I was nobody, I became desperate to prove I was somebody. I grabbed for things instead of letting them happen; I demanded approval; I had to be noticed. Starved for love, I became involved in one destructive relationship after another. Yet no amount of love, approval, or recognition ever filled the endless void of my being because I believed those lies about myself. The ultimate lie I believed was that the only way out for me was suicide.

Respecting God's Handiwork

Webster's New World Dictionary defines self-esteem as "belief in oneself and self respect." Low self-esteem, which is a lack of those two qualities, is the habit of accepting lies about oneself. When low self-esteem or lack of self-worth takes control of the personality it can be paralyzing. We're afraid to do anything because we might fail, so every action seems monumental.

We all want to be somebody. The truth is, God created each one of us to be somebody and no life is an accident or unwanted in His eyes. He has given us *each* a distinct purpose or calling. It is not humility to deny the Lord's extraordinary qualities in us, it's low self-esteem.

High self-esteem means seeing yourself as God made you, recognizing that you are a unique person in whom He has placed specific gifts, talents, and purpose unlike anyone else. Memorize this—cut it out, paste it on your hand, and say it aloud fifty times a day. Do whatever it takes to help you remember it. This is the absolute truth about you whether you can see it or not and whether or not anyone *else* recognizes it: "Each one has his own gift from God" (1 Cor. 7:7).

You have to be able to see that without money, without a job, without your talent, without having your hair done or make-up on, without being thin, without nice clothes, house, car, or family, *you are worth something.* When you allow God to show you what *He* thinks of you and let it sink in and penetrate every fiber of your being, whatever is added or taken away doesn't make or break you.

I have learned to value myself as God values me by deliberately thanking Him for any positive things I see. "Thank you, Lord, that I am alive, that I can walk, that I can talk, that I can see, that I can prepare a meal, that I can write letters, that I am neat, that I love my children, that I know Jesus. Thank you God that You have made me to be a person of worth and purpose." As we praise God for specific things, we are inviting His presence to bring transformation. It's the best medicine I know for believing lies about yourself.

That may seem like a difficult concept to understand, but actually it is very simple. You are choosing to thank God in the midst of the negative in faith that He will not leave you there for long. You are saying, "Thank you, God, that this negative thing I see in myself has a positive aspect that You are working in me." For example, like most people who have been scarred by verbal abuse in early childhood, I have been highly oversensitive to other people's comments. This is a negative trait. Someone who is easily hurt puts others in the uncomfortable position of having to walk on eggshells or be responsible for hurting them. By praising God in the midst of my oversensitivity, I have allowed Him to transform that negative quality into a positive one—that of being sensitive to other people instead of myself.

If you've been told, "You're hopeless. You can't make it. You don't have it!'' by a parent, brother, sister, friend, or stranger, take a long look at those words, and recognize who is behind them. Say to the devil, "Satan, I no longer will listen to lies about myself. I am not a cosmic accident as you would have me to believe. I have worth. I have purpose. I have gifts and talents. God says that about me and I will not contradict my heavenly Father. I rebuke your lies and I refuse to hear them."

The Bible says, "A house divided against itself will fall" (Luke 11:17 NIV). This means that a person who has turned against himself won't make it. A large amount of your emotional pain may be caused by believing untrue things about yourself. Many times God was the *only* one who believed in me, but that was enough. I know now that because I believe in Him and He believes in me, I *can* make it. So can *you!*

■————— *What the Bible Says About* —————■
Believing Lies About Yourself

He chose us in Him before the foundation of the world, that we should be holy and without blame before Him in love.
  Ephesians 1:4

Before I was born the LORD called me;
from my birth he has made mention of my name.
  Isaiah 49:1 NIV

The very hairs of your head are all numbered. Do not fear therefore; you are of more value than many sparrows.
  Luke 12:7

God does not show favoritism but accepts men from every nation who fear him and do what is right.
  Acts 10:34–35 NIV

But you are a chosen generation, a royal priesthood, a holy nation, His own special people, that you may proclaim the praises of Him who called you out of darkness into His marvelous light.
  1 Peter 2:9

■   ■

REJECT THE PITFALL OF BLAMING GOD

The lie we believe when we blame God is "God could have kept this from happening. He could have made things different." The truth is God has given us a free will, which He won't violate. As a result, *we all make choices, and things are often the way they are because of them.* He also gives us limitations and boundaries which are for our protection. If we will to violate that order, leaving our circumstances to chance or the work of the enemy, we breed destruction.

Before I came to know the Lord, I blamed Him for everything. I thought, *If God is so great why is there suffering? Why doesn't He lift me out of my misery and pain? Why was I born to an abusive mother? He certainly knew she was crazy. Why didn't He make me different? I'm a good person. I don't rob liquor stores. I haven't murdered anyone. Shouldn't I be rewarded?*

I was confused about who God is, and I ended up blaming Him for things that happened. I didn't understand that He is good, He is on my side, and His will is for my highest good. I didn't understand the importance of living God's way. I also didn't understand that the devil is an enemy who wants me destroyed. I blamed God for things Satan does. When I finally learned to distinguish between the heart of God and the work of the devil, I was set free of the bondage of blaming God.

No Way Out

Blaming God is far more common than most of us care to admit, especially for those who have been abused, neglected, or deeply disappointed by authority figures. The tendency is to think subconsciously of God as being like that abusive father, grandparent, teacher, or boss, projecting on Him attitudes and behavior that have nothing to do with who He really is.

We also blame God for anything negative our parents told us about ourselves. We feel God must have created us the way they say we are and we wonder why He was so careless. We also project human imperfections on to Him. For example, we blame Him if our parents didn't want or love us.

We may think of God as *authoritative* (mean, stern, exacting, merciless, expecting perfection). Or we think of Him as *distant* (cold, uncommunicative, uncaring). Or we might see Him as *weak* (passive, powerless, unable to help, an observer but not a doer in our behalf). Or we see Him as *super nice* (a sugar daddy, a holy Santa Claus). Such projections will make us angry at God.

To stop blaming God, we have to know what He's really like. And we can find out by looking to Jesus, who said, "He who has seen Me has seen the Father" (John 14:9). Unless we truly let Jesus penetrate every part of our lives, we won't ever really know what God is like.

When you truly know Jesus, you see that Father God is fair and compassionate. His love is unlimited and unfailing. He does not neglect, abuse, forget, or misunderstand. He will never disappoint or be imperfect. When we understand who God really is and stop blaming Him, we find peace and security.

My husband and I have a friend who is gifted in many ways but has shut God out of His life, blaming Him for a car accident in which his sister was killed and he was injured severely enough to end his promising sports career. Fifteen years later, he still bitterly questions why God didn't keep it from happening. The truth is, the accident was never part of God's plan. It was the devil who came to destroy because death *is* a part of *his* plan. This is a good man, but he is agonizingly frustrated and unfulfilled because he has shut God off from working powerfully in his life.

If you are mad at God, then you need to get to know Him better because there is a lot about Him that you don't fully understand. The best thing to do is to be honest with Him about it. You won't hurt God's feelings—He has known about it all along anyway. Pray to Him saying, "Father I have been angry at You because of this particular situation (be specific). I have hated this and I've blamed You for it. Please forgive me and help me to be released from it. Take away my misconceptions about You and help me to know You better."

Blaming God is a no-win attitude. We back ourselves into a corner with no way out, instead of recognizing God as the *only* way out. Blaming God produces misplaced anger that will be channeled inward—making you sick, frustrated, and unfulfilled—or outward, causing you to hate a husband or wife, to abuse a child, to treat a friend rudely, to be uncooperative with a fellow worker, or to lash out at strangers. People who are angry and belligerent are usually blaming God for something instead of understanding that Satan is their enemy.

The opposite of blaming God is trusting Him. Decide now whom you will trust. You can't move on into all God has for you if any bitterness and misplaced blame have a place in your heart.

■ ——————— *What the Bible Says About* ——————— ■
Blaming God

Surely God will never do wickedly,
Nor will the Almighty pervert justice.
  Job 34:12

The foolishness of a man twists his way,
And his heart frets against the LORD.
  Proverbs 19:3

The wicked plots against the just,
And gnashes at him with his teeth.
  Psalm 37:12

Do not trust in oppression.
  Psalm 62:10

Blessed are all those who put their trust in Him.
  Psalm 2:12

■ ——————————————————————————————————— ■

REJECT THE PITFALL OF CHILD ABUSE

The lie we believe when we abuse our children is "Because I'm a good person, because I know what child abuse is, and because I love my child, I will never do anything to hurt him." Unfortunately, good intentions will not be enough when the pressures of parenthood and the tidal wave of past hurts rise up and collide in a weak moment.

I had always thought of myself as the one who had been abused. It never occurred to me that I had the potential in me to abuse. But I did, and it had been built in from my childhood. When my first child was born, I subconsciously expected my child to comfort, love, and fulfill me, even though he couldn't (see Chapter 5). Years later Dr. Ross Campbell's *How to Really Love Your Child* (Wheaton, IL: Victor, 1982) helped me to understand those feelings. He says, "Role-reversal is the primary relationship in the frightening phenomenon of child abuse. An abusing parent feels his child must take care of the parent's emotional needs, that the parent has a right to be nourished and comforted by his child. When the child fails in this, the parent feels a right to punish him."

What I felt inside me at the time was beyond normal irritation or frustration with childish behavior. It was violent, out-of-control hysteria, fueled by supernatural energy that derives satisfaction from hurting someone else. At its extreme it is the same destructive force that causes remorseless rape and murder.

I had thought determination to be a good parent and love for my child were all I needed, but they weren't. The emotional damage of my past set me up to be a potential child abuser, and only the restoring love of God rescued me from that.

Forgiving Your Parents

Abuse is any unpleasant treatment that lowers self-worth—verbal abuse, neglect, a perceived lack of love—as well as beatings and molestation. If a child can't perceive his parents' acceptance of him, he grows up with a self-destructive hunger for love that can't be satisfied by any human being. The needs not met in childhood will be just as strong in adulthood, but they will be expertly camouflaged.

If you were abused as a child, don't be misled into saying to yourself, "I'm born-again—I shouldn't still hurt inside. There must be something wrong with me." The fact that you still hurt doesn't negate your born-again status or make you any less spiritual. Because people tend to view God the same way they viewed their parents, it takes a time of healing, deliverance, and getting to know the love of God before total trust comes.

Forgiving your parents is a big part of the healing (and crucial to avoiding the pitfall of abusing your own children). You have to forgive the father who never protected you, the mother who mistreated and abused you, the stepfather who didn't love you, the grandfather or uncle who sexually molested you, the parent who was never there or deserted you through death or abandonment, the weak parent who shut you out emotionally in order to drink, eat, or drug himself into oblivion, the selfish parent who reminded you that you were never wanted, or the emotionally deficient parent who didn't know how to properly nurture you.

These bitterly painful experiences will *continue* to hurt you if you don't cry out your pain to the Lord and ask Him to help you forgive. You will not only be hurt by your unforgiveness but, worse yet, you may well hurt your own children. For their sake, if not your own, you have to fully release the past. The Bible says,

> When my father and my mother forsake me,
> Then the LORD will take care of me. (Ps. 27:10)

Seeing your parent as the unloved, mistreated, or traumatized child he or she may have been helps you to forgive, yet most people know little about their parents' backgrounds. Most incidents, especially the bad ones, are seldom talked about, even by another relative. When you understand that your parent did not deliberately withhold love from you, but actually never had it to give in the first place, it's easier to forgive. Sometimes what one parent *didn't* do hurts as bad as what the abusing one *did*. A parent's non-involvement or unwillingness to step in and rescue you feels like betrayal. Unforgiveness for that uninvolved parent is more difficult to recognize but is more common than we think. Ask God to show you any unforgiveness toward a parent who didn't come to your rescue. If it's there, you have to deal honestly with your feelings about it.

I counseled one young woman whose father had sex with her on a regular basis. Because she was the only member of the family who was not beaten (it's common for an abusing parent to single out one child in this manner), she felt he had favored her. She was suffering from severe depression and suicidal thoughts when she came to me for help.

"You need to forgive your father, Cyndie," I suggested.

"What for? He was always good to me," she retorted immediately.

"Cyndie, he failed you. He didn't beat you, but he destroyed your self-worth by having sexual relations with you," I said, trying to cover my shock that she was deceived into thinking he had done no wrong.

I was never able to convince Cyndie of what I told her, but I sent her to a therapist who, after a year of therapy, helped her to admit that her father had failed her and she needed to forgive him. Her life has finally turned around.

We all need parents who will love us, encourage us, nurture us, be affectionate with us, believe for the best in us, and be interested in what we do. Those of us who did not have parents like that have needs that only God can meet. We can't go back in time and get someone to hold and nurture us, and we mustn't demand it from a spouse or friends because they can't do it. It has to come from our heavenly Father.

What If the Damage Is Already Done?

One of the questions I am asked most frequently is "How do I make up for the damage I have already done to my children?" If you feel you have abused, neglected, or failed to communicate love to your child, you can take a few basic steps to begin to rectify it. You can never change what has been done, but God can use you as an instrument of healing for the wounds you have inflicted and you can take the following steps to help restore the relationship.

1. *Confess to the Lord what you have done.* Ask God to heal and deliver you and make you into a loving, patient parent. Ask Him for wisdom in raising your children, and ask Him to help you speak words of restoration and healing to each one.

2. *Seek professional help immediately if you are abusing your child or feel he is in any present danger.* Call a child abuse hotline and *also* talk to a Christian counselor or pastor. If necessary, have a friend or family member care for your child for a few days.

3. *Go to the child and ask forgiveness.* Look him straight in the eye and say, "I love you, but I've failed to show my love appropriately." If there are specific incidents, name them. Tell him that God is showing you the truth about yourself and that with His help you intend to be different.

Even if your child is small and cannot understand, say it anyway. He will understand the spirit of what's being said, and it will bring healing. At a later time when he *can* understand, talk to him again. Don't be afraid of rejection. Most children will greatly appreciate your honesty and frank communication.

Continue to say you're sorry if you do anything else abusive. Tell the child that God is helping you, but you still have a lot to learn. Ask for the child's forgiveness, and encourage him to say, "I forgive you" to you. It's important for him to speak those words even if he doesn't feel it wholeheartedly. What we speak affects our souls.

4. *Pray for the child daily.* Say, "God, make this child all You created him to be. Don't let me do anything to damage him. Heal his scars and our relationship."

5. *Spend time with the child and strengthen the relationship.* Look the child in the eyes every day, and speak words that are encouraging and uplifting to him. Say, "I love you very much, and I think you're great." Do something with him or for him that clearly demonstrates your love.

6. *Seek healing for yourself.* One of the best things you can do for your child is become a whole person. It's difficult to nurture and love a child if you've never been nurtured and loved. Seek counseling from a Christian counselor or a pastor if you need it. The way you live will determine what your children and grandchildren will inherit. Your sin and disobedience will have a negative effect on their lives. You are choosing your spiritual legacy now.

7. *Praise God daily for His restoration power.* God is our only hope for restoring relationships damaged by abuse. Your praising God for His transformation of the situation is one of the avenues by which it will happen. Get to know Father God better. He is the perfect parental role model.

In times of weakness when life seems out of control, as can happen in dealing with children, you have to take charge and choose to put yourself under God's control. Surrender your weak places fully and honestly to Him so He can turn them around to be vessels of His strength. He is a God of restoration and redemption, so He can redeem whatever has occurred in your past with your parents. He can mend the breach between you and your children. Restoration doesn't happen overnight, but redemption can. Allow God to redeem your situation now, so it can be turned around and headed in the right direction.

■ ——————— *What the Bible Says About* ——————— ■
Child Abuse

And you, fathers, do not provoke your children to wrath, but bring them up in the training and admonition of the Lord.
Ephesians 6:4

Behold, children are a heritage from the LORD,
The fruit of the womb is His reward.
Psalm 127:3

When my father and my mother forsake me,
Then the LORD will take care of me.
Psalm 27:10

He sent His word and healed them,
And delivered them from their destructions.
Psalm 107:20

A good man leaves an inheritance to his children's children.
  Proverbs 13:22

■ ─── ■

REJECT THE PITFALL OF CONFUSION

The lie we believe when we feel confused is "The issues at hand seem too complex and overwhelming to grasp, so there must be something wrong with me." Sometimes we take action or make decisions based on this confusion, instead of recognizing it for what it is and looking for the source. While life in and of itself can be extremely complicated and unclear, life with Jesus at the helm is simple, orderly, and clear.

While writing this book, I was suddenly overwhelmed by confusion. I woke up one morning, and everything seemed disjointed. I saw no purpose or future. I felt distant and hopeless about my family as if I were unconnected to them. I felt dissatisfied with everything: where I live ("It's time to move"); my marriage ("Who is this person I'm married to?"); my friendships ("Does anyone really care?"); my writing ("How can I possibly have anything to say?"). Nothing was exciting. Everything seemed pointless. I couldn't get a handle on anything.

Why am I suddenly feeling this way? Where did it come from? I asked the Lord, *I know it's not from You, God. It has to be from the evil one. But how did the devil get in like that? What changed?*

I had been fine the day before. So what had happened in the night? I thought back. Both children had been invited to go out after dinner with friends for an evening's activities, prompting Michael and me to seize the opportunity to have a rare night out alone. We decided to go to a movie and glanced through the theater section of the newspaper.

"These have undesirable ratings. That one is too violent. This one is mindless. This one is filled with sexual garbage," I said as I eliminated one movie after another.

That left us with one possibility, but neither of us knew anything about it. I looked through all my reports on movies, which I collect to be informed on whether they are fit for human consumption, and found no information on this one.

"Well, it doesn't have an R rating. How bad can it be?" we concluded. "At least we'll be together."

The movie was a comedy that included an adulterous affair by the lonely wife of the workaholic husband. Even though that part of it wasn't shown explicitly on the screen, the idea of something so opposed to God's ways being made light of and acceptable made me uneasy.

Looking back, I believe that exposure to the values in that movie, even though I had not adopted them, opened the way for a spirit of confusion. Had we left the theater at the first prompting of the Lord, I'm sure I would have felt different the next day. As it was, the pure flow of the Holy Spirit I had been enjoying was tainted with the world's pollution, and my dissatisfaction with all God had given me was a clear indication that it had invaded my heart.

Was it just a coincidence? Was I merely too impressionable? I don't think so. Just like the bank teller who learned to recognize counterfeit money by feeling real money day after day, I have learned to recognize counterfeit spirits by spending time in the presence of the Holy Spirit. What invaded my soul was not of the Lord; it was the spirit of confusion that permeated that movie.

Confusion and the Worldly Perspective

Confusion is a lack of proper order, the indiscriminate mixing of dissimilar things, and being mentally mixed up. *Confusion is caused by mixing darkness with light.* It is anything out of the divine order or out of sync with God. There is every kind of confusion in the world today, because what is bad is now considered good, and what is good is disdained. Life has become bewildering, and the only thing that breaks through the confusion is the Lord's presence and the Word of His truth.

Confusion is a spirit, and everyone, even those who walk closely with the Lord, is susceptible to its attack. The Bible says, "God is not the author of confusion but of peace" (1 Cor. 14:33). If He is completely in charge of every area of your life and His order is brought to reign, clarity, simplicity, and peace are the immediate by-products. If not, life becomes jumbled, out of order, complex, confusing, and difficult to deal with.

How Do I Open Myself Up to Confusion?

You don't have to go to a bad movie in order to move into confusion. Too many outside opinions, when you should be listening only to God's, will cause confusion. Opposing God's Word in any way will invite spirits of confusion to dwell in your life. The Bible says drinking alcohol brings confusion, but also imbibing in *any-*

thing that is not of God, such as gossip, foul language, promiscuity, drugs, television, movies, and magazines tainted with world mind-edness, will bring confusion. When we try to put elements together in our lives that don't go together we get confused. For example, we attend church, we tithe, we fast and pray, and yet we entertain a little fantasy about the cute assistant pastor or that attractive person at work.

All lust of the flesh brings confusion: "Where envy and self-seeking exist, confusion and every evil thing will be there" (James 3:16). In fact, too much focus on ourselves always invites in a spirit of confusion.

How Do I Get Rid of Confusion?

When confusion does come in, it may cause you to make unwise or quick decisions based on a faulty frame of reference, or it can paralyze your thought processes so you won't be able to make any decision at all. In either case, it will help you remember that *you absolutely never have to live with confusion*. Take it to God. Pray about every aspect of it. Say, "I refuse to live in confusion. I know that confusion is *not* from God. I know that power, love, and a sound mind *are* from God. I know that God's ways are simple. It is *we* who make things complex. Lord, show me Your simple truth about what I'm feeling and thinking. Show me where I have opened the door to allow confusion to enter into my life so that I may confess it before You as sin and be cleansed. I rebuke the spirit of confusion and say it has *no* power in my life. By the authority I have in Jesus Christ I command you to be gone. I praise You, Lord, and thank You for the wisdom, clarity, and simplicity that are in Christ." Worship and praise God until you are thinking clearly again.

Confusion cannot coexist with God's presence. That's why worship, praise, and thanksgiving are the best weapons to dissolve it. Your emotional health and well-being and your growth in the Lord depend on your ability to identify this pit *before* you fall into it.

■ ————— *What the Bible Says About* ————— ■
Confusion

Evidently some people are throwing you into confusion and are trying to pervert the gospel of Christ.
Galatians 1:7 NIV

The one who is throwing you into confusion will pay the penalty.
  Galatians 5:10 NIV

But I fear, lest somehow, as the serpent deceived Eve by his craftiness, so your minds may be corrupted from the simplicity that is in Christ.
  2 Corinthians 11:3

Woe to those who call evil good, and good evil;
Who put darkness for light, and light for darkness;
Who put bitter for sweet, and sweet for bitter!
  Isaiah 5:20

Your eyes will see strange sights and your mind imagine confusing things.
  Proverbs 23:33 NIV

REJECT THE PITFALL OF CRITICISM

The lie we secretly want to believe when we criticize others is "I'm better than they are." But what we *really* fear is "*They* are better than *I* am." For the sake of ego we make ourselves look good by putting someone else down, and then we adopt an "I'm right and they're wrong" attitude to justify our criticism. The deception we come under is in thinking that anyone but God has the right to sit in judgment of another person.

I used to be very critical of people, dissecting them in my mind to see if they were as much better than I as I feared. Even then there was no enjoyment in it for me because I was just as critical of myself. But I read, "For with what judgment you judge, you will be judged; and with the same measure you use, it will be measured back to you" (Matt. 7:2). I also read in *My Utmost for His Highest*, "See that you do not use your limitations to criticize someone else" (131). I recognized then that my criticizing others meant I was judging them by my own limitations, not only limiting what God could do in my life, but inviting judgment back upon myself.

Crowding Out a Critical Spirit

Those of us who have been abused as children often grow up to be judgmental and critical. Being torn down when we were young makes tearing someone else down to build ourselves up very appealing. We become unmerciful because we were not shown mercy.

Criticizing others quickly becomes a bad habit that can backfire. Constantly criticizing, even only in the mind, invites a critical spirit. When you have a spirit of criticism, your every thought and word is colored by it. You eventually become cynical and then completely unable to experience joy. You can be reading the Word, praying, and obeying and still not have peace and joy in your life because you are critical. Being critical of circumstances or conditions can be as detrimental as criticizing people because it turns you into a grumbler and complainer—the type of person people generally like to avoid. It's difficult to find the love and support you need when no one wants to be around you.

Criticism crowds love out of our hearts. And "though I have the gift of prophecy, and understand all mysteries and all knowledge, and though I have all faith, so that I could remove mountains, but have not love, I am nothing" (1 Cor. 13:2). Without love in our hearts we cannot grow emotionally and we will always be at a standstill in our healing and development. But we can crowd out criticism by being constantly filled with the love of the Lord through a stance of praise and thanksgiving toward Him.

If you've learned to be critical from childhood, you must set a monitor over your mouth and heart. Learn to recognize the unrestful and distasteful quality of a critical spirit and deliberately replace critical thoughts and words with ones that recognize the good in that person or situation. Ask yourself, "Am I building up or am I tearing down and destroying?"

If you recognize a serious, almost compulsive tendency toward criticism in yourself, say, "I refuse to allow a spirit of criticism to control my thoughts and my mouth. I realize that You, Lord, are the only one who knows the whole story in any situation. I don't have the right to judge others. Make me a person who shows mercy, who doesn't criticize, grumble, or complain. Thank You for Your forgiveness of me. Help me to extend that same forgiveness to others."

I prayed that prayer, and now God helps me see the good, or potential for greatness, in everyone. It's not that I don't recognize someone's sin but that I realize I have no right to judge or criticize them for it. I can pray for, confront, and speak God's Word to them, but I can't be critical or faultfinding.

If you struggle with being critical of yourself or others, ask God to help you to be merciful. Having a critical spirit can cut off avenues of blessing and keep you from becoming the whole person you desire to be.

◼ ———————— *What the Bible Says About* ———————— ◼
Criticism

Let none of you think evil in your heart against your neighbor.
    Zechariah 8:17

So speak and so do as those who will be judged by the law of liberty. For judgment is without mercy to the one who has shown no mercy. Mercy triumphs over judgment.
    James 2:12–13

Let no corrupt communication proceed out of your mouth, but what is good for necessary edification, that it may impart grace to the hearers.
    Ephesians 4:29

He who is without sin among you, let him throw a stone at her first.
    John 8:7

And above all things have fervent love for one another, for "love will cover a multitude of sins."
    1 Peter 4:8

◼ ◼

REJECT THE PITFALL OF DENIAL

The lie we believe when we deny a problem is "If I pretend this isn't happening, it will go away" or "If I tell myself this is something else, it *will* be." This self-protective measure kicks in when things appear to be completely out of our control. We block the situation from our mind or deny its existence in order to survive. The problem with denial is that the truth eventually comes out, and if we don't take care of emotional bills now, we will pay more later.

Deception is *believing* a *lie* and not realizing you have done so. *Denial* is *knowing* the *truth* but choosing to live as if you don't. *Denial is deceiving yourself.*

My mentally ill mother believed *she* was normal and something was wrong with everyone else. She was deceived. My father knew she was not normal, but didn't know what to do about it. He was afraid to seek psychiatric help for fear she would be committed for life to a mental hospital like the ones in the horror movies he had seen in his youth. Hoping she would someday miraculously "snap out of it," he chose to ignore her problem. He lived in denial. His self-deception was a means of survival.

Cyndie, the young woman whose father frequently had sex with her but beat the other family members, believed he was her ally. She had learned to deny that sex between a father and a daughter is an abomination because that was the only way she could survive her experience. She was too weak and powerless to handle the truth. It was too painful to acknowledge what she could neither cope with nor change. Her healing didn't happen until she became stable enough to acknowledge the sinfulness of the relationship. This opened the way for forgiveness for her father, which she had adamantly denied was even needed, and God's restoration.

A Form of Survival

Living in denial is living a lie. We steadfastly refuse to be swayed by the facts, no matter how they add up. For instance:

Fact one: Dad frequently comes home drunk.

Fact two: At those times he becomes violent and beats me.

Those facts add up to Dad's being an alcoholic, yet we mask the truth by saying, "It's okay. It's not that bad. I can live with this situation." All the while it's really *not* okay, it *is* bad, and we *can't* live that way without paying severely for it. We have to be free of deception in every form—even the deception of knowing the truth and believing we can minimize it.

Because God's Spirit of truth is necessary to penetrate the darkness of self-deception, confronting someone living in denial doesn't often work. To rip this self-protective, self-imposed, false skin graft away is to rip flesh away from bone. The pain would be unbearable. It's not simply a matter of peeling away dead skin; this false skin is deeply attached and grown together with the real flesh. There has to be healing from within so that what has been attached from the outside will fall away. Any confrontation has to be preceded by much prayer and completely *led* by the Holy Spirit.

Facing the Truth

Many people don't want to spend any time at all dealing with the past. They often cite the passage in Scripture where the apostle Paul says we should be "forgetting those things which are behind and reaching forward to those things which are ahead" (Phil. 3:13).

But what he means is that we shouldn't be living in the past from which we've been set *free*. Yet we can't be set free from something we have not brought into the full light of God and exposed for what it is. Only when we do that will we find healing for it, and only then can we forget and move on.

If you live in denial about anything, you will keep coming around to the same problem over and over again. "Why doesn't this situation ever change? Why can't I ever get beyond it?" you'll ask. And the answer will be that the Spirit of truth has not been allowed to bear upon it.

We have to look at our lives as a counselor would and ask ourselves these questions:

1. The last time I felt unhappy, the following things were happening (for instance, my husband was gone on a business trip): _____
   _____.

2. The time before that, the following things were happening (for instance, my closest friends went away for the weekend and didn't include me): _____
   _____.

3. When I was a child, I was unhappy when (for instance, my dad was away and not able to attend my softball games):
   _____
   _____.

4. Is there anything similar about the events in all of these situations? (For instance, I tend to feel lonely and abandoned when my husband is gone or my friends are gone because my father was gone so often.) _____
   _____.

5. I may be unhappy because _____
   _____.

Now think about your relationships.

1. The last time I disagreed with my spouse or a friend was because (for instance, they questioned my judgment about something as if I couldn't make a sound decision) _____
   _____
   _____.

2. I feel unhappy with my boss at work when (for instance, he wants to know every detail of what I'm doing as if he's check-

ing up on me) _____

_____ .

3. As a child I became angry with my parents when (for instance, they quizzed me incessantly about where I'd been and what I was doing) _____

_____ .

4. Some of my anger at my spouse or my friend or my boss might relate back to (for instance, my dad's efforts to control everything I did) _____

_____ .

Now think about your relationship with God.

1. I think of God as (for instance, as a firm disciplinarian who expects me to be perfect) _____

_____ .

2. I think of my father or my mother as (for instance, I think of them as distant and always expecting too much of me) ____

_____

_____ .

3. My relationship with my father (or mother) might be influencing my relationship with God in the following ways:

_____

_____ .

As you work through this introspection, ask God to reveal any place in your life where you are denying the truth. Then bring the truth of God's Word to bear upon that situation. The Psalms tell us,

> The LORD is gracious and full of compassion,
> Slow to anger and great in mercy.
> The LORD is good to all. (145:8–9)

God is not a harsh disciplinarian, but we will not know this unless we test our opinion of Him against the truth in the Bible. Testing your beliefs against the truth is crucial to your healing because the longer you go on denying a problem, the longer it will take you to find wholeness. Had my father faced the problem of my mother head-on, a good psychiatrist might have helped her overcome her illness through counseling and medication. All those years of misery and destruction might never have happened.

Make No Room for Denial

Once we have moved out of denial, God is the only one who can keep us out. We have to continue to pray, "Lord keep me undeceived and help me to never deny Your truth. If there is any place in my life where I have been deceiving myself, shine the light of Your Word upon it and bring Your Spirit of truth to rule there. Show me where I have rationalized anything that I should have faced. Where have I swept something under the rug that should have been thrown out? Where have I justified myself when I should have simply confessed? Please show me everything because I truly want to know."

Remember, sin is missing the mark. "If we say that we have no sin, we deceive ourselves, and the truth is not in us" (1 John 1:8). If we think we are without error all the time, whom are we kidding? I know someone who, when confronted about possible denial in her life by several friends, went to other friends who did not know the situation as well and built a case for what she wanted to believe, instead of going to God and saying, "Show me the truth, Lord. If what these people are saying is right, help me to see it. If it isn't right, help *them* to see it. I release it into Your hands." As long as we depend on lies to insulate us from pain, we don't need to depend on God, and this will always keep us from experiencing all He has for us.

We are *all* victims of self-deception at one time or another. We do it expertly. That's why we can never be critical of another who lives in denial. We can recognize it and pray for their eyes to be opened, but we are just as easily able to fall prey to it if we are not seeking to have God's light shed on our life. Pray frequently for the power of God to penetrate any form of denial in you.

■ ——————— *What the Bible Says About* ——————— ■
Denial

You desire truth in the inward parts,
And in the hidden part You will make me to know wisdom.
   Psalm 51:6

I have no greater joy than to hear that my children walk in truth.
   3 John 4

You shall know the truth, and the truth shall make you free.
  John 8:32

For the wrath of God is revealed from heaven against all ungodliness and unrighteousness of men, who suppress the truth in unrighteousness.
  Romans 1:18

When He, the Spirit of truth, has come, He will guide you into all truth.
  John 16:13

REJECT THE PITFALL OF DEPRESSION

The lie that we believe when we feel depressed is "I cannot live with my situation the way it is, and I am powerless to change it." When the discouragement of that belief settles over us like a thick fog, we can't see any way out of the darkness. The deception is in thinking that our situation is hopeless. This thought can be so subtle that we don't even realize it until we fall into a full-fledged depression: "Hope deferred makes the heart sick" (Prov. 13:12). Losing hope is what causes depression.

Check the statements below that express your feelings in the last year:

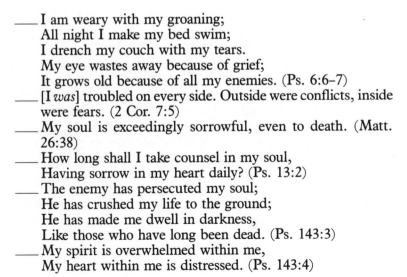

____ I am weary with my groaning;
  All night I make my bed swim;
  I drench my couch with my tears.
  My eye wastes away because of grief;
  It grows old because of all my enemies. (Ps. 6:6–7)
____ [I *was*] troubled on every side. Outside were conflicts, inside were fears. (2 Cor. 7:5)
____ My soul is exceedingly sorrowful, even to death. (Matt. 26:38)
____ How long shall I take counsel in my soul,
  Having sorrow in my heart daily? (Ps. 13:2)
____ The enemy has persecuted my soul;
  He has crushed my life to the ground;
  He has made me dwell in darkness,
  Like those who have long been dead. (Ps. 143:3)
____ My spirit is overwhelmed within me,
  My heart within me is distressed. (Ps. 143:4)

If you checked any of these statements, you have definitely suffered with depression. Sleepless nights, lying awake with your heart pounding. Feeling weak and crushed as if you're sinking into a deep, dark pit. When you look at yourself in the mirror the next morning, there is no light in your face, and your eyes are dull. You feel like people don't want to be around you. You feel like you can't emotionally connect with anyone. If you've ever been depressed, you know those feelings. So have many people who love God. Most of these Bible quotations were written by two great men who were dear to God's heart: David, the giant killer and king, and the apostle Paul. Both found God to be the ultimate answer to their depression. Obviously, depression is not unknown to the Lord.

One of the biggest deceptions about depression is thinking you are the only one who has ever felt depressed. Millions of people are depressed right now and feel exactly the way these people felt thousands of years ago. That fact may not reduce your depression, but at least you know you are not alone.

Some common symptoms of depression are troubled sleep, sleeping too much, constant fatigue, loss of weight, excessive weight gain due to compulsive eating, poor concentration and memory, high degree of self-criticism, extreme difficulty in making even the simplest of decisions, suicidal thoughts, inclination toward isolation, negative outlook, feelings of failure, not being able to finish anything, inability to cope with even the slightest pressure, being gripped with sadness and discouragement, or inability to handle the most menial of tasks.

Some of us live with these kinds of feelings so much we begin to accept them as a part of life. But they are not. Depression is not God's will for our lives. I battled depression until I was in my early thirties. Utter hopelessness about anything ever being any different in my life had led me to the point of suicide. After I came to the Lord, my first major deliverance was from depression due to enormous amounts of unconfessed sin, which had separated me from God's presence and power. Now when I'm threatened by depression, I recognize that something is out of order in my life or my mind, and I do an immediate examination before the Lord.

Taking Action Against It

Unless you take definite steps to stop depression, it snowballs. You feel worse and worse about yourself, others, and God, which further distances and depresses you.

If you struggle with occasional bouts of depression, or are depressed right now, I suggest that you go before the Lord and ask the same questions I ask:

1. *Is there any physical problem that could be causing this?* Depression can be caused by any number of physical situations such as hormone changes, menstrual period, PMS, menopause, lack of sleep, taking drugs, alcohol, certain medications, overexertion, disease, lack of exercise, fatigue, allergies, and poor eating habits. Ask God to show you if anything physical is causing or contributing to your depression.

2. *Is there anyone or any circumstance that is causing this depression?* There may be a tangible reason for your depression. For example, having someone living in your house who is extremely negative and depressed can affect you. If you can think of anything like that, ask God what you can do to alter the situation. Can you speak to the person or do something to change things? Is there some possibility you're not seeing or never imagined? Sometimes depression signals that a major change is needed. Ask God to show you the burdens you shouldn't be carrying and the changes that need to be made.

3. *Is there any sin I have not confessed?* Sometimes the cause of depression is external (being exposed to something ungodly). Sometimes it is an attack by the devil (especially when God is doing a powerful work in your life). But most of the time it is caused by wrong thinking or action (an inappropriate response to a person or situation). Any negative feelings or bad attitudes need to be confessed—*especially unforgiveness. You* are the one who will suffer depression because of them, so ask God to show you any area where repentance is needed.

4. *Have I prayed about my depression?* One of the biggest traps or deceptions of depression is thinking you have a right to hang onto it. You don't. Tell God exactly how you feel and ask Him to take your depression. Too often we don't pray because we accept the depression as being a part of life instead of recognizing it as an emotional sickness like a cold or the flu, which needs attention before it turns into a more serious infection.

This is a good time to remember that *God is on your side and the devil is your enemy.* It's important to keep from blaming God for your problems while listening to the devil as if he were a good friend supplying you with important information about your life. God is for *you.* His plan is for you to succeed, to be free, healed, whole, happy, and fulfilled and loved.

Pastor Jack taught us, "You have to wait at Jesus' feet through the darkness. There is no night so long or so dark but that if you

stay at the feet of the Lord, He will take care of it in the morning."
Psalm 30:5 says:

> Weeping may endure for a night,
> But joy comes in the morning.

If you wake up in the night with your heart pounding in fear or
depression, get up immediately and go to your prayer closet and
pray and read the Word. Go back to sleep when you can, and then
continue praying the next day. One of the pitfalls of depression is
that when people don't get an immediate answer to their prayers,
they stop turning to God and try to work it out on their own.

5. *What lies am I listening to?* If you are depressed, you probably
have accepted a lie as the truth—usually a lie about yourself:
"You're a failure. You're no good. You won't make it. You're ugly."
But all of this is in direct opposition to Scripture, which says you
have special gifts and talents. The fact that the world isn't recognizing your gifts at this moment doesn't mean they aren't there or that
you are worthless. Dispel lies with the truth of God's Word.

6. *Which of God's promises can I quote aloud to sum up His view of
me or my situation?* It says in God's Word that "anxiety in the heart
of man causes depression, / But a good word makes it glad" (Prov.
12:25). This good word may come from a pastor, a friend, a spouse,
a family member, or a nice person on the street, but we can't depend on human beings. The good word that will truly make your
heart glad comes from the Lord through *His* Word. There are an
abundance of them, but I have listed just a few on page 201. When
you find a promise or word from Him that speaks to your situation,
underline it or write it on paper and tape it to your bathroom mirror. Speak it aloud whenever you feel depressed. Even when you
feel nothing is happening, continue speaking God's Word aloud;
eventually your spirit and soul will respond to the hope and truth.

7. *How much have I praised, worshiped, and thanked God in the
midst of my depression?* Being depressed is a sign that your personality has turned inward and focused on itself. One of the healthiest
steps to take is to focus outwardly on God through praise. Stop
everything you're doing and say, "Lord, I praise You. I worship
You. I give thanks to You. I glorify You. I love You. I exalt Your
name. I refuse depression in my life and I praise You, Lord, that
Your joy is my strength." Thanking Him for everything you can
think of is the best way to stop the stream of self-abuse that goes
through your head.

Words of Encouragement from the Lord to Speak in the Face of Depression

The righteous cry out, and the LORD hears them;
he delivers them from all their troubles.
The LORD is close to the brokenhearted
and saves those who are crushed in spirit.
(Psalm 34:17–18 NIV)

When you pass through the waters, I will be with you;
And through the rivers, they shall not overflow you.
When you walk through the fire, you
shall not be burned,
Nor shall the flame scorch you. (Isaiah 43:2)

Those who wait on the LORD
Shall renew their strength;
They shall mount up with wings like eagles,
They shall run and not be weary,
They shall walk and not faint. (Isaiah 40:31)

So the ransomed of the LORD shall return,
And come to Zion with singing,
With everlasting joy on their heads;
They shall obtain joy and gladness,
And sorrow and sighing shall flee away. (Isaiah 51:11)

He sent from above, He took me,
He drew me out of many waters.
He delivered me from my strong enemy,
From those who hated me;
For they were too strong for me.
They confronted me in the day of my calamity,
But the LORD was my support.
He also brought me out into a broad place;
He delivered me, because He delighted in me.
(2 Samuel 22:17–20)

I've also found that clapping my hands and singing praise to the Lord is unbeatable for bringing relief from a spirit of heaviness. No doubt this is the last thing you feel like doing when you're depressed, but you have to decide that you *don't* want depression and you *do* want all that God has for you. Don't give up until you've won.

When Nothing Helps

If you've asked yourself these questions and done all that's been suggested and are still deeply depressed, then you need deliverance and counseling. Seek out a Christian counselor.

If even the smallest task seems overwhelming to you and you can't get a counseling appointment until a week from Tuesday, make yourself get up each day and do two things. Wash the dishes, make the bed, pull some weeds in the yard, put one load of clothes in the washing machine, wash your car, or clean out a drawer. Don't worry about anything else at this moment. Then take your Bible, sit down with the Lord, and take comfort that your life has some order and you have accomplished something.

Don't let not-so-well-meaning, self-righteous Christians convince you that if you were really born-again you wouldn't be depressed. And don't think that going for counseling is an admission of mental instability or something to be ashamed of. That attitude went out with the fifties. Today people realize the decision to improve their lives is in their hands, and they are choosing to seek the godly counsel of godly people.

Because of Jesus, you can win over depression.

■ ———— *What the Bible Says About* ———— ■

Depression

Then they cried out to the LORD in their trouble,
And He saved them out of their distresses.
He brought them out of darkness and the shadow of death,
And broke their chains in pieces.
  Psalm 107:13–14

If I say, "My foot slips,"
Your mercy, O LORD, will hold me up.
In the multitude of my anxieties within me
Your comforts delight my soul.
  Psalm 94:18–19 NIV

In my distress I called upon the LORD,
And cried out to my God;
He heard my voice from His temple.
    Psalm 18:6

■   ■

REJECT THE PITFALL
OF DESTRUCTIVE RELATIONSHIPS

The lie we believe when we are involved in destructive relationships is "I deserve to be treated the way this person is treating me." If you allow yourself to be treated in a way that is destroying you, you are buying into that lie.

People who were emotionally damaged early in life often have trouble understanding relationships, so when they fall into a destructive one, they're unable to see it. The more emotionally needy they are, the harder it is for them to recognize it. The more it destroys them, the harder it is for them to get out.

Some people can be cantankerous, mean, grumpy, and negative, and will not really hurt you deeply. In a *destructive* relationship, the abuser destroys the very core of your being. He (she) gradually wears away the very person you are until you no longer have a healthy image of who God made you to be. In the abuser's presence you are constantly made to feel depressed.

We must have a safe harbor in order to grow. If we don't have it, we can't develop properly. As long as I lived at home with my mother, my personhood was steadily eroded. Even after I moved out, started walking with the Lord, and enjoyed much healing and deliverance, I was back in the counseling office after every visit to her. When Mary Anne advised me to avoid being with her until I had time to be healed, I realized that as long as the relationship was destroying me, it had to be avoided. Removing myself for a time was crucial to my healing.

Refuse Codependency

One of the pitfalls of living with an alcoholic, a drug abuser, or a mentally ill person is letting your life and the lives of your family revolve around him (her). Allowing someone who cannot handle his own life to control the lives of others puts all family members in constant anxiety and stress. Failing to identify the problem and face it openly makes the problem worse.

The fact that my mother's mental illness was never dealt with openly as I was growing up was disastrous for me. I was shocked later to discover that her odd and frightening behavior was normal for her illness. If we had faced this problem as a family, instead of pretending nothing was wrong, we all would have been healthier. Instead, I spent years hating my mother for something she couldn't help. I took her actions personally and felt guilty and responsible for them.

When you are a child, you can't control how people treat you. As an adult you have a choice. Although you can't demand that people act a certain way, you *can* refuse to allow people to be destructive or negative in their treatment of you.

If a person in your life who is not your spouse causes you to feel depressed and worthless each time you are with him or her and you have tried repeatedly to do everything you know to save the relationship, then you need to ask God if it isn't time to release that person into His hands. Once you have done this, don't see the person until the Lord gives you peace about it.

If your marriage relationship is destructive, you need to do all you can to change it. Seek God. Seek counsel. Do what they both say to do and don't give up until it is resolved. Under no circumstances should you ever allow yourself to take physical abuse from *anyone*, including a spouse. If there is danger of bodily harm for you or your children, get away from that person immediately and get help. If you don't, you become an accomplice to the sin. It's bad enough to let yourself be destroyed; it's even worse to subject your children to abuse. Do something now! Don't let fear keep you in a destructive relationship. The Bible says,

> The fear of man brings a snare,
> But whoever trusts in the LORD shall be safe. (Prov. 29:25)

If you fear bodily harm, financial insecurity, loneliness, or rejection if you leave, know that the Lord will provide protection and provision as you pray for Him to do so. If you are too beaten down to make a move, ask someone to help. When you pray, God will prepare someone to do just that.

Can I Inherit Family Problems?

I used to be so afraid that one of my children or I would inherit my mother's mental illness. But the Bible teaches that we aren't trapped in our heritage: "You have given me the heritage of those who fear Your name" (Ps. 61:5). Praise God we are related to *Him* and inherit *His* qualities. I have been *born again* and am now growing to resemble my heavenly Father. When the devil tries to torment me about that I now say, "Leave me alone or I'll tell my Father on you."

If you have that fear, know that mental illness, alcoholism, drug dependency, and anything else your family faces are spiritual problems *before* they are ever manifested physically. They are solvable in the spirit realm. Bind any spirit that threatens you by saying, for example, "Spirit of insanity (alcoholism, drug dependency), I address you as an evil spirit. I (and my children) have no part of you and you have no claim on me (us). I (we) have been born into my Father's house and now have a heavenly inheritance, not an earthly one. My Father God has given me authority over you, so in the name of Jesus Christ I bind you and cast you out of my (our) life. I refuse you now and forever." Don't hesitate to have one or more strong believers pray with you, especially if the devil tries to threaten you again.

Friendship: Building Block or Battering Ram?

I had a friend years ago who gradually became critical and angry toward me for vague reasons I never understood. I couldn't do enough to please her, and in her presence I always felt inadequate, unacceptable, and depressed. Over several years I subconsciously thought, *I'm probably a substandard friend, so I'm sure she is justified in feeling the way she does.*

It wasn't until other friends pointed out that friendship is to build up, not destroy, that I realized I was involved in a destructive relationship. Trying to "work things out" accomplished absolutely nothing. After much prayer and counsel with my husband, I decided to discontinue the relationship and release my friend totally into the Lord's hands. People can get sucked into a destructive relationship for a number of reasons, but they only stay in them because they feel they deserve it.

Are you living in a destructive relationship? If you are trying to recover from emotional damage yourself, you need to protect yourself from having to swim through someone else's bondage. Cultivate positive, uplifting relationships.

This is not a license to run every time someone challenges or confronts you. But if you step back from the relationship, your objectivity will return, and you will be able to tell if the person is confronting in love or attacking with a spirit of criticism and control. Remember, laying down your life for another doesn't mean allowing the person to run over you. Ask God about any relationship that destroys the joy of life in you, and pray for Him to show you what you should do. If you can't leave this person, ask God to help you confront him. Ask Him to change both of you; then take the steps necessary to see restoration happen.

The Lord may ask you to lay down your life for a relationship. You let a part of you die so that something greater will be made alive. You will *know* when God is asking you to do that. You will *choose* to do it; it won't be inflicted on you. You will feel peace, not anguish. Until a time like that, examine any relationship that brings out the worst in you. Don't allow yourself to be battered— physically, mentally, or emotionally.

■ ─────── *What the Bible Says About* ─────── ■

Rejecting the Pitfall of Destructive Relationships

Make no friendship with an angry man,
And with a furious man do not go,
Lest you learn his ways
And set a snare for your soul.
    Proverbs 22:24–25

If a wise man contends with a foolish man,
Whether the fool rages or laughs, there is no peace.
    Proverbs 29:9

As charcoal is to burning coals, and wood to fire,
So is a contentious man to kindle strife.
    Proverbs 26:21

Let no corrupt communication proceed out of your mouth,
but what is good for necessary edification that it may impart
grace to the hearers.
    Ephesians 4:29

The LORD is on my side;
I will not fear.
What can man do to me?
    Psalm 118:6

■   ■

REJECT THE PITFALL OF DIVORCE

The lie we believe when we are tempted to leave our marriage is "There is no acceptable solution to the problems in this relationship, so divorce is the only way out." We play that tape over in the mind until we accept it and act on it. As long as we feel this way, we have little hope of building a strong marriage.

The deception of divorce is in blaming the other person or yourself for what's happening instead of blaming the devil. Part of Satan's plan is to infiltrate our lives with a spirit of divorce, separation, and disunity so we can never work on deep personal growth and fulfillment. While it's true that we start the problems with hurtful words or actions, which open the door for evil, we, too, often fail to recognize Satan's hand in it. We can be manipulated by him and turn on one another.

People who are suffering in the hell of a miserable marriage will not be helped by someone who insensitively hurls Bible verses in their faces. I'm not going to do that. But I *am* going to tell you that a good marriage is worth working to establish. In fact, the boundaries of a good, healthy marriage will provide an atmosphere that promotes emotional healing. The opposite is also true. It takes longer to find restoration in a marriage that keeps you angry, depressed, anxious, fearful, or insecure. A bad marriage brings emotional healing to a slow crawl.

The full bloom of a healthy, happy marriage doesn't happen without proper planting, careful cultivation, watering, tending, feeding, and the divine intervention of God. Even marriages made in heaven die here on earth without proper attention.

My first marriage was short and miserable, and I don't minimize my contribution to making it that way. We didn't know the Lord, so we lived far from His ways. On top of that, I was an emotional cripple. I was committed to stay with him as long as I could stand it. That marriage lasted less than two years.

By contrast, when I married the second time, Michael and I had several things going for us:

- We both loved the Lord and wanted to live His way.
- We felt the Lord had put us together.
- We were committed to staying married.
- We were in agreement in certain important areas of our lives (career, home, finances, children).

To maintain a marriage you have to give it to God and be determined to live His way:

> Unless the LORD builds the house,
> They labor in vain who build it. (Ps. 127:1)

Unless God is at the center of your marriage, your focus is solely on each other to fulfill your every need. This puts a lot of pressure on each individual. Also, when God is doing the building, divorce isn't an option. You have to roll up your sleeves and get down to the nitty-gritty work of exposing everything in the relationship to the light of the Lord.

When Michael and I married, we both had deep insecurities, emotional damage, and past bondage—emotional needs far too complex for either of us to handle alone. But with the help of the Lord, a good pastor, Christian counselors, prayer partners, and believing friends, we were able to overcome them.

Being the husband or wife of someone with deep emotional hurts requires a gift of patience and understanding as well as love. If you are not emotionally stable, the problem is compounded. In our case, we gritted our teeth and hung on when the other one fell apart. When we were both dealing with things at the same time, the strain on the relationship became the greatest. But through it all, divorce was not an option. We *had* to work things out, no matter how painful. Without a doubt, we would not each be enjoying the degree of wholeness we do today had we run from our marriage at the first sign of discomfort.

At times in the seventeen years of our marriage, the spirit of divorce hammered at me, and I thought, "Divorce is the only way out." Each time, I took my feelings before the Lord, who showed me that Satan was trying to pit Michael and me against one another. Instead of realizing that *we* were on the *same* side, and that *he* was our *enemy*, we were buying into his lies.

Breeding Ground of Growth or Battleground of Wills

You can count on undesirable personality traits surfacing when you are married—anger, impatience, selfishness, cruelty, jealousy, rage, or fear. It's important to realize that you both need to face these traits head-on and grow through them. When they surface, carefully monitor your attitude toward your mate. Watch out for thoughts like:

- "I'm not going to give anything to this relationship anymore."
- "I have no feelings for him (her)."
- "I see nothing good in him (her)."
- "I no longer care what he (she) does."
- "I don't love him (her) anymore."
- "I've had it."

These dangerous thoughts, although sometimes justified, cannot be tolerated. They will open the way to spirits of division, deception, and immorality.

Combat these feelings by being willing for the Lord to change you. You may be thinking, "What about him (her)?" "Doesn't he (she) need to change?" The answer is yes, but you have no control over that and you've got to start somewhere. Chances are it won't happen unless you take the first step. One of the best contributions you can make, outside of praying for your mate, is to do all you can to get rid of your own bondage.

A few months into our marriage I realized that one of us needed to change in order for there to be real harmony. It was at least two years before I realized that it wasn't going to be Michael, or at least he wouldn't be changing as quickly as I'd hoped. It was nearly five years before I conceded that my critical badgering wasn't motivating him to grow. It was seven years before I saw there was a good chance he'd never be molded into my image. It was a full *ten* years before I decided that for the marriage to be a breeding ground for growth, instead of a battleground of wills, *I* would have to change. (My husband tells the story a little differently.) As I was able to say, "God, change *me*," my eyes were really opened to the ploys of the devil.

Steps to Take to Avoid a Divorce

First, decide whether or not you want the will of God to be done in your life. If you do, then you have to commit whatever it takes to work things out. Communicate everything you feel about your relationship to the Lord and ask Him to make things right. If you can't do that, then you need to confess that you don't even want things to work out. Say, "Lord, I really don't care about this marriage anymore. Change my heart and give me the desire to see it made right." You don't have to feel the feelings in the beginning; you've just got to let God meet you where you are and work from there. When I finally began to do most of my battling in the prayer closet,

How to Pray for Your Husband (or Wife)

1. Pray continually for his (her) salvation, if that hasn't yet happened. If it has, pray for continued spiritual growth.

2. Pray that he (she) has a heart that hungers for more of the Lord and a desire for a closer walk with Him.

3. Pray for deliverance from whatever bondage he (she) struggles against (drugs, alcohol, anger, selfishness, irresponsibility, lust).

4. Pray that he (she) be filled with God's love.

5. Pray that he (she) respond to your love by being able to receive it.

6. Pray that his (her) work be blessed and his (her) name will be preserved from any suspicion or maligning.

7. Pray that he (she) becomes all that God created him (her) to be.

instead of with my husband, things started to really progress (see page 210).

Next, communicate your feelings to your mate. Ask your husband or wife to set a block of time to be alone with you and to talk. Ask him to be ready to air grievances and concerns. Tell him you are willing to make changes and ask him to be willing to do the same.

If the situation between you and your spouse is too volatile to handle between the two of you, you need a third unbiased party who is mature in the Lord and experienced in marriage counseling. Often both people have justifiable complaints that need to be heard without accusations, prejudgments, or angry outbursts.

If you are being abused, get out and get help. You are never asked to suffer physical or mental harm in order to remain married. In fact, by staying you are enabling your spouse to continue in sin, and he will never find healing and fulfillment.

Probably all couples experience a time when they feel they have fallen out of love with their mate. Paradoxically, at that time you have the opportunity to cultivate a deeper love and commitment. Be willing to pray, "Lord, work in this marriage and let the work begin in me in ways that are visible to my husband (wife). Help me to be more concerned with my husband (wife) than I am with myself. Help me to live in ongoing forgiveness. Resurrect feelings of love, romance, and closeness in us. Help us to communicate and meet each other's physical and emotional needs. I depend on You, Lord."

If you have seen great deliverance, healing, and wholeness happen in your life, you may come to a time when you think, "If I had been delivered before I met this person, I probably wouldn't have married him (her)." This appears to be a legitimate observation because this person filled all of the needs you had at that time and now, perhaps, your needs have changed. If that thought occurs to you, take it to the Lord immediately and ask Him to comfort your heart about it. He will do that. He may also show you that it's now time for *you* to be supportive while your mate finds deliverance and healing.

If you can manage to cultivate a good marriage, your restoration will have a solid base from which to develop. If, however, divorce cannot be avoided or has already happened, look into the face of Jesus, receive His love and forgiveness, and find release from the pain of the past. Don't let the devil forever tie you up in guilt over this. Just determine that there will be no divorce in your future.

■ ——————— *What the Bible Says About* ——————— ■
Divorce

But from the beginning of the creation, God "made them male and female. For this reason a man shall leave his father and mother and be joined to his wife, and the two shall become one flesh"; so then they are no longer two, but one flesh. Therefore what God has joined together, let not man separate.
  Mark 10:6–9

Love suffers long and is kind; love does not envy; love does not parade itself, is not puffed up; does not behave rudely, does not seek its own, is not provoked, thinks no evil; does not rejoice in iniquity, but rejoices in the truth; bears all things, believes all things, hopes all things, endures all things. Love never fails.
  1 Corinthians 13:4–8

A soft answer turns away wrath,
But a harsh word stirs up anger.
  Proverbs 15:1

Let all bitterness, wrath, anger, clamor, and evil speaking be put away from you, with all malice. And be kind to one another, tenderhearted, forgiving one another, just as God in Christ also forgave you. ·
  Ephesians 4:31–32
■ ■

REJECT THE PITFALL OF ENVY

The lie we believe when we are envious of someone is "I need and deserve to have what they have." The truth is that all we have comes from God. To have sorrow, discontent, or ill will over others' possessions or advantages is to reject what God *has* given us and what He is *able* to give to us. The deception of envy is thinking that God doesn't have enough to go around. What someone else has then becomes a threat to our well-being.

The New Bible Dictionary describes covetousness as "selfish desire" and "in essence the worship of self." It is the ultimate idolatry, and *idolatry is the root of envy.* The Bible says we are to put to death "covetousness, which is idolatry" (Col. 3:5) because it will undermine the purposes of God in our lives.

> A sound heart is life to the body,
> But envy is rottenness to the bones. (Prov. 14:30)

Covetousness destroys the very core of our being and causes our inner strength to crumble. If unforgiveness is the cancer of the soul, envy is the osteoporosis!

Envy was not part of my early life because I believed I didn't deserve anything anyway. I wanted more, and I felt sorry for myself when I didn't get it, but I didn't begrudge others for having it. However, I coveted other people's abilities to speak or sing. My own struggle with vocal problems from early childhood on never improved as much as I wanted it to, and I felt cheated.

One day as I read the Bible, the Lord spoke to my heart through a verse that says, "Where envy and self-seeking exist, confusion and every evil thing will be there" (James 3:16). It was as if the Lord pointed to my heart and said, "You have confusion in your life right now because of the envy and self seeking in your heart."

How embarrassed I felt. *Me? Have envy?* But I knew that constantly measuring myself against others was the seed from which envy grows. I couldn't live in peace if I hung on to it.

To be free I had to do four things:

- I had to take stock of all that God had given me and be thankful for it.
- I had to come to terms with my limitations and strictly avoid comparing myself with others.
- I had to make myself be thankful to God for other people's talents, gifts, and abilities.
- I had to remind myself of what *my* calling was from God and not demand to have someone else's.

It was a matter of being able to say, "Lord, You created me and You know what will fulfill me. Forgive me for coveting the gifts of other people. Release me from the bondage of envy, and set me free from the agony of desiring anything that is not mine to have. I realize that what You have for me is better than anything I could covet for myself."

Assess Your Motives

Years ago, I walked into a friend's house and was struck by how much I enjoyed the spaciousness and the light airy feel of the home. I thought, *That's what I would like someday.* I did not want *her* house. I did not feel sad or resentful that *she* had the house. I didn't go home and hate *my* house. I didn't say, "I must have a house like that immediately!" But I did think, *I like that quality in a house, and if I'm ever given a choice, I would choose that.* Ten years later when Michael and I were looking for another home to move into, we chose one with many skylights and windows, which created that same feeling of spaciousness. I acknowledged the good that someone else had, but I did not envy.

I aspire to be as good a writer as some authors I particularly enjoy. I do not want to be given credit for writing their books. I don't long for people to say I'm better than they are. I don't want to copy their style. I don't desire that they fail. I *do* want to be able to touch people with the depth and penetration of other writers. I admire, but I do not envy.

However, if I felt miserable every time I walked into another person's house that was better than mine or if I felt bad every time I read a great new book, then I would be envious.

To decide whether what you feel is envy or admiration you need to assess your motives honestly. Check the following statements that apply to your present attitudes:

_____"I constantly compare myself with others."

_____"I secretly feel good when someone fails or has something bad happen to them."

_____"When I see how good someone is at what they do, I don't appreciate it but immediately berate myself for not being as good."

_____"I don't like to be around a certain person because his goodness makes me feel inferior."

_____"I feel bad when my neighbor gets a new car."

_____"When I see someone get something new, I feel I must have the same thing."

_____"When I see bad qualities in a certain person, I want others to see them too."

_____"I don't like to visit people in a nicer house because it makes me feel as if my house is not as good."

If you've checked any of the above, envy is trying to get hold of your heart. Call a halt to it, repent, and let it go.

Envy will put great limitations on your life. If you are envious of what someone has, you will either never have that yourself or you will get it and will not be satisfied by it. Proverbs 27:4 says, "Who is able to stand before jealousy?" Who, indeed, can live with it and not feel its crushing weight? Whether *in* you or directed *at* you, envy is evil. Satan fell from heaven because he wanted what God had. Find the great peace of knowing that what you have is from the Lord.

◼ ——————— *What the Bible Says About* ——————— ◼
Envy

God gave them over to a debased mind, to do those things which are not fitting; being filled with all unrighteousness, sexual immorality, wickedness, covetousness, maliciousness; full of envy, murder, strife, deceit, evil-mindedness . . . that those who practice such things are worthy of death.
Romans 1:28–29, 32

For we ourselves were also once foolish, disobedient, deceived, serving various lusts and pleasures, living in malice and envy, hateful and hating one another.
Titus 3:3

For where there are envy, strife and divisions among you, are you not carnal and behaving like mere men?
1 Corinthians 3:3

Love does not envy.
1 Corinthians 13:4

You shall not covet your neighbor's house . . . nor anything that is your neighbor's.
Exodus 20:17

◼ ————————————————————————— ◼

REJECT THE PITFALL OF FEAR

The lie we believe when we are afraid is "God is not able to keep me and all that I care about safe." To be sure, there is much to be afraid of in this world, but when the strength of that fear outweighs our sense of God's presence, a spirit of fear can attach itself to our personality. If frightening or traumatizing things have happened to us in childhood, we believe this lie all the more. We think God is not in control of our situation.

The opposite of fear is faith, and we usually interpret the circumstances of our lives through one or the other. Fear causes us to live like we are emotionally paralyzed. We fear not having enough, so we don't give. We fear being hurt, so we hesitate to love. We fear being taken advantage of, so we don't serve others. We fear rejection, so we don't step out and do what God has called us to do.

Fear was the controlling factor of my life before I received Jesus: fear of failure, of bodily harm, of being emotionally hurt, of getting old, of being a nobody. An aching, paralyzing, all-engulfing spirit of fear had overtaken me, bringing with it companion spirits of suicide, despair, anxiety, and hopelessness. As I fought to keep from drowning in my fears, I ran out of strength. Gradually my fear of life overrode my fear of death, and suicide seemed as if it would be a pleasant relief.

I have heard it said many times that F-E-A-R stands for:

*F*alse
*E*vidence
*A*ppearing
*R*eal

The devil presents false evidence and makes it seem real. We can choose to listen to his falsehoods or believe God.

One of the biggest fears for anyone who has been emotionally damaged as a child is fear of the opinions of others. Our fears tell us, "People won't like me when they find out what I'm really like." But Isaiah 51:7 tells us,

> Do not fear the reproach of men,
> Nor be afraid of their revilings.

Because of Jesus, we *never* have to live in fear of the opinions of others.

Emotionally damaged people also often fear bodily harm. I used to be afraid to stay alone even in the daytime, and I could barely sleep at night because I feared that all the evil of the world would come upon me. I don't live with that kind of fear now that I've learned to live under God's protective covering.

What to Do When You Are Afraid

Realizing that fear doesn't come from God and you don't have to live in it is the first step in freeing yourself from it. Here are a few more things you can do when you are afraid:

1. *Confess your fear to the Lord and ask Him to free you from it.* Don't deny your fear; rather take it to God and pray for deliverance. As you draw close to Him, His love will penetrate your life and crowd fear out.

If you are being controlled by strong fear, you are probably beset by a *spirit* of fear, which has to be cast out. In that case say, "God, I confess my fear as sin before You and ask You to forgive me for it. Strengthen my faith in You and Your Word. I command you, spirit of fear, to be gone in the name of Jesus. Thank You, Lord, that You have not given me a spirit of fear, but of love, power and a sound mind. Flood me with Your love and wash away all doubt."

2. *Check to see if there is, in fact, a very real danger, and do what you can to remedy the situation.* Have others pray with you until the danger passes and you have peace about it.

3. *Commit to trust the Lord unquestioningly for seven days.* Decide that for one week you are going to believe that every promise in God's Word is completely true for you. Each day read the promises of God's protection in Psalm 91. Pick one verse to say aloud throughout the day and thank God for His promises to you in it. Each verse is full of God's love toward you. When you store them in your heart, they will crowd out fear.

4. *Worship the Lord out loud.* Praise is your greatest weapon against fear, so use it with great force. Clap your hands, sing, and speak praises to God. Thank Him for His great love. The more you do, the more you'll open up to receive it. God's love and fear can not reside in the same heart.

No matter what has happened to you in the past or what's happening in the world around you, God promises to protect you as you walk with Him now. In fact, He is committed to protecting you all the time. We don't understand how much evil the Lord protects us from every day, but I'm sure it's far more than we imagine. He is more powerful than any adversary we face, and He promises that no matter what the enemy brings into our lives, we will triumph in it.

The only fear you are to have is the fear of God, a respect for God's authority and power. Fearing God means fearing what life without Him would be and thanking Him continually that because of His love you'll never have to experience it.

■ ——————— *What the Bible Says About* ——————— ■

Fear

I sought the LORD, and He heard me,
And delivered me from all my fears.
  Psalm 34:4

Fear not, for I have redeemed you;
I have called you by your name;
You are Mine.
When you pass through the waters, I will be with you;
And through the rivers, they shall not overflow you.
When you walk through the fire, you shall not be burned,
Nor shall the flame scorch you.
  Isaiah 43:1–2

There is no fear in love; but perfect love casts out fear, because fear involves torment. But he who fears has not been made perfect in love.
  1 John 4:18

The LORD is my light and my salvation;
Whom shall I fear?
The LORD is the strength of my life;
Of whom shall I be afraid?
  Psalm 27:1

Fear not, for I am with you;
Be not dismayed, for I am your God.
I will strengthen you,
Yes, I will help you,
I will uphold you with My righteous right hand.
  Isaiah 41:10

■   ■

REJECT THE PITFALL OF LUST

The lie we believe when we are tempted to lust is "It doesn't hurt to think about it if I'm not going to actually do anything." But every lustful act begins as a simple thought. The deception of lust is believing that we are too strong or too good to ever be tempted. The truth is that temptation always presents itself where our resistance is low. Lust is a possibility in anyone's life if the soul is left unguarded.

Lust is an excessive desire to gratify *any* of the senses, but I am referring here to sexual desire, a specific spirit that comes to destroy by tempting you to think and do something you have already made a decision not to do.

I was attacked by a spirit of lust after I'd been married nearly five years and was about to enter a new phase in my ministry. I say attacked because it came out of nowhere—a sudden, overwhelmingly strong attraction to someone I had no interest in whatsoever. It was like being in an ocean wave that carried me away. I'm sure some people would interpret this same thing as fate or love or the perfect match. I already knew it was none of those because I was certain my marriage was right in the sight of God and I did not want to be with anyone else.

I literally got on my face before the Lord, confessed those feelings, rebuked the spirit of lust, and cried out to God for deliverance. I struggled for several days, remaining in the Lord's presence (prayer, praise, the Word) while He fought the battle. When I woke up on the morning of the third day, it was *completely* gone. The war had ended, the Lord had won, and I had been liberated. If it had gone on any longer, I would have gone to a Christian counselor for prayer. But I knew the victory was complete for whenever I saw that person again, there was absolutely no attraction. In fact, I thought, *How could I have even been tempted?* Not because he isn't attractive, but because only my husband is attractive to me.

Trust the Lord, Not Your Heart

The Bible says,

> He who trusts in his own heart is a fool,
> But whoever walks wisely will be delivered. (Prov. 28:26)

I would have been a fool to have trusted in my own heart then. I could have lost everything. I now believe the devil came to tempt me and the Lord allowed me to be proved, as He did Job. I'm convinced that the decision I made determined the course of my life and the release of my ministry.

I know from experience that a spirit of lust is powerful. People who are weak in the Lord don't have the strength to resist it. But if we handle it properly, the temptation will expose any weaknesses in ourselves and the marriage. I realized, for example, that my husband and I had become too busy to nurture ourselves as a couple. Michael's work was thriving, he was gone a lot and inattentive to my needs, and I was insecure and vulnerable. The atmosphere was ripe for the devil to move in.

Married people fall into adultery, and single people fall into sexual failure because a spirit of lust tempts them with lies like

- "No one will know."
  The truth is, God knows.
- "I can handle this."
  The truth is that the spirit of lust is too strong for human flesh to resist.
- "This is all in fun, it's nothing serious."
  The truth is, Satan is behind a spirit of lust, and he is always serious about your destruction.
- "I know what I'm doing."
  The truth is, anyone under the influence of lust is being deceived, so you can't possibly know what you are doing.

Watch out for these thoughts. Take an attitude check every once in a while so you can beware of this spirit. If you are married, check the *DANGER SIGNS FOR A MARRIED PERSON:*

____"I have even the slightest hint of a sexual or emotional attraction to someone other than my spouse."

____"I can't get that person out of my mind, and I daydream about what it would be like to be with that person in different settings (in a restaurant, walking together, etc.)."

____"I make decisions or dress with that person in mind."

____"I feel self-conscious when I'm in his presence."

____"I go out of my way to be with this person."

____"I imagine how that person might think of the way I look or what I'm doing."

____"I am extra nice to my husband (wife) so he (she) won't notice how attentive I am to the other person."

___"I imagine what it would be like to be married to that person."

___"I feel guilty about the thoughts I have toward this person."

If you are single, check the *DANGER SIGNS FOR A SINGLE PERSON:*

___"I am obsessed with sexual thoughts about a certain person."

___"I feel a sexual drive toward this person that I fear I will be unable to control."

___"I think of this person as a sexual object more than as a brother (or sister) in the Lord."

___"My primary goal for this person is to meet my needs, rather than helping him (her) become what God made him (her) to be."

___"I am unable to confess my deepest feelings about this person to the Lord."

___"When I come before the Lord, my thoughts about this person don't make me feel clean."

___"I rearrange Bible verses to justify my feelings about him (her)."

___"I doubt the validity of Scripture if it suggests that I restrict my relationship with him (her)."

___"I allow myself to venture into dangerous territory by being alone with this person, for example, when I know I shouldn't."

If you come in contact with someone for whom you feel a strong sexual attraction, immediately rebuke the devil. Say, "I bind you, Satan, and refuse to let you destroy my life with temptation. Sexual immorality is a sin against God, and I don't want any part of it. By the power of the Holy Spirit, I smash any hold the spirit of lust has on my life."

Then go before the Lord in prayer. And I mean lie down in your prayer closet on your face and cry out to God. Say, "Lord, I confess my attraction to this person and these sexual thoughts which come to my mind. Forgive me and set me free from them. Show me, God, why Satan thinks he can attack me in this area. Help me to not be deceived, but to see everything clearly. I praise You, Lord, that You are more powerful than any temptation I face." Stay there before the Lord, praising Him for His grace, love, and goodness until you feel the pressure lifted.

If you leave the safety of the Lord's presence before the battle is under control, you can step into dangerous territory and get shot down, seriously maimed, or even mortally wounded. Don't play around with this kind of fire. It's attached to an explosive with the power to do irreparable damage.

After the Fall

If you've already fallen into the devil's trap and acted on a spirit of lust, you need to receive deliverance. Don't try to handle it on your own. Get help. Go to a counselor, a Christian therapist, a pastor, church elders, a prayer group, or a strong believer who will keep your confidence. Have them pray for you to be free. If you don't, you won't be. After deliverance, expect an extended time of healing. Find help for that too.

Every time you feel tempted by this spirit again, confess it to whomever you have chosen to help you. Absolutely do *not* be with the person you are attracted to *alone*. It's best not to see him (her) at all, but if it cannot be avoided, be sure at least one other person is with you at all times.

We are to forsake even the appearance of evil, and so it is with lust. We can know when we have crossed from mere observation into the realm of attraction or desire. At that time, even a meeting of the eyes can be a manifestation of evil. You have to decide *now* that you will resist lust in every way until it no longer makes any appearance at all.

Check to see if this lustful situation has come from problems in your marriage, bondage in your life, or wounds from the past. Or is it that your ministry is about to advance further to destroy some of the devil's territory? If it is, he will be right there with a spirit of lust (either sexual or a quest for power or both) to try to stop you. Take it seriously. We have seen him succeed all too often. Lust is a pit waiting for all of us. Refuse to allow Satan the satisfaction of seeing you fall into it.

■ ——————— *What the Bible Says About* ——————— ■

Lust

For this is the will of God, your sanctification: that you should abstain from sexual immorality; that each of you

should know how to possess his own vessel in sanctification and honor, not in passion of lust, like the Gentiles who do not know God.
1 Thessalonians 4:3–5

No temptation has overtaken you except such as is common to man; but God is faithful, who will not allow you to be tempted beyond what you are able, but with the temptation will also make the way of escape, that you may be able to bear it.
1 Corinthians 10:13

Abstain from fleshly lusts which war against the soul.
1 Peter 2:11

The righteousness of the upright will deliver them,
But the unfaithful will be taken by their own lust.
Proverbs 11:6

Blessed is the man who endures temptation; for when he has been proved, he will receive the crown of life which the Lord has promised to those who love Him.
James 1:12

REJECT THE PITFALL OF LYING

The lie we believe when we lie to others is "It's okay to tell this little lie because it's not going to hurt anyone and nobody will know the difference." Yet *God always knows*. He also knows that He can't bring you into close communion with Himself and restore you to wholeness until His truth controls your heart.

The deception of lying is thinking that a lie will make things better for you. Actually, it does the opposite. Telling a lie means that you have aligned yourself with the spirit of lies, which is Satan. *Lying means you have just given the devil a piece of your heart.* Allowing Satan to have any part of you opens you to his kingdom. The more you lie, the greater his hold on you, and once you are bound by a lying spirit, you won't be able to stop yourself from lying. I learned to lie as a child because I felt the consequences of telling the truth were too great. Also I was so embarrassed about my life that lying to others was far more tolerable than admitting the truth.

One of the lies I frequently told was my age. In our small town in Wyoming, the one school was so crowded that unless you were six years old by the time school started on September 14, you had to wait until the following year to start first grade. (There was no kindergarten.) My birthday was on September 16, so I had to wait and start the next year. When we moved to California during the summer before I started fourth grade, I turned ten the day before school started. Everyone else in the class was nine. When the other children found out, I was teased mercilessly about having flunked a grade.

The next time we moved to a different city, I decided to lie about my age. Through high school, college, and working in television, I continued to lie. The entertainment business was so youth oriented I sometimes lopped off as much as five years off my age. I lived in terror that someone would find out. Once, when someone did, I was mortified.

When I came to know the Lord and started living His way, I realized I couldn't align myself with the author of lies and the Spirit of truth at the same time. I decided that I wanted people to know everything about me so they could accept or reject me on the basis of who I am. It was a big relief to be freed from the fear of people finding out I was lying to them, and as far as I know, no one has ever rejected me because of my age. Your feelings of self-worth rise sharply when you know you are living in truth.

Lying as a Means of Survival

People who have been physically or emotionally abused learn to lie to protect themselves or to make themselves feel better. Even though such lying is thoroughly understandable, it's still lying and can lead to emotional imbalance and even mental illness. Lies start becoming so real to the person telling them that they begin to believe them themselves.

This is what happened to my mother. When she was eleven, her mother died suddenly and tragically. Because her father was unable to care for her and her two sisters, they were sent to various homes to live. When my mother finally became attached to another family, the father in that family committed suicide. The deaths of her mother and then this foster parent several years later were so traumatic that she never recovered.

She told me many times that she was responsible for both deaths. She'd had an argument with her mother the night she went into the hospital and died, and my mother's guilt and remorse lasted for the rest of her life. She also believed her foster father killed himself because she came to live with them during the Depression and was an added burden. My mother's guilt was too unbearable for her to handle, so she created a world all her own, in which lies became her reality and she never had to face the truth. If she'd had good Christian therapy, or at least a family who prayed her through this time of trauma, she might have been spared from her tragic life of mental illness. She was an extreme example of the result of a lying spirit.

The Bible says,

> Getting treasures by a lying tongue
> Is the fleeting fantasy of those who seek death. (Prov. 21:6)

How could it be said more clearly? The consequences of telling the truth have to be better than death.

If you are aware of falling into the pit of lying, you must confess every lie to God immediately. The moment you discover you have lied say, "Lord, I confess before You I have lied and in so doing have aligned myself with Satan. God forgive me for that and cleanse me of all evil. Satan, I rebuke you. I refuse to be a part of your deception and evil, and I command your lying spirit to be gone in the name of Jesus. Praise You, Lord, that You are the God of truth and have the power to make all things new."

Next, immerse yourself in God's truth, His Word. Ask the Spirit of truth—the Holy Spirit—to flow through you and cleanse you from all lies. Ask God to show you any other lie that you are speaking or living. Remember that lying keeps you from enjoying healthy relationships (Prov. 26:28), and it separates you from the presence of the Lord: "He who tells lies shall not continue in my presence" (Ps. 101:7). You can't have emotional health and happiness without the presence of God in your life.

Remember every lie from your lips means you have given a piece of your heart to the devil who fills that hole with confusion, emotional and mental illness, and death. Don't allow him the pleasure. Instead, choose the way of truth.

— *What the Bible Says About* —
Lying

> Let not mercy and truth forsake you;
> Bind them around your neck,

> Write them on the tablet of your heart,
> And so find favor and high esteem
> In the sight of God and man.
>   Proverbs 3:3-4

> Lying lips are an abomination to the LORD,
> But those who deal truthfully are His delight.
>   Proverbs 12:22

> Deliver my soul, O LORD, from lying lips
> And from a deceitful tongue.
>   Psalm 120:2

> A lying tongue hates those who are crushed by it.
>   Proverbs 26:28

> My soul melts from heaviness;
> Strengthen me according to Your word.
> Remove from me the way of lying.
>   Psalm 119:28-29

■ ━━━ ■

REJECT THE PITFALL OF PERFECTIONISM

The lie we believe when we strive for perfection is, "I've got to be perfect in order to be acceptable to myself and to others." In reality, the more perfect we try to make ourselves, the more uncomfortable we are to be around. People aren't looking for perfection; they're looking for love. Our love for the Lord and others makes us acceptable to everyone—even ourselves. The deception of perfectionism is in thinking that anyone other than God can ever be perfect.

For years I wouldn't write anything for people to see or sing anything for people to hear because I knew what I wrote or sang wasn't perfect. I also wouldn't have people to my house for dinner because my house and my cooking weren't perfect. I wouldn't see people when I didn't look perfect, and I wouldn't talk to them on the phone when I wasn't feeling perfect. Living every day with the pressure to be perfect nearly suffocated me.

Perfect in Love

I once wrote a magazine article in which I said, "God never asks us to be perfect; He simply asks us to take steps of obedience."

Someone wrote to me afterward asking how I could say that when Matthew 5:48 says, "Therefore you shall be perfect, just as your Father in heaven is perfect."

In a responding article, I wrote that the definition of *perfect* in the *New World Dictionary* is "complete in all respects, flawless, faultless, without defect, in a condition of complete excellence." If we use this definition, Jesus is saying, "You must be faultless, without defect, and completely excellent! Now!"

People who feel God expects this level of performance put pressure on themselves to attain it. Then they feel like failures when they fall short. But the good news is that the Word of God doesn't say that at all.

According to W. E. Vine's *An Expository Dictionary of Biblical Words,* the word *perfect* in the Bible means "having reached its end, finished or complete"—in other words, having been brought to our fullest potential, being all that God made us to be.

The Bible also says we are born sinful; perfection is not inherent in us. The apostle Paul recognized his inability to be perfect on human terms when he said, "Not that I have already attained, or am already perfected" (Phil. 3:12). Instead he committed to pressing on further, recognizing that God's strength was made perfect in his weakness (2 Cor. 12:9).

So what does Jesus mean when He says, "Be perfect as your Father in heaven"? That verse is part of a Scripture passage that says, "You have heard that it was said, 'You shall love your neighbor and hate your enemy.' But I say to you, love your enemies, bless those who curse you, do good to those who hate you, and pray for those who spitefully use you and persecute you" (Matt. 5:43–44).

The passage goes on to say that if you love as God loves, you shall be perfect, just as your Father in heaven is perfect. In other words, if we are motivated in all we do by love for God, which overflows into love for others, we shall be perfected. *Being perfect has to do with the condition of the heart.*

One day my six-year-old daughter, knowing how much I love flowers, picked roses for me from our backyard. While she was getting my favorite vase down from the shelf, she dropped it on the tile floor, and it smashed into a hundred pieces. She was devastated and so was I, but I didn't punish her because I recognized her *heart* was perfect, even though her *performance* was *not.* She was doing what she did out of love, even though she was not able to accomplish it perfectly. The perfection God expects from us is just that. A heart that is pure in love toward God is a heart that desires to obey Him. God knows our actions can never be 100 percent perfect.

That's why He sent Jesus. Through Christ, He has given us access to the perfection only God can provide. Our hearts can be perfect even if our actions are not.

Oswald Chambers says, "The one marvelous secret of a holy life lies not in imitating Jesus but in letting the perfections of Jesus manifest themselves in my mortal flesh. . . . In Jesus Christ is the perfection of everything, and the mystery of sanctification is that all the perfections of Jesus are at my disposal" (*My Utmost for His Highest*, 149). That is the only perfection we should ever desire to attain.

We who were abused as children are already painfully aware of our imperfections. We need to know that God doesn't expect us to be perfect in *performance* but perfect in *heart*. We need to know that God *already* views us as perfect when He looks into our hearts and sees Jesus there. Failure to understand this can keep us forever striving for the unattainable and eventually giving up because we feel we can never be all we "should" be.

In our flesh we strive to succeed. We feel we're worth something when we win, worthless when we lose. What we demand of ourselves is always limited by the outer layer. Human perfection can only be as good as that. But God says He wants to make you something *more* than your human excellence. You will rise to the level and degree you sense His love in your life. That's why I can now invite people to my home, cook for them, speak to them, and write to them. I don't have to worry about being perfect because the perfection of Christ is manifested by His love flowing through me.

When you look in the mirror and see the excellence of Jesus reflected back, that's when you will have a sense of your true worth. The actual transformation takes place as you worship the Lord in and for *His* perfection.

■ —————— *What the Bible Says About* —————— ■
Perfectionism

But this Man, after He had offered one sacrifice for sins forever, sat down at the right hand of God, from that time waiting till His enemies are made His footstool. For by one offering He has perfected forever those who are being sanctified.

Hebrews 10:12–14

Him we preach, warning every man and teaching every man
in all wisdom, that we may present every man perfect in
Christ Jesus.
Colossians 1:28

Not that I have already attained, or am already perfected;
but I press on, that I may lay hold of that for which Christ
Jesus has also laid hold of me.
Philippians 3:12

But may the God of all grace, who called us to His eternal
glory by Christ Jesus, after you have suffered a while, perfect, establish, strengthen, and settle you.
1 Peter 5:10

It is God who arms me with strength,
And makes my way perfect.
Psalm 18:32

REJECT THE PITFALL OF PRIDE

The lie we believe when we are prideful is "I'm in control of my
life, I'm important, and I can make things happen the way I want
them to happen." The opposite—which is humility—says, "Without God I am nothing, but I can do all things through Christ who
strengthens me."

The deception of pride is thinking that our will is more important than God's will. This was Satan's downfall. He didn't want to
let God be God and do things God's way. His last words before he
was cast out of heaven were "I will exalt my throne above the stars
of God" (Isa. 14:13). He was perfect before pride took root in his
heart and he decided God's will was no longer as important as his
own.

Oddly enough, pride is one of the biggest problems for someone
who has been emotionally damaged. Because it is so hidden inside
and covered over with feelings of low worth, it is hard to spot. I
always believed I didn't have pride. In fact, I took pride in that.
But it wasn't true. When I was working as a television entertainer, I
feared failure even more than I desired success. This fear of failure
was not humility; it was pride. I felt I deserved to be prominent.
But my pride made me *more* susceptible to failure because I didn't
have God's help:

> God resists the proud,
> But gives grace to the humble. (James 4:6)

Pride leads to death because it doesn't allow for God's grace.

A Mask for Fear

Pride comes from being afraid that you have no value as a person. In a reaction against the beating down and scarring of life, pride says, "I have to be great because I fear I'll be nothing." At the opposite extreme is the thought, "If I can't be the best, then I'll be the worst. If I can't make people love me, then I'll make them hate me." Prisons are crowded with people who have felt that way.

Having self-worth is knowing your value in God's eyes, and that's very humbling. The stronger and more spiritually healthy we become, the more we see that without God we are nothing. It is *He* who gives us our worth: "For if anyone thinks himself to be something, when he is nothing, he deceives himself" (Gal. 6:3). Proverbs 3:7–8 says,

> Do not be wise in your own eyes;
> Fear the LORD and depart from evil.
> It will be health to your flesh,
> And strength to your bones.

It takes a lot of healing to come from feeling like a nothing to accepting your worth in Jesus, then to admitting that apart from God you are nothing. But when you can do that, it will be God *in* you that leads you to greatness.

One of the dangerous deceptions of pride is in our thinking we don't have any. No matter who we are or how long we've known the Lord, pride creeps into our lives if we don't watch for it. It keeps growing unless we beat it back. Worshiping the Lord is the best way to defeat pride, because we can't praise the God of the universe and still believe we will accomplish everything on our own. Ask God to give you a humble heart. He will.

■ ——————— *What the Bible Says About* ——————— ■
Pride

Pride goes before destruction,
And a haughty spirit before a fall.
   Proverbs 16:18

They have humbled themselves; therefore I will not destroy them, but I will grant them some deliverance.
2 Chronicles 12:7

He who is of a proud heart stirs up strife,
But he who trusts in the LORD will be prospered.
Proverbs 28:25

A man's pride will bring him low,
But the humble in spirit will retain honor.
Proverbs 29:23

Everyone who is proud in heart is an abomination to the LORD.
Proverbs 16:5

REJECT THE PITFALL OF REBELLION

The lie we believe when we rebel against God is "I think this is right for me, so I'm going to do it no matter what God or anyone else says." Rebellion is closely related to pride; it is preferring self-will to God's will. The deception of rebellion is in thinking that our way is better than God's. *Rebellion is pride put into action.*

The Bible says, "Rebellion is as the sin of witchcraft" (1 Sam. 15:23). Witchcraft is, of course, total opposition to God. The same verse says that stubbornness is idolatry. Stubbornness *keeps* us in rebellion. *There is an idol in the life of anyone who walks stubbornly in rebellion, and identifying and smashing it is the key to coming back into alignment with God.*

Before we give our lives to Jesus, we all walk in rebellion, but rebellion can happen *after* we've received the Lord, have our lives right with God, and are living in obedience. In fact, we can fall into rebellion without even realizing it.

One of the most common forms is spiritual apathy. We all know if we've just robbed a liquor store, murdered someone, or committed adultery. We're not as keen to recognize when we have drifted away from the mainstream of God's Spirit in our lives.

A number of years ago, I had corrective surgery for an old childhood injury. The doctor's instructions were, "Stay home for two months and do no lifting, no bending, no walking, no exercising, no quick movements, and no straining."

In the first couple of weeks I was too groggy to read the Bible very much or do any in-depth praying, so I resorted to something I never do, I watched a lot of television and looked through many secular magazines. None of them was objectionable, but all the messages were from the world, telling me how to think, to look, to buy and sell, and to structure my home and marriage.

When my convalescence ended, I slowly made efforts to get back into my normal routine. But things were different. I didn't read the Bible as much, and I was too busy for the prayer closet, opting rather to pray and run. Soon I was running on my own steam instead of being sustained and guided by the Lord.

Slowly I began to make decisions without God. I didn't think I was doing that, but the fruit of those decisions (or should I say lack of) made it apparent that I was. What seemed right led me to walking in rebellion by serving my own needs.

Spiritual Apathy

The danger once we know the Lord and have been walking His way is that we've learned the lessons. We've read the Bible, we're receiving the blessings, and now we think we can let things slide. We become lazy in what we have already learned to do. We let church attendance have a lower priority, allow giving to slack off, and look the other way when certain steps of obedience fall by the wayside—while the enemy sneaks up on our blind side.

Too many battles have been lost by just this sort of rebellion. Only we don't call it rebellion—not we seasoned Christians—we call it "maturity." *After* the fact, we call it "stupidity." Because all of us are susceptible to spiritual apathy, "we must give the more earnest heed to the things we have heard, lest we drift away" (Heb. 2:1).

Do you wonder if you are falling into rebellion by drifting spiritually? A number of warning signs can help you prevent such a fall. Periodically check the statements below that apply to you:

____"I am allowing outer sources like TV, magazines, movies, and books to mold me more than the Holy Spirit does."

____"I'm influenced more by what my friends say than by what the Lord is telling me."

____"I am becoming spiritually malnourished because I am not *daily* feeding on the Word of God or feasting in His presence in prayer and praise."

____"I am beginning to think I've heard it all so I have no reason to go to church or Bible study."

____"I've begun to do a few things I formerly avoided, ignoring what I've learned to be right, in favor of a new experience."

____"I've begun to make decisions without godly counsel because it *feels* right."

____"I haven't asked the Lord specifically about a major purchase, but it's something I've always wanted so it must be God's will."

____"I haven't done anything wrong so I don't need to ask God to reveal any unconfessed sin."

If you checked any item above, take it before the Lord in repentance immediately so you can be taken off the path that leads to destruction.

Walking in the Will of God

The Bible says,

> There is a way that seems right to a man,
> But its end is the way of death. (Prov. 16:25)

It can *seem* right but be totally wrong. We can never determine accurately the right path for ourselves because God alone knows it. We must look to Him to find the center of *His* will, for only there can we truly be safe. *Walking in His will is the opposite of walking in rebellion.*

When Michael and I were dating, I worried constantly that I might take matters concerning our relationship into my own hands and ruin everything. Over and over I prayed that God would keep me in His will about the relationship. I didn't want to make another mistake like my first marriage.

I did my best to keep from manipulating the outcome to what I thought would be my advantage. For example, when Michael didn't call me for a period of time, I resisted the temptation to contact him, no matter how lonely I felt. I didn't actively pursue him though my heart's desire was for this relationship to work out. When he finally did ask me to marry him, I was certain it was a prompting from the Lord and not the result of any sly maneuvers on my part.

The key to finding God's will, in this case, was to ongoingly give the situation entirely to the Lord, pray about it, praise Him for His perfect will in my life, and then wait on Him for the answer. Being in the center of God's will brings great security and confidence because there is something uniquely wonderful about knowing you are exactly where you're supposed to be. It is a guaranteed place of safety and peace.

Walking in God's will also makes your life simpler. Oswald Chambers says, "If we have purpose of our own, it destroys the simplicity and the leisureliness which ought to characterize the children of God" (*My Utmost for His Highest*, 159). This doesn't mean that there won't be storms in the center of God's will. Problems arise there too. But in the midst of them, there will be a simple and quiet peace that passes all understanding.

The wickedness of Jerusalem is a prime example of rebellion against the will of God. Four things led to her downfall:

- She did *not obey God's voice,*
- She did *not receive His correction,*
- She did *not trust in the Lord,*
- She did *not draw near to God.* (Zeph. 3:1–2)

We need to judge ourselves against these standards. We must obey. We must always be open to correction. We must have faith in God and His Word. And we must seek His presence constantly in prayer, praise, and communion with Him.

The will of God is greater than any one detail of our lives. If we miss the mark a few times, it doesn't forever sentence us to living outside God's best. If you know you've gotten off the mark by walking in rebellion, put every area of your life back into submission to the Lord, and by His grace He'll get you back on target.

Frequently ask God to show you if there is any rebellion in your life, and confess as it is revealed to you. If you don't, you will never be able to realize God's fullest blessing for you.

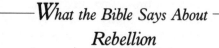

What the Bible Says About Rebellion

If you are willing and obedient,
You shall eat the good of the land;
But if you refuse and rebel,

You shall be devoured by the
   sword.
    Isaiah 1:19–20

Let them fall by their own counsels;
Cast them out in the multitude of their transgressions,
For they have rebelled against You.
    Psalm 5:10

Those who sat in darkness and in the shadow of death,
Bound in affliction and irons—
Because they rebelled against the words of God,
And despised the counsel of the Most High,
Therefore He brought down their heart with labor;
They fell down, and there was none to help.
    Psalm 107:10–12

Nevertheless they were disobedient
And rebelled against You . . .
Therefore You delivered them into the hand of their ene-
mies,
Who oppressed them.
    Nehemiah 9:26–27

REJECT THE PITFALL OF REJECTION

The lie we believe when we feel rejection is "I'm not worth anything so it's completely understandable that someone would reject
me." A spirit of rejection convinces you that you will be rejected,
and then every word and action of other people is interpreted
through the eyes of rejection.

Each of us has been rejected—by a family member, a friend, a
teacher, a stranger, or a casual acquaintance. When we're emotionally healthy, such an incident won't set us back much. We are soon
able to put it in perspective and brush it off. But if we have deep
emotional scars from incident after incident of rejection, each small
thing will feel like a knife to the heart.

My earliest memory of rejection is of being locked in that closet
by my mother. Had it been an isolated incident, it might not have
been so bad. But it wasn't. As a result I grew up feeling rejected,

and the feelings of rejection grew in me until no amount of affirmation and encouragement could overcome them.

I became an overachiever to gain approval. I worked hard so people would notice me and say I did a good job. When they did, the good feeling only lasted for the moment. I was certain that if people really knew the truth about me and my limitations, they would not have such a favorable opinion.

Just a few years ago I ran into the best friend of a young man I had dated seriously when I was working in television. We talked briefly about old times together and my old boyfriend.

"Ron was devastated when you severed the relationship so abruptly," he told me.

"He was?" I asked in amazement. "I thought he didn't care that much and it was best that we just get on with our lives."

"Oh, no," the friend said, "he felt you were the girl for him. In fact, he planned to ask you to marry him that summer. He could never figure out why you walked out on the relationship."

I was shocked. It was not that I wished I had stayed with Ron or felt that I'd made a foolish mistake by leaving him, but I was amazed at how my feelings of rejection had blinded me.

Years after Michael and I were married, our relationship struck an impasse because of chronic missed communication, so we searched for a qualified third person to help us.

"You've allowed a spirit of rejection to color everything you've heard each other say," Tim Davis, our marriage counselor and assistant pastor at our church, told us. "Every time one of you said or did something, a spirit of rejection interpreted it for the other. You both have to learn to relate to one another, not expecting rejection and listening to it, but expecting acceptance and receiving it."

I had never thought of rejection as a spirit, but the more I pondered what Tim told us, the more I began to identify that spirit rising up in me. I interpreted Michael's working long hours and being gone all of the time as rejection of me. When he went golfing with his friends on his one day off, I interpreted that as rejection. When he was short with me, I interpreted it as rejection instead of attributing it to his being under pressure. My responses came out of my own feelings of rejection. "Rejection is a spirit that has to be fed to stay alive," Tim continued, "and it has to be starved in order to kill it. It is fed with negative thoughts about yourself. It is starved by refusing to give it the destructive food it wants and instead building and nourishing yourself on the love and acceptance of God.

"It's not that the power of this spirit is greater than the Lord's power to cast it out, but you can't be delivered from something you are giving place to. If you feed a stray dog, he's going to stay. If you are feeding a spirit of rejection, it's going to stay also. The best way to starve a spirit of rejection is to fill yourself with the knowledge of God's acceptance."

He sent us home with an assignment to find all the verses in the Bible about God's acceptance. We compiled a long list over the next few weeks. By the sixth and final week of our counseling, we had a much deeper understanding of God's love and how to receive it. Tim prayed for us each to be released from the spirit of rejection, and our relationship never went back to that point of missed communication.

Living Like a Chosen One

If there is a sin behind every evil spirit, then the sin behind a spirit of rejection is not believing that Jesus died for you. Even when you have been born with a spirit of rejection due to family curses, such as having a parent who didn't want you or tried to abort you, *the power of that evil spirit can be broken the minute you receive Jesus and truly believe He died for you.*

One of the Scriptures I found while doing Tim Davis's assignment was "I chose you out of the world" (John 15:19). The realization that we did not choose Him first, but He chose *us*, was releasing. On the cross, Jesus was rejected by God. Because Jesus took upon Himself all the sin of the world, God, who is holy, could not look upon him who is not holy. *Because Jesus bore this rejection, we don't have to live in rejection.* We can live like the chosen ones we are.

When I first read in the Bible that the good shepherd laid down His life for His sheep, I thought about Science of Mind and the Eastern religions I had followed in the past. No one in any of them had laid down his life for me. No one else bore my rejection in life so that I could be free of it. No one else had paid for my mistakes. These religions said, "Do it yourself." This sounded good to me because I had already learned I couldn't depend on anyone else anyway. But hard as I tried, I was never able to change myself or my circumstances.

I once heard a gifted pastor named Jerry Cook describe how God views us. He said, "God views us through our future. We view ourselves from our past." We look at our failures and the way we are at this moment. God looks at us the way He made us to be. He sees the end result. If we think of it that way, it's easier to comprehend God's acceptance of us.

People who have been rejected all their lives, especially by a parent, can accept themselves more easily when they realize that God accepts them just as they are. But He isn't going to leave them that way. Because He loves us so much, He is going to help us become all He created us to be. If something in us needs to be changed, *He* changes us as we surrender ourselves to Him.

When you sense the red light of rejection flashing off and on in your brain over some word or action someone has said or done, remember that *the voice of God always encourages. The voice of the devil always discourages. If you can't see anything good about yourself, it's because the devil has covered up your future with the past.*

Every time you feel rejection in any way, refuse to accept it no matter how much your flesh wants to agree with it. Say, "Spirit of rejection, I reject *you!* God accepts me and loves me just the way I am. Even if no one else on earth can accept me that way, I know that *He* does. I refuse to live in the pain of rejection any longer. I have been chosen by God and I choose to live in the full acceptance of the Lord. Thank You, God, for loving me. Praise You, God, for transforming me into all You made me to be."

Open up to God's love and acceptance and accept it for yourself. Your emotional health depends upon it.

■ ——— *What the Bible Says About* ——— ■

Rejection

I have chosen you and not cast you away:
Fear not, for I am with you;
Be not dismayed, for I am your God.
I will strengthen you,
Yes, I will help you,
I will uphold you with My righteous right hand.
 Isaiah 41:9–10

For the LORD will not reject his people;
He will never forsake his inheritance.
 Psalm 94:14 (NIV)

For you are a holy people to the LORD your God; the LORD your God has chosen you to be a people for Himself.
 Deuteronomy 7:6

God from the beginning chose you for salvation through sanctification by the Spirit and belief in the truth.
2 Thessalonians 2:13

For the LORD will not forsake His people, for His great name's sake, because it has pleased the LORD to make you His people.
1 Samuel 12:22

REJECT THE PITFALL OF SELFISHNESS

The lie we believe when we are selfish is "It doesn't matter what anyone else wants because there is nothing more important than what I want, what I need, and what I feel." The ultimate deception is believing "My needs must be met at all costs." This always leads to destructive behavior. We are all inclined to be selfish from the time we're born, but if we're parented well, we learn to be loving and giving. If not, preoccupation with self is one of the devil's tools designed to paralyze us. For example, if he can get us so focused on the way we appear to others that we can't function at our best, then he has control of our lives.

People who have been emotionally damaged early on in life often end up negatively self-focused. Frequently they begin with the thought, "Poor me. The worst things always happen to me." When we rehearse the misery day after day, we open ourselves up to an evil spirit. This spirit of self-pity makes you feel bad for yourself *all the time* about *everything*. The smallest negative incident, like losing your car keys or spraining your ankle, becomes a sign that God is not on your side.

Oswald Chambers says, "Beware of allowing self-consciousness to continue because by slow degrees it will awaken self-pity and self-pity is Satanic" (*My Utmost for His Highest*, 170). Self-pity is a work of the devil, who is intent upon stealing life away from you to destroy you. Remember that. It may seem right to be sorry for yourself because of bad things that happened, but allowing yourself to feel that way all the time means you are ignoring the power of God in your life now.

Focusing on God

The opposite of focusing *inward* on self is focusing *outward* on God. Oswald Chambers says, "The initiative of the saint is not towards self-realization, but towards knowing Jesus Christ" (*My Utmost for His Highest*, 140). How opposite this is from what the world promotes today! We mistakenly think that an intense focus on ourselves will contribute most to our happiness and fulfillment, when actually the opposite is true. Dwelling on ourselves leads to emotional sickness. *Instead of being filled with thoughts about what we need and feel, we must be full of the Lord and thankful to Him that He meets all our needs better than we can.*

The only focus inward we *are* to have is sincere self-examination, to see if we are living and thinking the Lord's way. Even then, that should be done in the Lord's presence because He will be the only one who can reveal the truth in a way that convicts but does not condemn.

Our complete focus must be on God alone. The Bible says, "The backslider in heart will be filled with his own ways, / But a good man will be satisfied from above" (Prov. 14:14).

The best way to focus on God is to thank Him continually for all He has given, praise Him for all He has done, and worship Him for all He is. It's impossible to be self-absorbed or self-obsessed while you are glorifying God in that way.

Also, resolve with your mouth that you will not sin with your mind. Say aloud, "I refuse to sit around and think about what I need and want and feel. I refuse to mourn and moan about the past, present, and future. I refuse to become a giant ego with only thoughts of myself. I deliberately choose to think about You, Lord, and Your goodness. I look to You to meet all my needs. You know what they are even better than I do. I realize it's not confidence in myself that will make things happen for me, but confidence in *You*."

Deliberately avoid the pitfall of self-centeredness by focusing on the Lord in thanksgiving and praise to your Creator. Your emotional health depends on it.

■ ———————— *What the Bible Says About* ———————— ■
Selfishness

I have been crucified with Christ; it is no longer I who live, but Christ lives in me; and the life which I now live in the flesh I live by faith in the Son of God, who loved me and gave Himself for me.
Galatians 2:20

Examine yourselves as to whether you are in the faith. Prove yourselves. Do you not know yourselves, that Jesus Christ is in you?—unless indeed you are disqualified.
2 Corinthians 13:5

But you, beloved, building yourselves up on your most holy faith, praying in the Holy Spirit, keep yourselves in the love of God, looking for the mercy of our Lord Jesus Christ unto eternal life.
Jude 20–21

There are many plans in a man's heart,
Nevertheless the LORD's counsel—that will stand.
Proverbs 19:21

Whoever has no rule over his own spirit
Is like a city broken down, without walls.
Proverbs 25:28

■   ■

REJECT THE PITFALL OF SUICIDE

The lie we believe when we contemplate suicide is "There is no way out." We first believe that our situation is hopeless; then we accept the next lie: Death is the only means of escape. In the Lord, this is *never* true, no matter how painful and agonizing our circumstances. God *in* you is stronger than anything you are facing, and with Him comes freedom and deliverance.

When I was fourteen I was so overcome with emotional torment that I could not envision a future without it. I felt ugly, worthless, stupid, unwanted, and unloved, especially by my parents. One night when I had done nothing to provoke it, my mother unleashed a venomous verbal attack, accusing me of things I had not done. I was helpless to defend myself against her rage, and I suffered such extreme loneliness, depression, and hopelessness that I felt crushed and emotionally mutilated by it. I saw no possibility for things to ever be any different, and I decided I didn't want to live. I took an overdose of drugs that night, but it was not to attract attention or make people feel sorry for me. I didn't leave a note or phone for help. I simply did not want to wake up again.

The Mental Torment of Suicidal Thoughts

Nearly everyone with any serious emotional damage will at one time or another consider suicide; when that happens the most important thing to remember is that those thoughts come from Satan. A desire to die is not from God and is not from you. You may want to be free of physical and emotional pain, and rightly so, but the thought of killing yourself to do it comes from a spirit of death sent from hell to destroy you. *It is not you!* The Spirit of God in you *always* has a solution that leads to life.

If you are contemplating suicide, and I know some who read these pages may be, I want to tell you that I have been in the bottomless pit you're in and I've known its anguish, despair, and pain. I've heard and believed the lies of the devil saying:

- "Death would be better. Go ahead and do it."
- "End this agony. Put a stop to this emptiness."
- "Don't worry about what it would do to anyone else. Nobody really cares anyway. Actually, you'll be doing them a favor."
- "You can't live with this pain another moment. Get it over with and kill yourself now."

I know that many people think of suicide as selfish—and it *is* the final act of a person focused intently upon self—but I know from experience that when you're suicidal, something beyond selfishness overtakes you. I know that down deep you really *do* want to live, but you don't want to live the way you've been living. A voice in your mind tells you you'd be better off dead. You really do want to have hope, but you have a voice in you telling you it's hopeless. Because you're mentally tormented and emotionally weak, you believe it. But the truth is *you want to live.*

Fortunately I didn't take enough drugs when I was fourteen, so I ended up sick instead of dead. When I did wake up I felt different, even though nothing in my circumstances had changed. I wasn't sure why I had been spared from death, but somehow I didn't feel like dying anymore. Why my perception changed, I don't know. Perhaps someone prayed for me, although I never knew that anyone did. But for some reason only God knows, my life was spared and I felt differently. I felt like fighting back, and I decided to do it by taking steps to get out of my miserable situation.

The second important thing to remember in the midst of suicidal thoughts is that *at any moment in our lives things can change.* In fact, change is inevitable. The only thing that doesn't change is God: "For I am the LORD, I do not change" (Mal. 3:6). He will always be working on your behalf. *You may feel like killing yourself now, but tomorrow afternoon you could feel differently.*

Resisting Suicidal Thoughts

A suicidal spirit gains control over you when you say, "I don't want to live any more" a few times to yourself, as I did, without repentance before God. That invites an all-too-willing spirit of death in to assist you in fulfilling that desire to escape life.

Even after I became a Christian I contemplated suicide, and so have countless others. Don't think that because you receive Jesus you are free from enemy attack. And just because you've considered suicide, it doesn't mean you're a failure. It means you need prayer and counseling and deliverance.

Whether you feel suicidal at this moment or not, you need to confess before the Lord any time in your life that you ever said or thought that you wanted to die. After you do that, then say aloud, "I recognize the desire to die as coming from you, Satan, and I renounce you in Jesus' name. I refuse your lying spirit and the only truth I accept is the truth of God, which says His plans and purposes for me are for good. Therefore my future is not hopeless. I want to live and glorify my Father God. By the authority given to me in Jesus' name, I smash the spirit of suicide and refuse any voice that tells me I deserve to die. Thank You, Lord, that *You* died to break any hold death wants to have on my life. Praise the name of Jesus."

If you have to say this prayer twenty times a day, do it. I was freed from a spirit of suicide in the counseling office with Mary Anne, so I was never gripped by it again. However, several times I have been taunted by that spirit over the last fifteen years, and when I said that prayer the spirit left. Don't give the spirit of suicide a place for even one moment.

Once you renounce wanting to die, you will have to deal with why you wanted to die in the first place. You may need to forgive certain people, or God, or yourself for not being what *you* think you should be. Be sure to confess anything that needs to be confessed so you can know that you have received the release of God's full forgiveness toward you.

Never attempt to handle suicidal thoughts without help. Seek out someone who can counsel you now. A Christian psychologist would be best, but if you can't get to one try a suicide hotline, a psychiatrist, a pastor, a counselor, a friend, or strong believer in the Lord. Throughout your counseling get-together with other believers who can pray with you and for you, and make sure you go to church regularly for extensive times of worship and prayer. You must be built up from the inside.

The Best Is Yet to Come

Pastor Jack always taught us that the best part of our lives is ahead, and in the twenty years I've walked with Jesus, that has proven true. The little girl who spent so much time locked in the closet now has a loving husband who provides well for his family, a son and daughter who love the Lord, and a fulfilling and fruitful life. I never imagined these blessings, *especially* when I was contemplating suicide, and had I carried out my suicide plans, I never would have experienced any of it.

It doesn't matter that you can't see it or even imagine it at the moment—God has great things in store for you. You have to take it on faith. You have to know that there is no pit so deep Jesus can't pull you out. The devil *has* blinded you. God has *not* forsaken you. Things *always* change. God is able to transform your circumstances overnight, and this may be the time. If you kill yourself, you will never know the great things that He has waiting for you. Why miss the greatest part of your life by ending it? Know that because Jesus lives, life *is* worth living.

■ ────────── *What the Bible Says About* ────────── ■

Suicide

The fear of the LORD is a fountain of life,
To avoid the snares of death.
  Proverbs 14:27

For You have delivered my soul from death,
My eyes from tears,
And my feet from falling.
I will walk before the LORD
In the land of the living.
  Psalm 116:8–9

The thief does not come except to steal, and to kill, and to destroy. I have come that they may have life, and that they may have it more abundantly.
  John 10:10

The pangs of death encompassed me,
And the floods of ungodliness made me afraid.
The sorrows of Sheol surrounded me;
The snares of death confronted me.
In my distress I called upon the LORD,
And cried out to my God;
He heard my voice from His temple,
And my cry came before Him, even to His ears.
   Psalm 18:4–6

He drew me out of many waters.
He delivered me from my strong enemy.
   Psalm 18:16–17

CHAPTER 8

Step Seven:
Stand Strong

When the phone rang, I leaped to answer it. Diane's tests were to be back, and we would find out what had been causing her pain and failure to recover from what we thought must be a bad case of the flu. Since we'd met in drama class in high school twenty-eight years before, we'd been best friends. We quickly discovered how much we had in common, including our similar family situations. After I received Jesus, I led her to the Lord and she started coming to church with me every Sunday. We became steady prayer partners, praying four or five times a week together on the phone. In those years I did not make an important decision without her prayers.

Two years prior to this phone call, she discovered she had breast cancer. After having both breasts removed, she'd been found cancer free at each checkup. Still we always were concerned that it might come back.

"Stormie," the voice on the other end of the line sounded uncharacteristically small and shaken.

"What did the doctor say?"

"It's not good—" Her voice broke.

"What do you mean? What happened on the tests?"

"The cancer is back."

"Back where?" I held my breath in anticipation of the answer.

"It's everywhere—in my glands, my stomach, my bones, possibly my brain."

"Oh, dear Jesus, help us," I said as we both broke into tears. I don't know how many seconds or minutes passed with just the sound of muffled sobs. When we could talk again, we discussed her eight-year-old son, John.

"I just want to see him grow up," she cried.

We talked about the treatment the doctor had suggested for her. The megadoses of chemotherapy and radiation she described sounded like a death sentence. We prayed together for a miracle from God.

This happened in June, and during the summer months that followed, John stayed with us while his father took care of Diane. She suffered terribly, always growing weaker and more miserable, and by September 13 she went home to be with her heavenly Father.

The grief seemed unbearable to me, especially after the funeral. During Diane's decline and in the months after her death, I struggled with my own physical problems (caused by serious mistreatment of my body in my early twenties), which resulted in a total hysterectomy. A few weeks after the surgery, we sold our house and business, packed up, moved to a new location, and built a new studio. Then an unforeseen turn of events in the music business put us under severe financial strain, which in turn inflicted tremendous strain on our marriage. Dealing with all of these difficulties at once left me physically and emotionally drained.

"God, it feels as if my life is coming to an end," I cried to the Lord one night. "What can replace these losses? Why won't this sadness over Diane's death go away? I can't function well with it. And, God, help Michael and me. We're not living the way You want us to in our relationship. And did we hear You right about buying the house and building a new studio? We prayed for a year about it, and I thought we were clearly directed by You. All this is overwhelming, Lord, and I can't handle it anymore."

"Good. Now let *Me* take this burden for you," I heard the Lord instruct my heart. "You just stand strong in all you know of My truth, and I will take care of everything."

In spite of that word of comfort from God, that whole season was like being in a terrible storm. As the winds tossed the branches of my life, I held tight to my roots, just as He said. I lived with a sense of purpose, no matter how I ached inside or how shaky things felt around me. I stayed in the Word, I prayed, I praised, I surrendered more of myself and my life to Him, I lived God's way even when I felt like giving up. When the storm was over and I was still standing, I knew more than ever that I had chosen solid ground upon which to grow.

Eventually things turned around. I received deliverance from my grief over Diane's death as God gave me deeper relationships with others and with Him. I recovered from the hysterectomy and felt better than I had in years. Miracles happened in my husband's business, our studio and house were saved, and our marriage became stronger than ever. It sounds as if I should say I lived happily ever after, but the truth is that all this could just as easily have gone the other direction. My life could have been washed away by bankruptcy, divorce, and emotional and physical sickness. These kinds of things happen to good people all the time. But I hung on to the Lord, and not only did I get through it, I came out stronger. Only God can bring us back from hell and make us better for it. *But the key was standing strong in Him and doing what was right, no matter what.*

Trusting God for Every Step

If we are to have total deliverance, healing, wholeness, and restoration, there comes a time when we have to say, "This is what I believe; this is the way I will live; this is what I will and will not accept—and that's the way it is." We have to decide to stand strong and do what we know is right to do no matter what happens around us. Oswald Chambers says, "An average view of the Christian life is that it means deliverance from trouble. It is deliverance *in* trouble, which is very different" (*My Utmost for His Highest*, 157).

The Bible doesn't say we won't have problems. In fact, it says quite the opposite:

> Many are the afflictions of the righteous,
> But the LORD delivers him out of them all. (Ps. 34:19)

We don't need to fear because God uses our problems for good when we commit them to prayer and are obedient to His ways. Bad things do happen to good people. God never said they wouldn't. He didn't say life is fair. He said *He* is fair, and He will bring life out of our problems.

Growing Up in the Lord

One of the last times I saw Mary Anne, my counselor, before she moved away, I went to her for some problem that I don't even remember the details of now. What I *do* remember was her wise counsel, which amounted to two words: "Grow up," she said lovingly.

"What?" I asked.

"It's time to grow up, Stormie," she repeated in her patient voice. When my mother screamed those words at me for years, it felt like a beating. When Mary Anne said them, it felt like the Holy Spirit.

"Grow up?" I repeated, hoping she would give me just a little more information.

"Yes, Stormie. You need to get alone with the Lord and ask Him the questions you're asking me. Then tell me what He's saying to you."

Everything she said felt right to me, and I laughed about it later when I told Michael. "You've got to admit that when you go to a counselor for help and she tells you to grow up, it's a sign of emotional health to see how funny that is."

I did ask the Lord, just as she said, and I did hear the answer, just as she predicted. It was then I knew without a doubt that I had everything I needed for my life within me. I just had to stand strong in it. I think I walked a little taller after that.

A point comes in our walk with the Lord when we've had enough teaching, enough counseling, enough deliverance, and enough knowledge of God's ways to be able to stand on our own two feet and say, "I am not going to live on the negative side of life any more." We can't depend on someone to hold our hand and make difficult times go away. We have to "grow up" and take responsibility for our lives. We have to decide we won't be the victims of our circumstances because God has given us a way out. We are not to stand in our own power but to stand strong in Him.

When everything you've learned in the first six steps is put to the test, this last of the Seven Steps to Emotional Health will be the most crucial. This is when you stand strong in Him. The Bible says, "Let the weak say, 'I am strong'" (Joel 3:10). You do *not* say, "I think I can" or "Maybe I'll try." You say, "This is it. I will stand firm in the Lord and strong against the enemy. I will not cry, complain, and lament over what isn't. I will rejoice over what is and all that God is doing." This means standing strong in what you know and in whom you trust. It means growing up, and that's what emotional health is all about.

■ ────────── *What the Bible Says About* ────────── ■
Standing Strong

Be strong in the Lord and in the power of His might.
Ephesians 6:10

By standing firm you will save yourselves.
Luke 21:19 NIV

But as for you, continue in the things which you have learned and been assured of, knowing from whom you have learned them.
2 Timothy 3:14

Do not be deceived, God is not mocked; for whatever a man sows, that he will also reap. For he who sows to his flesh will of the flesh reap corruption, but he who sows to the Spirit will of the Spirit reap everlasting life. And let us not grow weary while doing good, for in due season we shall reap if we do not lose heart.
Galatians 6:7–9

Watch, stand fast in the faith, be brave, be strong.
1 Corinthians 16:13

■ ———————————————————————————— ■

STAND STRONG WHEN THE ENEMY ATTACKS

There will be times when you are doing everything you know to do and things are going well, and then suddenly depression will cloud your mind or low self-esteem will dominate your actions. Or unforgiveness will return in full force, or all hell will break loose in a relationship. Or you'll have problems in an area where you've found deliverance and healing. Suddenly things will seem worse than they have ever been. This means that you are under an attack from the devil. Don't be frightened. It happens to everybody at one time or another.

At those times you have to understand without a doubt that *when you walk with Jesus, you never walk backwards*. God has made it clear in His Word that if we have our eyes on Him, we will go from glory to glory and strength to strength: "But we all, with unveiled face, beholding as in a mirror the glory of the Lord, are being transformed into the same image from glory to glory, just as by the Spirit of the Lord" (2 Cor. 3:18). The psalmist tells us,

> They go from strength to strength;
> Every one of them appears before God in Zion. (Ps. 84:7)

To go backward, you would have to deliberately turn your back on God and walk in the other direction. As long as you are looking to Him, you are moving forward. It doesn't matter how it *feels;* that's the way it is.

Don't get confused. God is on *your* side. He is not responsible for the death of a loved one, the divorce, the husband who drinks, the loss of your job, the accident, the strife in your family, the illness, the feelings of inadequacy. Satan is responsible. Satan is your enemy and wants you to believe his lies. He comes to you at your weakest (especially physically) and mixes his lies with just enough truth that you believe them.

Along with my grief after Diane died came a sudden frightening feeling that I would die too. I had so closely identified with her for twenty-eight years that her death made life seem fragile and fleeting.

I was gripped by that thought until one Sunday morning during church worship, as I was voicing praise and thanksgiving to God for the life He had given me, I saw clearly I had been under satanic attack. I was weak physically and emotionally. The devil had bombarded my mind with the thought that my mother had died of cancer, that my best friend who was my age had died of cancer, and that therefore I could soon die of cancer too.

During that church service God presented me with the *whole* truth: I'm not my mother or Diane. If God chooses to call me home, it will not be on the basis of what happened to them. It will be in *His* timing. Tears of joy welled up as I thanked God for my life with renewed hope and zeal.

This story is just one small incident of many that you or I or any other believer could tell of enemy attack. If you recognize that this kind of attack has happened to you, don't let the devil push you around. If he has kept you in poverty or sickness or tragedy upon disaster, stand up with courage, knowing that God has given you authority over him. Yes, we do have times of suffering. But they do not go on and on. And when the Lord is attending the suffering, you become stronger in Him.

If you are moving forward in Jesus and the enemy attacks from behind, don't be afraid. Just be still and know that the Lord is God. Get quiet in your spirit, and remember all that God has taught you and what He has done for you. We too easily forget everything we've learned at the first sign of attack from the devil.

Four Ways to Recognize Enemy Attack

When God is working in your life, things that you are attached to are being shaken loose, and parts of your flesh are being crucified. This doesn't feel good. But neither does the attack of the devil. The only way you can know for sure which is happening is to let the Spirit of God reveal it to you through His Word, by being in His presence in praise and worship, and asking Him in prayer, "Is this You, God, or is this the devil?" He is faithful to show you.

Too many people do as I did and assume that they deserve what's happening to them. They don't question that it could be a shot directed at them from enemy territory. That's why it's important to know how to identify the enemy's attack.

I don't want to reduce everything to steps and formulas, but sometimes we need simple guidelines. This is one of those times. Often the attack is of such magnitude that we can hardly see straight, let alone figure out clear direction for ourselves. This is especially true of anyone who has been abused or rejected. Because Satan will always attack your self-worth, you can be shaken violently. With that in mind, I have four suggestions that will help you navigate those rough times.

1. *Know God well enough to understand His heart.* If I had not been so exhausted emotionally and physically in the year of Diane's suffering and death, I would have recognized the voice of the devil more quickly. But in my weakened state, I listened. Looking back, I wonder why I thought God would even say to me, "Your mother and your best friend died of cancer; you're going to die that way too." This does not sound like the God I know. The realization of the truth came when I was in the Lord's presence.

Soon after this happened, a friend called to tell me her young son was very ill and asked if it might be the Lord punishing her for not being in church.

"You don't understand the heart of the Lord, Mary," I countered. "The Lord *never* makes someone sick, and He certainly never punishes us for things we neglect to do by allowing something to happen to our children. In fact, He doesn't have to punish us at all because our punishment is built in to our sin. The kind of misery you're speaking about comes from the devil. He's the one we need to do battle against. And you're assured victory over his attack when you depend on God. In fact, you can't lose."

You have to be willing to let your knowledge of the Lord and your desire for His presence be so strong that you won't give the devil any ground. Satan will always try to push your back to the wall, but don't let him. Push *his* back to the wall by saying, "I will *not* allow defeat! My God is my defender and I refuse you entry into my life."

Get clear in your mind the things that are always true about God and hold them alongside what is happening in your life to see if they line up. Mary's fear that God was punishing her for not going to church does not line up with God's goodness. Don't focus on what's going on *around* you, but rather focus on what's *in* you. Check off the following statements that you know for certain are always true about God:

Seven Things That I Know Are Always True about God

___*I know God is a good God.*
Good and upright is the LORD. (Ps. 25:8)
___*I know God is on my side.*
The LORD is on my side. (Ps. 118:6)
God is for me. (Ps. 56:9)
___*I know God's laws and ways are for my benefit.*
The judgments of the LORD are true and righteous altogether . . . / And in keeping them there is great reward. (Ps. 19:9, 11)
___*I know God is always with me.*
I will never leave you nor forsake you. (Heb. 13:5)
___*I know God wants me restored.*
For You have delivered my soul from death. (Ps. 116:8)
___*I know God's promises to me will never fail.*
Your faithfulness endures to all generations. (Ps. 119:90)
___*I know God is always the winner.*
He shall prevail against His enemies. (Isa. 42:13)

If you left any of these statements unchecked, read the entire chapter from which the Scripture below it was taken, and ask God to make the truth of it real to your heart.

2. *Know who Satan is.* You may be thinking, "I don't want any part of a battle with the devil. In fact, I prefer not to even think about things like that." Yet God and Satan are in a battle for your life. The war is real, and denying it will not change that reality. If you are a believer, you're already on the side that wins. But if you aren't where you're supposed to be (in God's will, in His presence, in His truth, in obedience to Him), then you've come out from under His covering, and you can get shot down in the crossfire. People who lose the battle often do so because they believe victory just happens. It doesn't. We must identify the enemy and the battle lines and make sure we're marching in the right army.

As I was worshiping the Lord that day in church, I realized again that *Satan* was my enemy and *he* wanted me dead. I could now see how *he* had been relentlessly trying to undermine what God was doing to give me renewed life. I remembered that *he* is the loser, not God, and *I* am the winner because I belong to the Lord.

Learn the eternal truths about the devil so that you are constantly aware of the nature of his intentions. Check off the following statements that you know are always true about Satan:

Seven Things That I Know Are Always True about the Devil

_____*I know Satan is my enemy.*
For we do not wrestle against flesh and blood, but against principalities, against powers, against the rulers of the darkness of this age, against spiritual hosts of wickedness in the heavenly places. (Eph. 6:12)

_____*I know Satan robs, kills, and destroys.*
The thief does not come except to steal, and to kill, and to destroy. (John 10:10)

_____*I know Satan is a deceiver.*
When he speaks a lie, he speaks from his own resources, for he is a liar and the father of it. (John 8:44)

_____*I know Satan disguises himself.*
For Satan himself transforms himself into an angel of light. (2 Cor. 11:14)

_____*I know Satan never rests from doing evil.*
Be sober, be vigilant; because your adversary the devil walks about like a roaring lion, seeking whom he may devour. (1 Peter 5:8)

_____*I know Satan will always try to undermine what God does in my life.*
And when they hear, Satan comes immediately and takes away the word that was sown in their hearts. (Mark 4:15)

_____*I know Satan is a loser.*
Now is the judgment of this world; now the ruler of this world will be cast out. (John 12:31)

If you left any of these statements unchecked, look up the reference below it in the Bible and read the entire chapter from which it was taken. Ask God to make the truth of it real to your heart.

Sometimes we blame ourselves for what's happening. If we are sick or poor or have some bad things happen to us, we think it's all our fault. Yet there is a difference between taking responsibility for your life and blaming yourself for everything. Sometimes we have met the enemy, and it is *not* us. One of Satan's plans is to keep people weighted down with guilt over things *he* is doing. He disguises himself and sometimes even comes to you as *you*. The devil is out to crush us whenever and wherever he can, and we have to decide whether we're going to go along with his plans or not.

3. *Know what makes you most susceptible to satanic attack.* Often we give Satan unintentional invitations to attack us by what we do or don't do. For example, during those weeks after Diane died, I became so worn out emotionally and physically that I neglected to spend much time with the Lord. I felt too tired to read more than a verse or two of Scripture a day. Because I had lost my dear prayer partner, I prayed much less than I had when she was alive. I had a lump in my throat over her death, and I didn't feel like praising God nearly as much. I went to church regularly, but I was not in fellowship with other believers. It was a time when my life was about to make a new beginning in every area (marriage, friendship, writing, home, finances), but I saw just the opposite. I felt my life was over. Yet because I was in church when I was supposed to be, God made His truth alive to my heart and revealed the enemy's attack to me.

We can fend off much enemy attack by simply paying attention to the reasons he gains access to our lives. Check the reasons the enemy can attack below, and see if you are weak in any area:

Seven Reasons the Enemy Can Attack

____I have neglected to read the Word, so I have no frame of reference for the right way to live.

____I have neglected to pray, so I have lost all power.

____I have neglected times of praise and worship, so I have forfeited the opportunity for God's presence to dwell powerfully in my life.

____I have not lived in all the ways of the Lord, so my enemy has found an entry point.

____I am due for a major breakthrough of some kind in an area of my life, but I struggle with doubt that it could actually happen for me.

____I am walking in disobedience to what God has directed me to do.

____I am moving out in a new area or dimension of ministry without proper prayer covering.

If you checked any of the statements above, confess it to God, and ask Him to show you what to do about it.

4. *Know the signs of satanic attack.* If you learn to recognize the

signs of satanic attack, you will be better able to establish your own defense and to counterattack. If you don't, you may end up aiding the enemy. The devil can attack you through your mind, your emotions, your body, your relationships, or your circumstances. If you can immediately recognize negative emotions such as fear, guilt, depression, confusion, and lack of peace as coming from the enemy, instead of accepting them as truth, you can protect yourself better.

Check the seven signs of satanic attack to help you identify enemy threats upon your life:

Seven Signs of Satanic Attack

_____I experience sudden paralyzing fear that leaves me incapacitated.

_____I have guilt that is overwhelming and doesn't respond to confession or a corrected walk.

_____I have recurring depression or depression that lasts a long time.

_____I have what feels like hell breaking loose in my mind, body, emotions, or situation, especially in an area where there has already been deliverance.

_____I have no peace about specific things that are happening to me.

_____I have great confusion at a point where I once had clarity.

_____I am receiving ideas in my mind that are in direct opposition to God's ways.

If you have checked any one of the above, pray against this attack of Satan upon you. Praying with one or more believers about this is very important, also.

What to Do When the Enemy Attacks

When you first sense you are under enemy attack, go immediately back to the basics.

1. *Check to see that you are proclaiming the Lordship of Jesus in every area of your life.* Sometimes we exclude Him without realizing it. Say, "Jesus is Lord over my mind." "Jesus is Lord over my finances." "Jesus is Lord over my relationships." Specifically name the area the enemy is threatening.

2. *Saturate yourself with God's Word.* Read especially any promises from God concerning enemy attack, and speak them aloud in the face of your circumstances. For example:

- Therefore submit to God. Resist the devil and he will flee from you. (James 4:7)
- But the Lord is faithful, who will establish you and guard you from the evil one. (2 Thess. 3:3)

3. *Be much in prayer.* Ask God to reveal the truth of your situation to you. Ask Him for guidance, protection, and strength for whatever you are facing. Remember there is no unity in the realm of darkness. That's why the two weakest Christians have more power, if they are in unity, than all the power of hell.

4. *Continue to praise God in the midst of whatever is happening.* Remember God inhabits the praises of His people, and you will always be safe in His presence.

5. *Check to see if there are any points of obedience that you have not taken.* Lack of obedience always opens us up to enemy attack.

6. *Fast and pray.* This is a powerful weapon for breaking down enemy strongholds that have been erected against you.

7. *Resist Satan.* Don't run from the enemy, but instead face him with all the spiritual weapons at your disposal, knowing that because of Jesus in you, you have full authority and power over him.

8. *Rest in the Lord.* Once you have done all you know to do, be still and know that Jesus is the victor and the battle is the Lord's. Gain strength in that knowledge.

When the heat is on and the battle is raging, know that as long as you are standing strong in the Lord, you won't be shot down or burned up by your circumstances. If it looks like all hell is breaking loose in your life, know God will bring heaven to rule in your situation. *Think in terms of God's power and not your own weakness.* A clear picture of His power will settle everything in your mind. Don't give the devil the pleasure of seeing you give up.

■ ——————— *What the Bible Says About* ——————— ■
Standing Strong
When the Enemy Attacks

Blessed is the man who endures temptation; for when he has been proved, he will receive the crown of life which the Lord has promised to those who love Him.
James 1:12

When the storm has swept by, the wicked are gone, but the righteous stand firm forever.
Proverbs 10:25 NIV

Resist him, standing firm in the faith, because you know that your brothers throughout the world are undergoing the same kind of sufferings.
1 Peter 5:9 NIV

Escape the snare of the devil, having been taken captive by him to do his will.
2 Timothy 2:26

He delivered me from my strong enemy.
Psalm 18:17

■   ■

STAND STRONG WHEN YOUR PRAYERS HAVEN'T BEEN ANSWERED

There will be times when your prayers will not be answered—at least not exactly the way you prayed them or according to your timetable. If that happens, trust that God knows what is best.

Until Diane died, I and all who knew her never stopped praying for her healing. Hundreds of strong believers in two congregations who didn't even know her prayed for her continually. If her healing depended on prayer and faith, she was covered. But those specific prayers were not answered, at least not the way we wanted them to be.

We all have lived through the painful consequences of unanswered prayer. Sometimes what seems like unanswered prayer is actually a matter of patient waiting. Other times the prayers are answered so differently from what we expect that we can't even see they've been answered until much later. Sometimes our prayers are not answered at all as we have prayed them. The key is standing strong in the Lord whether we see that our prayers are answered or not.

When getting an answer to prayer takes a long time, we sometimes begin to lose hope. We become discouraged and fear the Lord has forgotten us. We stop praying, stop going to church, stop reading the Bible, stop doing certain steps of obedience because we think "What's the point?" Sometimes we get mad at God. We don't like waiting the two weeks, two months, two years, or as long as it takes for the answer to come. And what if the answer never comes? That's miserable and we don't like to suffer.

The Purpose of Suffering

Everyone, without exception, suffers at one time or another. No one is exempt. Sometimes we do stupid or sinful things that lead to misery. Sometimes it's satanic attack. Sometimes we suffer because we are not doing what God is directing us to. Sometimes people think that if there is no *immediate* suffering when they stray from God's ways, they are getting away with something. Later on, when they're miserable, they don't connect the two.

Sometimes suffering is used by God to refine us. He doesn't put the suffering upon us, but He allows us to be in it for our own purifying. And no matter how hard we pray, there is still a season of it in our lives because through it His purposes are worked in us.

No one suffers willingly. Even Jesus asked God for His suffering on the cross to be eliminated if at all possible in the Father's will. The good news is that what comes out of suffering is so far above what we endure that it more than compensates for our misery: "The sufferings of this present time are not worthy to be compared with the glory which shall be revealed in us" (Rom. 8:18). God is not minimizing our suffering in that Scripture, He's putting it in perspective. The great things ahead for those who stand strong are so far superior to what we can imagine that our suffering will seem momentary when weighed against the entirety of our lives here on earth and in heaven.

I was miserably sick throughout both of my pregnancies. I have never before or since experienced such physical suffering and have no desire to repeat it. But the rewards of having my son and daughter are so superior to my suffering that I can't even compare the two. Even knowing my prayers for an easy pregnancy would not be answered, I would choose to go through it again. The changes that will be birthed in our lives after a time of suffering will be well worth it.

When you are suffering (which is what you feel when your prayers are not answered), God reveals two things to you: *His grace* and *His power*—His grace to sustain you and keep you, and His power to deliver you. God wants us to see without a doubt that *we are limited* in our power. He also wants us to see that *He is not*. He waits until all hope outside of Him is dead so that we will know it is He who brought life where there was none. Sometimes He takes things out of our lives so that we will turn to Him to supply our need. No matter how much God blesses us, He wants us to acknowledge that we depend on Him. He uses the storms of our lives to accomplish that purpose.

Treasures of Darkness

God is God when things are bad as well as when they are good, when it is dark as well as when it is light. Sometimes the darkness around us is not a darkness of death but rather a darkness like in a womb, where we are growing and being made ready for birth. Just as a child in the womb knows nothing of the world waiting for him, so we do not realize the greatness of God's purpose for us. The Bible says, "I will give you the treasures of darkness" (Isa. 45:3). Certain valuable experiences in the Lord can *only* be found in the dark times.

If it's true that God never leaves us or forsakes us, then when we are in darkness, He is there also. And wherever He is, there is healing and growth. Some of my closest encounters with the Lord have happened in the dark times when I turned to Him and found a more powerful presence of His Spirit than I had known before. Those times have been precious, unforgettable, and life changing. Through them I have found a larger portion of Him in me, and I wouldn't trade that now for anything.

Don't worry. This time of darkness, waiting, and unanswered prayer is not going to become a way of life. It's only a season of the soul.

How to Grow in the Dark

So what do you do when you've believed and praised and prayed and now you're disillusioned and afraid your dreams and hopes are gone? First of all, don't be consumed in guilt. Don't feel that this is all your fault and therefore God won't answer your prayer. If your prayers are unanswered because of sin, confess it, stop doing it, and pray. God will turn things around.

Secondly, allow no situation to make you turn your back on Him. Know that He sees where you are, He has not forgotten you, and He will sustain you through it. Rest in the fact that He is in control and more powerful than your problems. It's at this time that we either turn away from the Lord's ways or determine to live them even more diligently. We can give up too soon and say, "This obviously isn't working so why bother doing it this way?" We can try to make things work on our own steam instead of turning it all over to

God and doing what's right until we see Him move. We can choose to try to ride the storm out by ourselves, or we can align with the God who either calms the storm or sets our feet on solid ground in the center of it where we won't be harmed. Far too many people have given up when the answer to their prayer was just around the corner.

Part of standing strong in times of unanswered prayer is waiting, and waiting produces patience. The Bible says, "In your patience possess your souls" (Luke 21:19). When you are patient, you're able to take control of your very being and place yourself in God's hands. He, then, is in control whether it is night or day in your soul. He becomes God to you in every season of your life—the good and the bad. And because you know Him that way, you become unshakable.

Since we have no choice but to wait, our attitude makes a lot of difference. We can either shake our fist at God and scream, "Why me?" Or we can open up our hearts to God and pray, "Lord, change this situation. Perfect Your life in me as I wait on You. Help me to do the right thing, and let it all work out for my greatest good."

You may have to wait for God to move, but you don't have to sit twiddling your thumbs until it happens. The best way to sustain a good attitude while you wait is to spend much time in praise and worship of God. Say, "Lord, I praise You in the midst of this situation. I confess I'm afraid that my prayers may never be answered. I'm weary and discouraged from the waiting, and feel I'm losing the strength to fight. Forgive me, Lord, for not trusting You more. I pray my weariness would end and there would be renewed hope in my spirit. Help me to feel Your presence and Your love, and help me to hear Your voice and follow Your lead. Thank You that You are in full control."

Don't stop praying even if you've been doing it for a long time and it seems as if God must not be listening. God hears your every prayer. You may feel like nothing is going on, but in God's kingdom, God's love, healing, and redemption are always going on. You tap into it by prayer and by surrendering yourself and your life to Him on a daily basis.

Remember that no matter how much freedom, deliverance, and victory you receive, you will still have times of dryness, conflict, and suffering. Don't be shaken, for when God is in charge, these times will have an end, and He will use them to perfect you. Don't sin in reaction to them so that you limit the blessings that can come out of them. Stay close to God so that He can reveal the way you should go.

─── *What the Bible Says About* ───

Standing Strong When Your Prayers Haven't Been Answered

Beloved, do not think it strange concerning the fiery trial which is to try you, as though some strange thing happened to you; but rejoice to the extent that you partake of Christ's sufferings, that when His glory is revealed, you may also be glad with exceeding joy.
1 Peter 4:12–13

In this you greatly rejoice, though now for a little while, if need be, you have been grieved by various trials, that the genuineness of your faith, being much more precious than gold that perishes, though it is tested by fire, may be found to praise, honor, and glory at the revelation of Jesus Christ.
1 Peter 1:6–7

But may the God of all grace, who called us to His eternal glory by Christ Jesus, after you have suffered a while, perfect, establish, strengthen, and settle you.
1 Peter 5:10

STAND STRONG WHEN YOUR PRAYERS *HAVE* BEEN ANSWERED

One of the big surprises for people who come out of the wilderness of their past and enter the promised land of answered prayer is that there are giants in the land and they have to fight against them in order to possess it. Because Satan never has a day when he is feeling friendly toward us, our prosperity, success, breakthrough, deliverance, and healing will not go unchallenged. We have to remember to stand strong against the work of the enemy in the easy times as well as the difficult.

During the year Diane died, Michael and I were finally brought to the realization that the devil had designed a plan to destroy our marriage, our business, and our health through our finances. Worse than that, we were allowing him to do it. Things had been going along well in the area of our finances, so we hadn't prayed much about them. Suddenly, they started to get very shaky. One evening, on the brink of what could have been financial ruin, Michael and I knelt before God and repented of our failure to cover our finances in prayer. We had not stopped tithing but had neglected to be prayerful about the stewardship of our income. We asked God to be in charge and bless us with restoration. *Every* morning we diligently prayed about it, and immediately the strain on our marriage and health showed signs of improvement. Soon the business and finances began to turn around also.

When a certain contract that we had been praying for came through, along with a large check, the pressure was off. We cheered, we praised God, we danced, we whooped, and we screamed. The very next day we slept later than usual, got up in a rush, and left the house before we had time to pray. The next few days brought situations that kept us from praying together as we had when things were tough. As it turned out, we were able to catch ourselves before disaster struck again, but our experience shows how we do not naturally turn to God when things are going well. And *we* knew better.

How Quickly We Forget

The truth about human flesh is that when we come to a place of comfort, we tend to forget God. As I read through the Old Testament from beginning to end, what impressed me most was how the Israelites struggled, strained, cried, sought God, repented, and prayed when things were bad, and God heard and answered their prayers. Once all was going well, they forgot where they had come from, forgot what God had done, and lived their own way. In bad times, they remembered God and did the right thing. In good times, they forgot God and sinned—time and again.

You and I are no different. How many of us can say that we pray as fervently when all is well as we do when all hell is breaking loose? Not many, I'm sure. If we could serve the Lord just as faithfully and fervently when our prayers *have* been answered as when they haven't, we might never have to suffer as we do. I'm not saying that life would be pain-free because life doesn't work that way, but we do sometimes suffer needlessly. The Bible says, "Let him who thinks he stands take heed lest he fall" (1 Cor. 10:12). When things are going well, beware!

Watching Out for Giants

"The promised land the Bible talks about is a place of restoration," Mary Anne, my counselor, explained. "It's a time of renewing all that has been destroyed, stolen, or lost from our lives. When we enter the promised land, we don't think about the giants; we think about the milk and honey, about how good this feels and what life will be like now that we've been set free and are being renewed. We know that evil lurks about, but we don't want to think about that now, not when things are good. That's why when an attack comes, we are so unprepared. When we enter the promised land we need to know there are giants we must face."

"Who are these giants?" I asked.

Mary Anne named certain enemies that were in the promised land as described in the book of Exodus. She said she found that the meanings of their names correlated with areas of our flesh in which we struggle, such as fear, confusion, discouragement, pride, rebelliousness, and condemnation. These were exactly the ones that threatened me when I came into my time of restoration, and ones we must be ready to battle, even in time of peace.

Keep It Written in Stone

Years ago Pastor Jack instructed each family unit in our church, single or married, to go out and find a rock large enough to write the words, "As for me and my house, we will serve the LORD" (Josh. 24:15), and then put it in a prominent place in their home. Michael and I found a five-pound gray stone with a flat enough surface on one side to print that Scripture. We placed it next to the fireplace in the living room, and every time we see it we remember our commitment to serve God and stand strong in Him. Everyone who comes in the house sees it, and I believe the devil knows it's there too. It's a good reminder for him—and for you. In fact, I'm giving you an assignment. Go find yourself a decent-sized rock, print that Scripture on it with an indelible marker, and place it in the heart of your home. Whether you live in a one-room trailer, a forty-room mansion, or a corner of someone else's apartment, make sure those words are visible to you somewhere. It's a scriptural proclamation of where you stand, and it helps you to stand taller in the presence of giants.

Don't ever be fooled into believing that when all is going well, you don't need to read, pray, praise, and obey as carefully as you did before. Resolve to stand strong in the Lord, even when your prayers have been answered, and you will live safely in the promised land of God's restoration.

What the Bible Says About

Standing Strong When Your Prayers Have Been Answered

Be steadfast, immovable, always abounding in the work of the Lord, knowing that your labor is not in vain in the Lord.
1 Corinthians 15:58

But each one is tempted when he is drawn away by his own desires and enticed. Then, when desire has conceived, it gives birth to sin; and sin, when it is full-grown, brings forth death.
James 1:14–15

Watch and pray, lest you enter into temptation.
Matthew 26:41

Rejoice always, pray without ceasing, in everything give thanks; for this is the will of God in Christ Jesus for you.
1 Thessalonians 5:16–18

As you therefore have received Christ Jesus the Lord, so walk in Him, rooted and built up in Him and established in the faith.
Colossians 2:6–7

CHAPTER 9

Becoming All God Made You to Be

Y ou've just gone through the Seven Steps to Emotional Health, and if you have taken even one step in each area, there are bound to be noticeable positive changes in your life. You may not see as many as you'd like yet, but don't give up. You will. God promises that "He who has begun a good work in you will complete it until the day of Jesus Christ" (Phil. 1:6).

I'm going to assume that if you've read this far, you've already decided you want all God has for you. This is good because becoming all He created you to be begins with a deep desire in the heart. When that longing turns into a hunger for more of the Lord than can ever be completely satisfied until you are in His presence, then you are on your way to becoming all you can be. Now it's time to make your commitment to the Lord a solid one. It's time to start living what you believe and walking in the wholeness to which you plan to become accustomed. You'll be able to do that more effectively if you stay emotionally current and mindful of the truth about yourself.

BECOMING ALL GOD MADE YOU TO BE
BY STAYING EMOTIONALLY CURRENT

Once you are on the road to emotional health, remain sensitive to what is currently happening inside of you. That doesn't mean you sit around all day thinking about how you feel. The focus stays on Jesus. But now because your focus *is* so much on the Lord and living His way, you can deal with your emotions as they surface. In *The Road Less Traveled* (New York: Simon and Schuster, 1980, 51), Scott Peck says, "Mental health is an ongoing process of dedication to reality at all costs." Covering up our emotions is the opposite.

If you have unexplained negative emotions, don't just push them below the surface because you think that's what good Christians do. Find out where they're coming from. Realize that you don't have to put up with them, and interrogate yourself to get to the bottom of why you feel the way you do.

Every one of us has countless tears buried inside. We've pulled back from crying because it didn't seem socially appropriate or because we were afraid that if we shed one tear, the floodgates would open and we wouldn't be able to regain control. Often there has been so much hurt we've had to harden our hearts to dull the pain. When we no longer feel the pain, we don't cry. This is a survival method, but it isn't healthy. The Bible says,

> To everything there is a season,
> A time for every purpose under heaven:
> . . . a time to weep,
> And a time to laugh;
> A time to mourn,
> And a time to dance. (Eccl. 3:1, 4)

We would be wise to remember that.

I once heard a doctor say, "Colds are a result of uncried tears that back up and clog the system." I don't know if that can ever be scientifically proven, but I believe our emotions overflow onto our physical self more than we dream possible. We must stay current with our need to cry and feel free to let ourselves do it. Crying in the presence of the Lord brings much healing and should not be restricted.

Whatever has been lost to you must be mourned completely, whether it is the loss of a dream, a childhood, a part of your body, a marriage, a loved one, or a period of time in your life. Grief comes in stages, so don't let getting through one stage close you off to further stages. Each one is a different aspect of the loss that you are coming to terms with. Don't avoid it out of fear. You won't be consumed by it; you will be released.

Our emotions should not rule our lives, nor should we make decisions based on them, but we shouldn't ignore them either. Part of letting go of the past involves facing the present. Listen to what you are feeling and ask God to help you to identify it and deal with it. Don't let the devil cover over anything that should be brought to the light of God. It could be something coming up from the past because God is bringing you to a new level of deliverance. Allow yourself to be emotionally current at all times.

BECOMING ALL GOD MADE YOU TO BE
BY REMEMBERING THE TRUTH ABOUT YOURSELF

Total wholeness and restoration was God's plan for your life from the beginning, and you are to live in confidence about that. He has said many wonderful things in His Word about you, and I have listed seven very important ones below. Check to make sure you are living as though you believe each one of them.

Seven Things That God Says Are Always True about Me

___*I am a child of God, and my inheritance comes from Him.*
But as many as received Him, to them He gave the right to become children of God, even to those who believe in His name. (John 1:12)
___*I have a special, God-ordained purpose.*
Eye has not seen, nor ear heard, nor have entered into the heart of man
The things which God has prepared for those who love Him. (1 Cor. 2:9)
___*I have been created with a specific calling.*
Let each one remain with God in that calling in which he was called. (1 Cor. 7:24)
___*I am never alone.*
I am with you always, even to the end of the age. (Matt. 28:20)
___*I am never forgotten.*
God has not cast away His people whom He foreknew. (Rom. 11:2)
___*I am loved.*
As the Father loved Me, I also have loved you. (John 15:9)
___*I am a winner.*
In all these things we are more than conquerors through Him who loved us. (Rom. 8:37)

From the time I decided to receive the Lord, to the day I finished this book, a little over twenty years has gone by. In that time, God has kept His promises, and He has always come through. Many times it didn't feel as if He was going to, but He did. It certainly hasn't been the way I was directing Him each time or as quickly as

I wanted to see things happen. And, thank God, it wasn't to the degree I envisioned. It was always far *better*. His timing was perfect and His way was right! Everything I have received from the Lord and more, I want for you.

If at any time you become overwhelmed by how much you think you have to do to arrive at emotional wholeness or if you have doubts about whether you can do all that's necessary, then *you need to remind yourself that the Holy Spirit accomplishes wholeness in you, as you allow Him.* Let *Him* do it. All *you* have to do is tell God that you want *His* ways to become *your* ways, and then take one step at a time in the right direction as it is revealed to you. *You only need to be concerned with the step you're on.*

■ ————————— *What the Bible Says About* ————————— ■

Becoming All God Made You to Be

If anyone is in Christ, he is a new creation; old things have passed away; behold, all things have become new.
2 Corinthians 5:17

Do not remember the former things,
Nor consider the things of old.
Behold, I will do a new thing,
Now it shall spring forth;
Shall you not know it?
I will even make a road in the wilderness
And rivers in the desert.
Isaiah 43:18–19

Most assuredly, I say to you, he who hears My word and believes in Him who sent Me has everlasting life, and shall not come into judgment, but has passed from death into life.
John 5:24

The LORD shall preserve your going out and your coming in
From this time forth, and even forevermore.
Psalm 121:8

You are complete in Him.
Colossians 2:10

Arise, shine;
   For your light has come!
And the glory of the LORD is risen upon you.
   Isaiah 60:1